MODERN FANTASY WRITERS

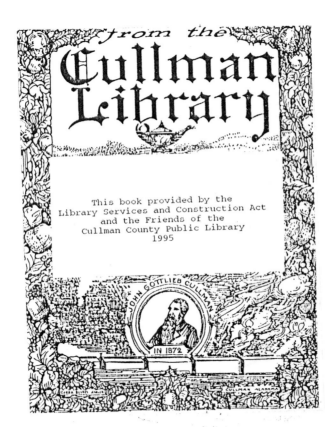

Writers of English: Lives and Works

MODERN FANTASY WRITERS

Edited and with an Introduction by

Harold Bloom

CHELSEA HOUSE PUBLISHERS
New York   Philadelphia

Jacket illustration: Max Ernst (1891–1976), *Gypsy Rose Lee* (Private Collection; © ARS, NY; courtesy of Art Resource, NY).

CHELSEA HOUSE PUBLISHERS

Editorial Director Richard Rennert
Executive Managing Editor Karyn Gullen Browne
Picture Editor Adrian G. Allen
Copy Chief Robin James
Art Director Robert Mitchell
Manufacturing Director Gerald Levine
Assistant Art Director Joan Ferrigno

Writers of English: Lives and Works

Senior Editor S. T. Joshi
Series Design Rae Grant

Staff for MODERN FANTASY WRITERS

Assistant Editor Mary Sisson
Research Peter Cannon, Stefan Dziemianowicz
Picture Researcher Pat Burns

Printed and bound in the United States of America.

First Printing

1 3 5 7 9 8 6 4 2

Library of Congress Cataloging-in-Publication Data

Modern fantasy writers / edited and with an introduction by Harold Bloom.
    p.   cm.—(Writers of English)
    Includes bibliographical references.
    ISBN 0-7910-2223-4.—ISBN 0-7910-2248-X (pbk.)
  1. Fantastic fiction, American—History and criticism. 2. Fantastic literature, English—
History and criticism. 3. Fantastic literature—Bio-bibliography. 4. Fantastic fiction—Bio-
bibliography. I. Bloom, Harold. II. Series.
PS374.F27M63 1994
813'.0876609—dc20   94-5890
[B]   CIP

▨ Contents

User's Guide	vi
The Life of the Author	vii
Introduction	xi
Ray Bradbury	1
John Collier	16
L. Sprague de Camp and Fletcher Pratt	29
E. R. Eddison	43
Robert E. Howard	57
Fritz Leiber	71
C. S. Lewis	85
David Lindsay	98
A. Merritt	110
Mervyn Peake	123
M. P. Shiel	137
Clark Ashton Smith	151
J. R. R. Tolkien	165
Charles Williams	180

◼ User's Guide

THIS VOLUME PROVIDES biographical, critical, and bibliographical information on the fifteen most significant modern fantasy writers. Each chapter consists of three parts: a biography of the author; a selection of brief critical extracts about the author; and a bibliography of the author's published books.

The biography supplies a detailed outline of the important events in the author's life, including his or her major writings. The critical extracts are taken from a wide array of books and periodicals, from the author's lifetime to the present, and range in content from biographical to critical to historical. The extracts are arranged in chronological order by date of writing or publication, and a full bibliographical citation is provided at the end of each extract. Editorial additions or deletions are indicated within carets.

The author bibliographies list every separate publication—including books, pamphlets, broadsides, collaborations, and works edited or translated by the author—for works published in the author's lifetime; selected important posthumous publications are also listed. Titles are those of the first edition; variant titles are supplied within carets. In selected instances dates of revised editions are given where these are significant. Pseudonymous works are listed, but not the pseudonyms under which these works were published. Periodicals edited by the author are listed only when the author has written most or all of the contents. Titles enclosed in square brackets are of doubtful authenticity. All works by the author, whether in English or in other languages, have been listed; English translations of foreign-language works are not listed unless the author has done the translation.

The Life of the Author
Harold Bloom

NIETZSCHE, WITH EXULTANT ANGUISH, famously proclaimed that God was dead. Whatever the consequences of this for the ethical life, its ultimate literary effect certainly would have surprised the author Nietzsche. His French disciples, Foucault most prominent among them, developed the Nietzschean proclamation into the dogma that all authors, God included, were dead. The death of the author, which is no more than a Parisian trope, another metaphor for fashion's setting of skirt-lengths, is now accepted as literal truth by most of our current apostles of what should be called French Nietzsche, to distinguish it from the merely original Nietzsche. We also have French Freud or Lacan, which has little to do with the actual thought of Sigmund Freud, and even French Joyce, which interprets *Finnegans Wake* as the major work of Jacques Derrida. But all this is as nothing compared to the final triumph of the doctrine of the death of the author: French Shakespeare. That delicious absurdity is given us by the New Historicism, which blends Foucault and California fruit juice to give us the Word that Renaissance "social energies," and not William Shakespeare, composed *Hamlet* and *King Lear*. It seems a proper moment to murmur "enough" and to return to a study of the life of the author.

Sometimes it troubles me that there are so few masterpieces in the vast ocean of literary biography that stretches between James Boswell's great *Life* of Dr. Samuel Johnson and the late Richard Ellmann's wonderful *Oscar Wilde*. Literary biography is a crucial genre, and clearly a difficult one in which to excel. The actual nature of the lives of the poets seems to have little effect upon the quality of their biographies. Everything happened to Lord Byron and nothing at all to Wallace Stevens, and yet their biographers seem equally daunted by them. But even inadequate biographies of strong writers, or of weak ones, are of immense use. I have never read a literary biography from which I have not profited, a statement I cannot make about any other genre whatsoever. And when it comes to figures who are central to us—Dante, Shakespeare, Cervantes, Montaigne, Goethe, Whitman, Tolstoi, Freud, Joyce, Kafka among them—we reach out eagerly for every scrap that the biographers have gleaned. Concerning Dante and Shakespeare we know much too little, yet when we come to Goethe and Freud, where we seem to know more than everything, we still want to know more. The death of the author, despite our current resentniks, clearly was only a momentary fad. Something vital in every authentic lover of literature responds to Emerson's battle-cry sentence: "There is no history, only biography." Beyond that there is a deeper truth, difficult to come at and requiring a lifetime to understand, which is that there is no literature, only autobiography, however mediated, however veiled, however transformed. The events of Shakespeare's life included the composition of *Hamlet,* and that act of writing was itself a crucial act of living, though we do not yet know altogether how to read so doubled an act. When an author takes up a more overtly autobiographical stance, as so many do in their youth, again we still do not know precisely how to accommodate the vexed relation between life and work. T. S. Eliot, meditating upon James Joyce, made a classic statement as to such accommodation:

> We want to know who are the originals of his characters, and what were the origins of his episodes, so that we may unravel the web of memory and invention and discover how far and in what ways the crude material has been transformed.

When a writer is not even covertly autobiographical, the web of memory and invention is still there, but so subtly woven that we may never unravel it. And yet we want deeply never to stop trying, and not merely because we are curious, but because each of us is caught in her own network of memory and invention. We do not always recall our inventions, and long before we age we cease to be certain of the extent to which we have invented our memories. Perhaps one motive for reading is our need to unravel our own webs. If our masters could make, from their lives, what we read, then we can be moved by them to ask: What have we made or lived in relation to what we have read? The answers may be sad, or confused, but the question is likely, implicitly, to go on being asked as long as we read. In Freudian terms, we are asking: What is it that we have repressed? What have we forgotten, unconsciously but purposively: What is it that we flee? Art, literature necessarily included, is regression in the service of the ego, according to a famous Freudian formula. I doubt the Freudian wisdom here, but indubitably it is profoundly suggestive. When we read, something in us keeps asking the equivalent of the Freudian questions: From what or whom is the author in flight, and to what earlier stages in her life is she returning, and why?

Reading, whether as an art or a pastime, has been damaged by the visual media, television in particular, and might be in some danger of extinction in the age of the computer, except that the psychic need for it continues to endure, presumably because it alone can assuage a central loneliness in elitist society. Despite all sophisticated or resentful denials, the reading of imaginative literature remains a quest to overcome the isolation of the individual consciousness. We can read for information, or entertainment, or for love of the language, but in the end we seek, in the author, the person whom we have not found, whether in ourselves or in others. In that quest, there always are elements at once aggressive and defensive, so that reading, even in childhood, is rarely free of hidden anxieties. And yet it remains one of the few activities not contaminated by an entropy of spirit. We read in hope, because we lack companionship, and the author can become the object of the most idealistic elements in our search for the wit and inventiveness we so desperately require. We read biography, not as a supplement to reading the author, but as a second, fresh attempt to understand what always seems to evade us in the work, our drive towards a kind of identity with the author.

This will-to-identity, though recently much deprecated, is a prime basis for the experience of sublimity in reading. *Hamlet* retains its unique position in the Western canon not because most readers and playgoers identify themselves with the prince, who clearly is beyond them, but rather because they find themselves again in the power of the language that represents him with such immediacy and force. Yet we know that neither language nor social energy created Hamlet. Our curiosity about Shakespeare is endless, and never will be appeased. That curiosity itself is a value, and cannot be separated from the value of *Hamlet* the tragedy, or Hamlet the literary character. It provokes us that Shakespeare the man seems so unknowable, at once everyone and no one as Borges shrewdly observes. Critics keep telling us otherwise, yet something valid in us keeps believing that we would know Hamlet better if Shakespeare's life were as fully known as the lives of Goethe and Freud, Byron and Oscar Wilde, or best of all, Dr. Samuel Johnson. Shakespeare never will have his Boswell, and Dante never will have his Richard Ellmann. How much one would give for a detailed and candid *Life of Dante* by Petrarch, or an outspoken memoir of Shakespeare by Ben Jonson! Or, in the age just past, how superb would be rival studies of one another by Hemingway and Scott Fitzgerald! But the list is endless: think of *Oscar Wilde* by Lord Alfred Douglas, or a joint biography of Shelley by Mary Godwin, Emilia Viviani, and Jane Williams. More than our insatiable desire for scandal would be satisfied. The literary rivals and the lovers of the great writers possessed perspectives we will never enjoy, and without those perspectives we dwell in some poverty in regard to the writers with whom we ourselves never can be done.

There is a sense in which imaginative literature *is* perspectivism, so that the reader is likely to be overwhelmed by the work's difficulty unless its multiple perspectives are mastered. Literary biography matters most because it is a storehouse of perspectives, frequently far surpassing any that are grasped by the particular biographer. There are relations between authors' lives and their works of kinds we have yet to discover, because our analytical instruments are not yet advanced enough to perform the necessary labor. Perhaps a novel, poem, or play is not so much a regression in the service of the ego, as it is an amalgam of *all* the Freudian mechanisms of defense, all working together for the apotheosis of the ego. Freud valued art highly, but thought that the aesthetic enterprise was no rival for psychoanalysis, unlike religion and philosophy. Clearly Freud was mistaken; his own anxieties about his indebtedness to Shakespeare helped produce the weirdness of his joining in the lunacy that argued for the Earl of Oxford as the author of Shakespeare's plays. It was Shakespeare, and not "the poets," who was there before Freud arrived at his depth psychology, and it is Shakespeare who is there still, well out ahead of psychoanalysis. We see what Freud would not see, that psychoanalysis is Shakespeare prosified and systematized. Freud is part of literature, not of "science," and the biography of Freud has the same relations to psychoanalysis as the biography of Shakespeare has to *Hamlet* and *King Lear*, if only we knew more of the life of Shakespeare.

Western literature, particularly since Shakespeare, is marked by the representation of internalized change in its characters. A literature of the ever-growing inner self is in itself a large form of biography, even though this is the biography of imaginary beings, from Hamlet to the sometimes nameless protagonists of Kafka and Beckett. Skeptics might want to argue that all literary biography concerns imaginary beings, since authors make themselves up, and every biographer gives us a creation curiously different from the same author as seen by the writer of a rival *Life*. Boswell's Johnson is not quite anyone else's Johnson, though it is now very difficult for us to disentangle the great Doctor from his gifted Scottish friend and follower. The life of the author is not merely a metaphor or a fiction, as is "the Death of the Author," but it always does contain metaphorical or fictive elements. Those elements are a part of the value of literary biography, but not the largest or the crucial part, which is the separation of the mask from the man or woman who hid behind it. James Joyce and Samuel Beckett, master and sometime disciple, were both of them enigmatic personalities, and their biographers have not, as yet, fully expounded the mystery of these contrasting natures. Beckett seems very nearly to have been a secular saint: personally disinterested, heroic in the French Resistance, as humane a person ever to have composed major fictions and dramas. Joyce, self-obsessed even as Beckett was preternaturally selfless, was the Milton of the twentieth century. Beckett was perhaps the least egoistic post-Joycean, post-Proustian, post-Kafkan of writers. Does that illuminate the problematical nature of his work, or does it simply constitute another problem? Whatever the cause, the question matters. The only death of the author that is other than literal, and that matters, is the fate only of weak writers. The strong, who become canonical, never die, which is what the canon truly is about. To be read forever is the Life of the Author.

◈ Introduction

DAVID LINDSAY'S *A Voyage to Arcturus* is, to me, the most eminent of modern fantasy narratives. I prefer it even to Mervyn Peake's marvelous *Gormenghast* trilogy, let alone to the Neo-Christian moralizings of the Oxford group who called themselves "the Inklings": J. R. R. Tolkien, C. S. Lewis, Charles Williams. *Arcturus* was Lindsay's first and much his best book. His later efforts tended to be formless, and frequently are shrouded in a dank obscurantism. In *Arcturus*, Lindsay wrote the one authentic book he had in him, an uneven but frequently sublime vision of the ultimate quest-romance, in which a Promethean protagonist attempts to steal divine fire on a distant planet, a realm pervaded by alarming beings, demonic or semidivine, and by as varied and peculiar a fauna and flora as imaginative literature affords. *Arcturus* has its enthusiasts—including my favorite contemporary fantasy writers, Ursula K. Le Guin and John Crowley—but it seems to repel as many readers as it attracts. About half of those to whom I have recommended it have found it scarcely readable, while the other half reread it incessantly, as I do. Temperament seems the governing factor; *Arcturus* is an extreme work, pushing fantasy or romance to its limits, where it threatens to turn into Gnostic scripture.

Lindsay is overtly influenced by Novalis and by Carlyle, but his deepest mythopoeic affinities are with Blake, though Blake would not have approved of the theology of pain in *Arcturus*. Psychic cartography is Lindsay's mode, as it is Blake's. Maskull, the Promethean quester, is akin to Orc, the fallen form of the titan that Blake named Luvah, while Krag parallels Blake's Los, the hammering prophet of the imagination. Lindsay's Crystalman is like Blake's Urizen, a deceptive demiurge of the fallen world. The most mysterious of *Arcturus's* questers, Nightspore, has its affinities with Blake's Tharmas, the fallen sense of taste and of touch. The most difficult aspect of Blake's mythology, which is that his four primal titans, put together again, would constitute one Human Form Divine, a Hermetic pre-Adamic god-man, is hinted at throughout Lindsay's book, though perhaps without Lindsay's own full awareness. One of the curious aesthetic strengths of *Arcturus* is Lindsay's relative freedom from self-consciousness. He gives the impression of never quite knowing where his book is going: Maskull marches always north, in a hidden, intuitive drive toward the Muspel light, while Krag vanishes and reappears with a sublime willfulness. The effect is of Schiller's "naive" rather than "sentimental" romance; episodes proliferate and throw off long shadows of significances, which sometimes consolidate into a profound visionary meaning, and sometimes fall away as mythic exuberances in excess of the story's demands.

I find frequently that *Arcturus* comes back to me by involuntary recall, even in my reveries or in dreams and nightmares. The book works upon one like a trauma, that is, like the action of the Muspel light, which is both destructive and benign. Nightspore, in the extraordinary conclusion of *Arcturus,* returns with the death of Maskull, in order to face the ordeal of rebirth, which in Lindsay's cosmos is more horrible than death. Enduring the physical and psychic distress of clambering up the final tower, Nightspore finally pulls his body up and stands on the stone-floored roof, expecting to gaze upon Muspel, the divine light, for the first time. He sees *nothing,* until he realizes that the darkness around him, on every side, is mocking him, grinning in its apparent triumph:

> As soon as that happened, he understood that he was wholly surrounded
> by Crystalman's worlds, and that Muspel consisted of himself and the
> stone tower on which he was sitting . . .

This seems to me one of the pure visions of a modern Sublime, with the Promethean quester replaced by a consciousness that learns the negativity of the gnosis still possible in a ruined universe: there is only oneself, the empty roof of the tower, and a demiurgical darkness obscenely rejoicing against one. After that confrontation, the stoical Nightspore bleakly returns to the struggle, descending from the tower to push off on Krag's raft into the dark waters of what the ancient Gnostics called the *kenoma,* the sensible emptiness of our lives.

—H. B.

Ray Bradbury
b. 1920

RAYMOND DOUGLAS BRADBURY was born on August 22, 1920, in Waukegan, Illinois, the first child of Leonard Spaulding Bradbury, an electrical lineman whose family tree included an ancestor hanged as a witch during the Salem witch trials, and Esther Moberg Bradbury. Bradbury lived a happy childhood soaking up the sights and atmosphere of his rural midwestern town. His love of fantasy began with a viewing of *The Hunchback of Notre Dame* with Lon Chaney in 1923 and was reinforced by his discovery of the science fiction magazine *Amazing Stories* in 1929. His interest in writing was stimulated by family members reading the works of L. Frank Baum and Edgar Allan Poe to him, and later by his acquaintance with the work of Thomas Wolfe.

In 1934 Bradbury moved with his family to Los Angeles, where he was introduced to science fiction fandom through new friends Leigh Brackett and Henry Kuttner. Upon graduating from high school he supported himself selling newspapers and wrote prodigiously. His first professional fiction sale, a collaboration with Henry Hasse entitled "Pendulum," appeared in *Super Science Stories* in 1941. Shortly thereafter Bradbury became a regular contributor to *Weird Tales*, where his evocative tales of the dark side of small-town life were hailed as a turning point in weird fiction, hitherto dominated by excesses of the Gothic style. The best of these stories were collected in his first book, *Dark Carnival* (1947), the contents of which were modified and reprinted as *The October Country* (1955). In 1947 he married Marguerite McClure, with whom he would have four children.

In the late 1940s Bradbury began sending *Planet Stories, Thrilling Wonder Stories*, and other pulp science fiction magazines interplanetary adventures more concerned with human conflict than the scientific extrapolation by which the genre was defined. In 1950 he assembled many of these stories into *The Martian Chronicles*, an episodic first novel about mankind's colonization of Mars that helped to bring science fiction to the attention of the literary mainstream. Although Bradbury's collections *The Illustrated Man* (1951) and *The Golden Apples of the Sun* (1953) and his dystopic novel

1

Fahrenheit 451 (1953) were reviewed enthusiastically in the leading periodicals of the day, they were often scorned by science fiction purists.

Bradbury continued to branch out in his writing, adapting his stories for comic books, editing the contemporary fantasy anthologies *Timeless Stories for Today and Tomorrow* (1952) and *The Circus of Dr. Lao and Other Improbable Stories* (1956), producing a children's book, *Switch On the Night* (1955), and writing the screenplay for John Huston's film of *Moby Dick* (1956). In 1957 he turned a number of his nonfantastic stories into the novel *Dandelion Wine*, a nostalgic paean to childish innocence and imagination. *Something Wicked This Way Comes* (1962), about a sinister traveling carnival that almost steals the souls of two young boys on the brink of manhood, further explored many of the themes addressed in *Dandelion Wine*. With the later novels *Death Is a Lonely Business* (1985), *A Graveyard for Lunatics* (1990), and *Green Shadows, White Whale* (1992), these books constitute a fictional autobiography in which Bradbury traces the persistence of youthful imagination into adulthood.

Since the 1960s, Bradbury has concentrated increasingly on poetry and drama. His many adaptations of his stories to the stage have been collected as *Ray Bradbury on Stage: A Chrestomathy of His Plays* (1991) and his poetry has been published in several volumes, beginning with *When Elephants Last in the Dooryard Bloomed* (1973) and culminating in *Complete Poems* (1982). His screenplays include *It Came from Outer Space* (1963) and the Oscar-nominated *Icarus Montgolfier Wright* (1962); screen adaptations of Bradbury's work by others includemn François Truffaut's 1966 film of *Fahrenheit 451*, several episodes of Rod Serling's "The Twilight Zone," and the 1980 television miniseries based on *The Martian Chronicles*. Bradbury is a recipient of numerous awards, including the Science Fiction Writers of America's Nebula Grand Master Award and the World Fantasy Award for lifetime achievement. His literary influence can be found in the writing of Richard Matheson, William F. Nolan, Charles Beaumont, Dennis Etchison, and many other leading fantasists of the day.

▨ *Critical Extracts*

RAY BRADBURY   Some of my first memories concern going upstairs at night and finding an unpleasant beast waiting at the next to the last step. Screaming, I'd run back down to mother. Then, together, we'd climb the stairs. Invariably, the monster would be gone. Mother never saw it. Sometimes I was irritated at her lack of imagination.

I imagine I should be thankful for my fear of the dark, though. You have to know fear and apprehension in some form before you can write about it thoroughly, and God knows my first ten years were full of the usual paraphernalia of ghosts and skeletons and dead men tumbling down the twisting interior of my mind. What a morbid little brat I must have been to have around. ⟨. . .⟩

My urge for the unusual was stimulated first by the Oz books, then by Tarzan, then Buck Rogers, and finally the weird and fantasy publications. Every action of my life thereafter seemed to point inevitably to my writing the more outré kinds of fiction.

I'd like to continue along the line where I've begun my story series. I don't particularly care about ghosts, vampires or werewolves; they've been killed by repetition. Lovecraft, Poe and C. A. Smith are the rare ones who did a splendid job by them. There are plenty of good stories in neurotic psychology ready to be used. There are good stories in everyday things. Trains, crowds, motor-cars, submarines, dogs—the wind around the house. I'd like to use them more. And there's much good stuff buried in the green leafs of childhood and the heaped dead leafs of old age. I want to get at that, too. I want to write about humans; and add an unusual, unexpected twist.

Ray Bradbury, "The Eyrie," Weird Tales 37, No. 2 (November 1943): 109–10

WILL CUPPY   Are you a scoffer at the weird, as they call it? Have you ever become fatigued when reading childishly bad imitations of the most regrettable side of Edgar Allan Poe? Well, here's a big helping of the stuff that may hold you in spite of your mean disposition, by a fairly new writer of same who has obviously been tapped by leaders of the cult for the mantle of the late H. P. Lovecraft. Ray Bradbury, a youth of twenty-seven, who has already achieved publications in several magazines outside the pulp field, is something special, perhaps the first of the high-pressure weirdists suitable for general consumption. You'll see what we mean if you peruse "The Homecoming," the first of the twenty-seven tales in the volume.

If "The Homecoming" strikes your funny bone, indeed sounds like libretto to the drawings of Charles Addams, think no harm. There is more than the hint of a smile in Mr. Bradbury's fantastic exhibits and don't tell us it is unintentional. Exclusive prediction about this author: Mr. Bradbury will gradually move away from the weirder weird, having already dropped much of the piffle pertaining thereunto, in accordance with the fine art of omission and a robust sense of fun which will one day turn on those protoplasmic blobs and annihilate them. The weird fans will then hate him as a traitor to the cause and he will move serenely onward and up in the general direction of the John Collier bracket. But it will take practice. For one thing, he'll have to make his critters, human or diabolical, stop staring like rubber stamps (they can stare, too) in the lower depths of whodunitism. Please, Mr. Bradbury!

> Will Cuppy, [Review of *Dark Carnival*], *New York Herald Tribune Books*, 25 May 1947, p. 30

CHRISTOPHER ISHERWOOD   The best of this new generation of science-fiction writers are highly sensitive and intelligent. They are under no illusions about the prospective blessings of a machine-age utopia. They do not gape at gadgets with adoring wonder. Their approach to the inhabitants of others worlds is anthropological and nonviolent. They owe more to Aldous Huxley than to Jules Verne or H. G. Wells. Insofar as the reading public is turning to them and forsaking the cops and the cowboys, the public is growing up.

This is not to suggest, however, that Ray Bradbury can be classified simply as a science-fiction writer, even a superlatively good one. *Dark Carnival*, his earlier book of stories, showed that his talents can function equally well within comparatively realistic settings. If one must attach labels, I suppose he might be called a writer of fantasy, and his stories "tales of the grotesque and the arabesque" in the sense in which those words are used by Poe. Poe's name comes up almost inevitably, in any discussion of Mr. Bradbury's work; not because Mr. Bradbury is an imitator (though he is certainly a disciple) but because he already deserves to be measured against the greater master of his particular genre.

It may even be argued that *The Martian Chronicles* are not, strictly speaking, science fiction at all. The most firmly established convention of science fiction is that its writers shall use all their art to convince us that their stories *could* happen. The extraordinary must grow from roots in the ordinary. The scientific "explanations" must have an authoritative air. (There are, as a matter of fact, some science-fiction writers whose work is so full of abstruse technicalities that only connoisseurs can read it.) Such is not Mr. Bradbury's practice. His brilliant, shameless fantasy makes, and needs, no excuses for its wild jumps from the possible to the impossible. His interest in machines seems to be limited to their symbolic and aesthetic aspects. I doubt if he could pilot a rocketship, much less design one.

Christopher Isherwood, [Review of *The Martian Chronicles*], *Tomorrow* 10, No. 2 (October 1950): 56–57

AVRAM DAVIDSON   This most recent of Bradbury's novels ⟨*Something Wicked This Way Comes*⟩ combines two of Bradbury's favorite themes: his deep and undoubtedly sincere love for the Midwestern small town of bygone years, and his fascination with the sideshow (rather, perhaps, than the circus or carnival *per se*) as an antic mirror of the human and inhuman scene. I might really say it weaves in a third favorite Bradbury motif, that of Boyhood. "A three-fold cord is not easily broken," observes Proverbs, and those multitudes who love Ray Bradbury's writings on any theme with a warm and uncritical love, will certainly be enchanted and swept away. I would hazard that this is true of Bradbury-prone reader-types. Both groups will probably devour it whole at one ensorceled sitting. Those to whom Ray Bradbury's name is like bandilleras to a bull will, of course, charge and trample the book down with shouts of triumph to the effect that he is repeating himself, that he has become the prisoner of his own style, that he comes perilously close to self-parody. But there is a third alignment, in which I find myself. I would gladly be once again in the first category, if I could. I acknowledge some measure of truth in the shouts of the second. But there remains so much that is rich and strange, so much that awakens echoes of the uncritical, magical, Bradburian past, in this book—this book about thirteen-year-old comrades Jim Nightshade and Will Halloway, and of the devilish and timeless travelling show—and it is so much of an improvement in construction over *Dandelion Wine* (the previous Bradbury novel) that I justify my pleasure and allay my discomfort with this: Bradbury has not yet mastered the technique of the novel, as he has more than mastered that of the short story, but there is hope and evidence

here that he will. It would be more than a shame if we were to be disappointed.

Avram Davidson, [Review of *Something Wicked This Way Comes*], *Magazine of Fantasy and Science Fiction* 25, No. 1 (July 1963): 105–6

RUSSELL KIRK   In Bradbury's fables of Mars and of the carnival,
fantasy has become what it was in the beginning: the enlightening moral
imagination, transcending simple rationality. The everyday world is not the
real world, for today's events are merely a film upon the deep well of the
past, and they will be swallowed up by the unknowable future. The real
world is the world of the permanent things, which often are discerned more
clearly in the fictional dead cities of Mars or the fictional carousel of Cooger
and Dark than in our own little private slice of evanescent experience.
And—what is a wondrous thing in itself—the new generations of Americans
are not blind to the truth of the fabulists, for Bradbury is their favorite
author.

The trappings of science fiction may have attracted young people to
Bradbury, but he has led them on to something much older and better:
mythopoeic literature, normative truth acquired through wonder. Bradbury's
stories are not an escape from reality; they are windows looking upon
enduring reality. As C. S. Lewis remarks, those who attack the fantasy
of moral imagination as trifling or baneful "escape literature" have shut
themselves up in Bentham's Panopticon. The ideologue, in particular,
denounces "escape"; for he is the prisoner of his own political obsessions,
and misery loves company. Lewis writes that he never fully understood this
denunciation of "escape," this hatred of mythopoeic literature, "till my
friend Professor Tolkien asked me the very simple question, 'What class of
men would you expect to be most preoccupied with, and most hostile to,
the idea of escape?' and gave the obvious answer: jailers . . . But there is
perhaps this truth behind it: that those who brood much on the remote
past or future, or stare long at the night sky, are less likely than others to
be ardent or orthodox partisans."

Bradbury, with Lewis and Tolkien and Collier and some few others, is
nobody's prisoner and nobody's jailer. For our modern fabulists have made
a breach in Giant Despair's castle.

Russell Kirk, "The World of Ray Bradbury," *Enemies of Permanent Things* (New Rochelle, NY: Arlington House, 1969), pp. 123–24

BRIAN ATTEBERY   The horror story depends on things remaining one sided, but fantasy demands both black magic and white. What Bradbury did, in *Something Wicked*, was use the conventions of gothic horror as a doorway to fantasy. All that needed to be done was to turn the fallible protagonist of horror fiction into a true fairy tale hero, someone the readers can root for and someone capable of striking back against dark gods, of stealing away a few of their prerogatives like the working of wonders.

One has the sense that the invasion of the dark carnival has results not intended by its owners. Its arrival throws things off balance, disturbs the established fabric of life. When the Tarot witch works her spells, when the carousel plays with time, they create a negative electric charge, as it were, like the charge the lightning-rod man senses building up in Jim Nightshade's house at the book's beginning. Because nature abhors imbalance, a corresponding charge begins to build in answer to the negative. The witch wakes inanimate objects to their potential power to do her bidding, but the waking proves contagious, spreading to objects not in her control. Evil gestures and incantations serve to bring out the magic in kindly acts and words. *Dandelion Wine* pointed out a great many of the rituals that develop in families and among friends: some of the same kinds of rituals reappear in *Something Wicked* with an added aura of the supernatural.

Will's father discovers that the carnival draws its strength from fear and sorrow, leaving it vulnerable to smiles and laughter. Those become the weapons of good, lent potency by the very evils they combat. A smile carved on a wax bullet kills the witch. The laughter of Will and his father brings Jim back from the edge, or beyond the edge, of death.

The book's happy ending, though not arrived at by the route followed in fairy tales, is appropriate to the characters involved, to the plot and to the meanings carried on the plot. The greatest threat to the confidence-man, says Bradbury through his fantasy, is the confidence to resist his lures, and death is most terrible when we try hardest to deny it. High themes can grow from humble memories, if one has the trick of it. Bradbury's memories, with help from Lovecraft, Burroughs, Melville, and especially Baum, shape themselves into stories with the authority of archetypes.

Brian Attebery, *The Fantasy Tradition in American Literature from Irving to Le Guin* (Bloomington: Indiana University Press, 1980), pp. 139–40

STEPHEN KING   More clearly than any other book discussed here, *Something Wicked This Way Comes* reflects the differences between the Apollonian life and the Dionysian. Bradbury's carnival, which creeps inside the town limits and sets up shop in a meadow at three o'clock in the morning (Fitzgerald's dark night of the soul, if you like), is a symbol of everything that is abnormal, mutated, monstrous . . . Dionysian. I've always wondered if the appeal of the vampire myth for children doesn't lie partly in the simple fact that vampires get to sleep all day and stay up all night (vampires never have to miss Creature Features at midnight because of school the next day). Similarly, we now know that part of this carnival's attraction for Jim and Will (sure, Will feels its pull too, although not as strongly as Jim feels it; even Will's father is not entirely immune to its deadly siren song) is that there will be no set bedtimes, no rules and regulations, no dull and boring small town day after day, no "eat your broccoli, think of people starving in China," no school. The carnival is chaos, it is taboo land made magically portable, traveling from place to place and even from time to time with its freight of freaks and its glamorous attractions.

The boys (sure, Jim too) represent just the opposite. They are normal, not monstrous. They live their lives by the rules of the sunlit world, Will willingly, Jim impatiently. Which is exactly why the carnival wants them. The essence of evil, Bradbury suggests, is its need to compromise and corrupt that delicate passage from innocence to experience that all children must make. In the rigid moral world of Bradbury's fiction, the freaks who populate the carnival have taken on the outward shapes of their inward vices. Mr. Cooger, who has lived for thousands of years, pays for his life of dark degeneracy by becoming a Thing even more ancient, ancient almost beyond our ability to comprehend, kept alive by a steady flow of electricity. The Human Skeleton is paying for miserliness of feeling; the fat lady for physical or emotional gluttony; the dust witch for her gossipy meddling in the lives of others. The carnival has done to them what the undertaker in that old Bradbury story ⟨"The Handler"⟩ did to his victims after they had died.

On its Apollonian side, the book asks us to recall and reexamine the facts and myths of our own childhoods, most specifically our small-town American childhoods. Written in a semipoetic style that seems to suit such concerns perfectly, Bradbury examines these childhood concerns and comes to the conclusion that only children are equipped to deal with childhood's myths and terrors and exhalations.

Stephen King, *Danse Macabre* (New York: Everest House, 1981), pp. 310–11

DAVID MOGEN   *The Halloween Tree* is a quest story overtly designed to dramatize mythological history and to advance a theory asserting the fundamental importance of Halloween, horror stories, and fantasy in general. The boys themselves, caught up in the pageantry of the Mexican festival, draw part of the moral. Though Green Town still celebrates Halloween much of its meaning and spirit have been lost, and the loss is profound: "Up in Illinois, we've forgotten what it's all about. I mean the dead, up in our town, tonight, heck, they're forgotten. . . . Boy, that's lonely. That's really sad. But here—why, shucks. It's both happy and sad. It's all fireworks and skeleton toys down here."

Through visceral experience of the meanings of the symbols and rituals from which their costumes originated, through direct exposure to the cultural contexts that created them, the boys now know that symbols of death and horror stories actually help humanize our relationship with the unknown. More appalling than any of the grisly and haunting images they encounter is the spiritual poverty of simply denying Death's presence. Not actually death itself but a symbol to represent strategies for emotionally coping with death, Moundshroud inspires both awe and affection. Representing the power of mythology in the figure of a teacher, he helps them face and penetrate the overwhelming mysteries of that "unknown country" from whose bourne no real traveler returns, but from which harrowed mythic travelers return in mythologies throughout history. ⟨. . .⟩

Bradbury proposes two major arguments to support his defense of our symbols of evil, both dramatized in *The Halloween Tree*. One argument is aesthetic: these symbols are intrinsically powerful; they move our souls to awe and wonder. But the other derives from "practical hair-ball psychology"—for knowledge of death is a loathsome hair-ball in all our throats, and only through imaginative encounters with it do we digest what we can and purge ourselves of the rest. The mythical, fantastical tradition of horror inoculates us to endure contact with the reality and survive emotionally intact. "To fantasize is to remain sane," he maintains, contrasting the wondrous horror and release provided by stories of Dracula and the Wolf Man with the unrelieved horror of such modern realist films as *Our Man Flint*, where we see toilet paper pile up around the feet of the dying victim, where there is no imaginative release from the tyranny of gruesome reportage. "Instead of imagination, we are treated to fact, to pure raw data, which cannot be digested." Ultimately, Bradbury's defense of fantasy is an undoctrinal defense of the role of mythologies and religions in general: "Our religions, our tribal as well as personal myths, tried to find symbols then for the vacuum, the void. . . . We had to know. We had to lie, and accept the lie of labels and names, even while we knew we lied. . . . Thus we gave gifts of names to ward off the night."

David Mogen, *Ray Bradbury* (Boston: Twayne, 1986), pp. 60–62

WILLIAM F. TOUPONCE   The plot ⟨of "Pillar of Fire"⟩ is fantastic in construction, made so that readers hesitate between a supernatural and a scientific explanation of the uncanny events that happen when William Lantry is reborn in the year of 2349 A.D. Is Lantry really one of the walking dead, or is he an extraordinary case of suspended animation? Appropriately, the answer to this question (the former) is set in Salem where the last graveyard had been preserved as a tourist attraction by the government as a reminder of a barbaric custom. Now this graveyard is scheduled by the government for destruction as well. The government seeks thereby to make its control over the world of darkness, death, decay (and of all writers whose imaginations are attracted to it) absolute. The society Lantry is reborn into is, therefore, an extreme Apollonian culture, as is evident from the symbolism it employs. It worships the sun of rationality, emblazoned everywhere on public buildings. The dead of this society are burned in "Incinerators," which are warm cozy temples where soothing music plays and the fear of death is abolished through ceremonies that deify fire. As Lantry watches, slowly the golden coffins of the dead roll in covered with sun symbols, and after a brief ceremony, they are cast into a flue. On the altar are written the words "We that are born of the sun return to the sun," a fantastic reversal of the words normally spoken at Christian burials.

It is these gigantic Incinerators as myths of an Apollonian culture that Lantry wants to explode, and does, killing hundreds of people in the surrounding towns. He hopes thereby to effect a revolution, to win converts to his cause by creating more walking dead. But in this rational world the dead remain dead. Because they never believed in vampires while living, they cannot be resurrected by Lantry's magical procedures later (he draws symbols of long-dead sorcerers on the floor of the makeshift morgue and chants his own formulas, to no avail). Eventually, he is picked up by the authorities and is interrogated by a man named McClure who is this century's representative of psychoanalysis and something of a detective as well.

McClure tries to analyze Lantry's mortified behavior, his paleness and lack of breath, as a self-induced psychosis but is himself slowly unnerved when he finds that Lantry is the real thing, one of the walking dead. Lantry is a logical impossibility to a mind such as McClure's. Lantry is, therefore, condemned to a second death by the State, a death which is the death of every fantastic writer in history, since only Lantry remembers them. If this were a Christian fantasy in the mode of J. R. R. Tolkien or C. S. Lewis, the evident compassion of McClure for his victim would have resulted in his conversion to the imagination at the end, thereby saving it. But no, Bradbury really wants us to feel the shock of seeing the imagination die forever, and on this level of response, the story is quite effective. The second death, the death of the imagination, becomes more terrible than real death.

> William F. Touponce, *Ray Bradbury* (Mercer Island, WA: Starmont House, 1989), pp. 87–88

STEFAN DZIEMIANOWICZ   In the two dozen stories he wrote for *Weird Tales* between 1942 and 1948, Bradbury shifted the focus of horror from monster-driven tales of the supernatural to dark fables that turned the everyday into the stuff of myth: in "The Scythe", he imagined a farmer harvesting his crops as the grim reaper incarnate; in "Emissary", a faithful dog becomes an agent for resurrecting the dead; in "Skeleton", he reminded us that we all carry a prop of Gothic horror inside us. The process by which Bradbury wrought these transformations, his fictionalized self reminds us in *Death Is a Lonely Business*, is simple recognition of the fantastic possibilities in ordinary things that most people take for granted ⟨. . .⟩

Bradbury achieved this interpenetration of the fantastic and the familiar by infusing his stories with an almost childish sense of wonder that blurs the boundaries between the natural and supernatural. *Death Is a Lonely Business* (originally published in 1985) and *A Graveyard for Lunatics* (originally published in 1990) are, after *Dandelion Wine* (1957) and *Something Wicked This Way Comes* (1962), the third and fourth installments, respectively, in his fictional autobiography (the fifth installment, *Green Shadows, White Whale*, was published in 1992), which is concerned in large part with how he has managed to preserve that childish imagination over the decades.

Both novels are mysteries with supernatural overtones. In the former, a writer of pulp horror stories nicknamed "The Crazy" must figure out why all his friends—a Dickensian cast of eccentrics that includes a 380-pound opera buff and an ageing actor with the face of a codger and the body of a young Adonis—are dying under mysterious circumstances. The latter, about a movie studio where characters manipulate Hollywood make-believe to carry on an intrigue that seems to be equal parts *The Phantom of the Opera* and *The Hunchback of Notre Dame*, is something of a riff on Bradbury's short story "The Night Sets", in which a man who takes refuge in an abandoned movie backlot actually turns into a prop. Neither novel has much of a plot, but then one doesn't turn to Bradbury for plot; one turns for passages like this:

> The long chattering clack and grind, the ascending slow clang, rattle, and roar, like some robot centipede of immense size scaling the side of a nightmare, pausing at the top for the merest breath, then cascading in a serpentine squeal, rush, and thunderous roar, in scream, in human shriek down the abysmal span, there to attack, more swiftly this time, another hill, another ascending scale rising yet higher and higher to fall off into hysteria.

That, in case you didn't know, is a rendering of the Venice Beach roller coaster. Descriptions like this, or of telephone booths seen by night as "unlit caskets, waiting to be taken away", abound in both books. They're not really enough to sustain the two novels, but in quantity they infuse sufficient magic into the stories to divert reader attention from their self-indulgent style and puerile moralizing.

Stefan Dziemianowicz, "Back to the Future," *Necrofile* No. 9 (Summer 1993): 24

❖ *Bibliography*

Dark Carnival. 1947.
The Martian Chronicles. 1950.
The Illustrated Man. 1951.
Timeless Stories for Today and Tomorrow (editor). 1952.
No Man Is an Island. 1952.
The Golden Apples of the Sun. 1953.
Fahrenheit 451. 1953.
Switch On the Night. 1955.

The October Country. 1955.

The Circus of Dr. Lao and Other Improbable Stories (editor). 1956.

Sun and Shadow. 1957.

Dandelion Wine. 1957.

A Medicine for Melancholy. 1959.

The Essence of Creative Writing. 1962.

Something Wicked This Way Comes. 1962.

R Is for Rocket. 1962.

The Anthem Sprinters and Other Antics. 1963.

The Machineries of Joy. 1964.

The Pedestrian. 1964.

The Vintage Bradbury: Ray Bradbury's Own Selection of His Best Stories. 1965.

Twice Twenty-two ⟨*The Golden Apples of the Sun, A Medicine for Melancholy*⟩. 1966.

The Day It Rained Forever. 1966.

The Pedestrian (drama). 1966.

S Is for Space. 1966.

Teacher's Guide: Science Fiction (with Lewy Olfson). 1968.

I Sing the Body Electric! 1969.

Bloch and Bradbury (with Robert Bloch). Ed. Kurt Singer. 1969.

Old Ahab's Friend, and Friend to Noah, Speaks His Peace: A Celebration. 1971.

The Wonderful Ice-Cream Suit and Other Plays. 1972.

The Halloween Tree. 1972.

Zen and the Art of Writing and The Joy of Writing: Two Essays. 1973.

When Elephants Last in the Dooryard Bloomed: Celebrations for Almost Any Day in the Year. 1973.

That Son of Richard III: A Birth Announcement. 1974.

Ray Bradbury. Ed. Anthony Adams. 1975.

Kaleidoscope. 1975.

Pillar of Fire and Other Plays for Today, Tomorrow, and Beyond Tomorrow. 1975.

1984 Will Not Arrive: A Prediction for the Greening of Scripps. 1975.

Long After Midnight. 1976.

That Ghost, That Bride of Time: Excerpts from a Play-in-Progress Based on the Moby Dick Mythology and Dedicated to Herman Melville. 1976.

Something Wicked This Way Comes: Second Draft Screenplay. 1976.

Where Robot Mice and Robot Men Run Round in Robot Towns: New Poems, Both Light and Dark. 1977.

Man Dead? Then God Is Slain! A Celebration. 1977.

The God in Science Fiction. c. 1977.

The Bike Repairman. 1978.

Twin Hieroglyphs That Swim the River Dust. 1978.

The Mummies of Guanajuato. 1978.

The Poet Considers His Resources. 1979.

Beyond 1984: A Remembrance of Things Future. 1979.

To Sing Strange Songs. 1979.

About Norman Corwin. 1979.

This Attic where the Meadow Greens. 1979.

The Aqueduct: A Martian Chronicle. 1979.

The Stories of Ray Bradbury. 1980.

The Last Circus and The Electrocution. 1980.

Imagine. 1981.

The Haunted Computer and the Android Pope. 1981.

The Ghosts of Forever. 1981.

The Flying Machine. 1981.

Complete Poems. 1982.

The Love Affair: A Short Story; and Two Poems. 1982.

Dinosaur Tales. 1983.

October. 1983.

Forever and the Earth. 1984.

A Memory of Murder. 1984.

The Last Good Kiss. 1984.

Novels ⟨Fahrenheit 451, Dandelion Wine, Something Wicked This Way Comes⟩.
     1984.

Death Is a Lonely Business. 1985.

A Device out of Time. 1986.

Death Has Lost Its Charm for Me. 1987.

Fever Dream. 1987.

The Other Foot. 1987.

The Veldt. 1987.

The April Witch. 1988.

The Toynbee Convector. 1988.

The Fog Horn. 1988.

The Dragon. 1988.

The Fog Horn and Other Stories. 1989.

Classic Stories. 1990. 2 vols.

A Graveyard for Lunatics: Another Tale of Two Cities. 1990.
Zen in the Art of Writing. 1990.
Ray Bradbury on Stage: A Chrestomathy of His Plays. 1991.
The Smile. 1991.
Yestermorrow: Obvious Answers to Impossible Futures. 1991.
Green Shadows, White Whale. 1992.
The Stars. 1993.

John Collier
1901–1980

JOHN HENRY NOYES COLLIER was born in London on May 3, 1901, the son of John George and Emily Mary Noyes Collier. Although Collier's father had connections with royalty, he was very poor and was forced to work as a clerk. Collier's formal education was sporadic and he was largely tutored by his uncle, the minor novelist Vincent Collier. Because of his love of books, however, he gained a considerable self-education in English literature, especially of the eighteenth century.

Collier initially wished to be a poet, and in 1922 he was the recipient of a poetry prize by *This Quarter* magazine. By this time he had also become a reviewer and journalist for *Time and Tide,* the *Daily Telegraph,* and other magazines and newspapers. By the end of the decade, however, Collier had wearied of London and he moved to the country. Here he wrote *His Monkey Wife* (1930), his first novel, a curious light fantasy about a man who marries a chimpanzee. Although well received in English literary circles, the novel garnered mixed reviews in America.

Collier's one volume of poetry, *Gemini,* was published by a small press in 1931, and *Just the Other Day: An Informal History of Great Britain Since the War,* written in collaboration with Iain Lang, appeared in 1932. Collier's second novel, *Tom's a-Cold* (1933; published in the U.S. as *Full Circle*), describing an England following a devastating war, was a critical success, as was his next novel, *Defy the Foul Fiend* (1934), a picaresque novel written in an eighteenth-century style.

At this point in his career Collier turned his attention to two literary forms that would bring him the greatest renown: short stories and screenplays. He had begun writing short stories as early as 1926, and a few of them were published separately as chapbooks in the early 1930s. Collier's first collection of tales is *The Devil and All* (1934). In 1935 Collier left England and, after a brief stay in France, came to Hollywood. For the next seven years he lived alternately in England, France, New York, and California until finally settling down in California in 1942. He remained there for the next eleven years, writing the screenplays for *Sylvia Scarlett* (1936), *Elephant Boy* (1937), *Deception* (1946), and other films. Collier wrote the original script for *The African Queen*, but it was not used and the final version bears little resemblance to his.

Meanwhile Collier's short stories had been appearing regularly in the *New Yorker*, *Playboy*, and other prestigious and well-paying magazines. The collection *Presenting Moonshine* (1941) introduced to an American audience a writer of tales of mystery, horror, and fantasy full of dry wit, pungent misanthropy, and an enviable command of short story technique. Other collections include *The Touch of Nutmeg* (1943), *Fancies and Goodnights* (1951), and *Pictures in the Fire* (1958).

In 1953 Collier, wishing to avoid the anti-Communist witch-hunts of the McCarthy era and tiring of the lack of respect accorded his screenplays, left Hollywood for Mexico, where he married Harriet Hess in 1954; they had one son. The next year he purchased an estate in Grasse, France, where he lived for the next twenty-four years. *The John Collier Reader* (1972), a large collection of his short stories, fleetingly revived interest in his work; and the next year he published the eccentric *Milton's Paradise Lost: A Screenplay for Cinema of the Mind*. In 1979 Collier moved back to California to work on a stage version of this work, but he died in Pacific Palisades on April 6, 1980. Much of Collier's work has fallen out of print, but his short stories and *His Monkey Wife* retain a following among readers of fantasy and horror.

▧ *Critical Extracts*

UNSIGNED   Although this modern satirical rendition of the story of Cinderella ⟨*His Monkey Wife*⟩ has been hailed as vastly amusing by English critics, it is doubtful whether many Americans will split their sides over it. It is a curious mixture of the burlesque and the extravaganza, satirizing "this age, when men are what they are, and when so few women are what they were." Like most humorists, the author is measurably misanthropic, and when he casts his eyes on England's "first-class Nordic chivalry, on brave women and fair men," he finds them all very vulgar. ⟨. . .⟩

The subject of his mockery, in this case, is literary rather than social. *His Monkey Wife* takes a crack in passing at that broad but empty school of English literature, which is based on the sentimental love-in-the-jungle theme, the shopgirl school of virtue-triumphant-down-the-ages, and the precocious chatter of Mayfair and Chelsea. The mood is, however, nowhere sustained, and the greater part of the book is simply amusingly silly. It is a light-hearted reductio ad absurdum of the whole "struggle-of-the-sexes" idea which underlies far too much of Western fiction. Mr. Collier takes one of the elements of the eternal triangle, turns her into a chimpanzee, and tries out the result in all the stock literary equations.

Unsigned, "War of the Sexes," *New York Times Book Review,* 19 April 1931, p. 7

JOHN COLLIER   As a writer, my position is a difficult one. I cannot see much good in the world, nor much likelihood of good. There seems to me to be a definite bias in human nature towards ill, towards the immediate convenience, the vulgar, the cheap: a sort of stick whose fall into darkness must be the end of every rocket-like ascent from pleasant, grunting savagery. I cannot therefore believe very enthusiastically in myself or in my fellow men, for we are past the starry stage. I would rather probe the beating heart of humanity with a bodkin than with a pen. And, as the love borne to Mary by her lamb is said to have been of the responsive kind, it is hardly to be expected that the sheep will love one who bears them no sort of good-will. In fact, to be perfectly frank, I have become so ill-natured, that, looking on their Press, their pylons, their picture-palaces, their politics, I no longer feel in earnest remonstrative mood, like a little self-constituted good shepherd, nor inclined to the brisk satirical bark, like the frisking dog; but I rub my hands, and say, "Hurry up, you foulers of a good world, and destroy yourselves faster. Flock to be clerks and counter-jumpers and factory hands. Eat your tinned food. Build yourselves more of the houses, reach-me-downs, faces, lives, which express your single soul so well. Read your newspapers: they will tell you you are all right, that you should breed. They would tell the rats so, if they grew up to be certified readers. Spoil every good thing that stands in the way of trade, and praise every ill thing that can be made and sold, for, for the time being, it gives you license to spawn the more. You evil sheep, whom Shakespeare would have led, and Swift barked back from destruction, you choose your nasty progress into comfort, a swinish choice, and you have become swine, suicidal swine, thank God! on the Gadarene cliff of self-deception. Rush down it, into the sea, and, as swimming pigs are said to do, cut your own (or each other's) throats and be forgotten."

⟨. . .⟩ There are two sorts of prose: the impressionistic, in which you give yourself up to the subject, the human heart or the light on the tree, and the other sort, Burton's sort, Fielding's sort, in which you hold your puppet-subject at arm's length, give it a jerk or two, then, laying it down, you lean across the table, and with smile or leer address your ideal auditor direct, as one good fellow to another. Impressionistic prose has been most worked on lately: too much worked on. ⟨. . .⟩ The other sort is capable of quite a lot of development, and anyway I like it best. I wonder if, supposing I work hard for ten years, I shall find myself at forty in a position to write it well. That would be worth doing. Meanwhile I'll put some plots and things into my experiments, and by that means get some money.

John Collier, "Please Excuse Me, Comrade," cited in John Gawsworth, *Ten Contemporaries: Notes toward Their Definitive Bibliography: Second Series* (London: Joiner & Steele, 1933), pp. 109–11.

DAVID GARNETT   When I had read a few pages of *Tom's a-Cold*, by John Collier, I thought that the author of that highly original book *His Monkey Wife* had given us another *After London*. For Mr. Collier has taken the alarmists, who predict the collapse of civilisation, at their word and has drawn England in the nineteen nineties when, after wars, plagues, and famines have done their worst, what is left is almost exactly like what ⟨Richard⟩ Jefferies described in the Relapse into Barbarism, the first part of *After London*. The towns are in ruins, the rivers have been choked up in swamps, the forests have extended to twenty times their size; the cats have reverted to the grey brindled wild cat; dogs, horses and cattle are all wild. There is a talk of wolves, which shows that Whipsnade has been working well, and man himself has become a savage beast. But where Jefferies presented us with a sentimentalised feudalism, Mr. Collier shows us verminous and lonely groups of outlaws, who subsist on rabbits, and when undisturbed are able to grow a few potatoes. The more sordid and hopeless the surroundings, the more necessary it seems to give the reader a really heroic hero. Here we are given a magnificent young aspirant to the chiefdom who is coached by the oldest member of the clan—who, it is odd to reflect, must be living amongst us somewhere and just beginning to study Greek.

Mr. Collier says in an Introduction:

> To describe emotions and events totally incompatible with
> present-day life here it was absolutely necessary to choose some
> other scene: the question was—When or where?

He looked about—to Neolithic times and to savage islands, but these had their drawbacks, so he chose the setting of this tale. Thus the book is not written out of a deep emotion of hatred as Jefferies wrote, nor out of a deep conviction such as H. G. Wells would have brought to it. This is fatal. The clan has a tradition of the finer things of life, represented by the memories and the knowledge of the classics, of the old man. Unfortunately when it comes to a test, the finer things of life come to mean no more than the ability to murder a sick man under the pretence of healing him, and primitive contraptions for staging a terrific massacre of the Swindon folk which would have looked well in a book by Rider Haggard, but which is out of place here. The entire absence of nobility nullifies the sympathy we are expected to feel for the father. The descendants of a curate and a girl-guide would have been worth all this ignoble clan and we might have wept on seeing them kneeling on the rabbit-bitten turf. It was a mistake to leave out religion and morality; they were necessary, and the conditions would have produced them. It was also a mistake to let the second generation revert to the Intelligentsia and begin to discuss each other's motives as though they were hikers who had been reading Shaw. *Tom's a-Cold* is therefore a disappointing book from the author of that beautiful and brilliantly comic story, *In a Green Shade*. The description of the Swindon girl, Rose, and the attack on the tower, is very good indeed. But if Mr. Collier was a cat this is not what he would have drawn.

David Garnett, "Books in General," *New Statesman and Nation*, 8 April 1933, p. 448

STRUTHERS BURT   ⟨. . .⟩ John Collier has an infallible instinct for horror. The best contemporary one there is—far out in the lead. So much so, that I think frequently, and abruptly, he must frighten himself. Not on lonely roads or in haunted houses. Nothing as commonplace as that. But the far worse feeling of horror that creeps over you like a sudden paralyzing chill with a lot of people around; at cocktail parties, or something like that, when for a moment you are objective, and look into someone's eyes, or metaphorically speaking, into your own. That's dry-as-dust, desert horror. John Collier takes his horror more seriously than his wit, and that's why, it seems to me, his murder stories are practically perfect, while his fantasies, mostly diabolic, usually break down right at the end like a delicate bamboo rod with too big a fish on it. ⟨. . .⟩

Like the devil, or the jinn, or the bad-fairy, the author also is completely powerful in a fantasy. Moving in a never-never land, he can do exactly what he pleases, and therefore most exactly cannot do what he pleases. Released from any necessity of the rational, or the realistic, or the human, he must use his freedom with discrimination and, if anything, become more human. Faust had to turn against the world and undergo a long period of degeneration before the devil got him, and Dr. Jekyll did the same. You can't take any old scrubby human being and turn him over. If you do, it's like some undergraduate joke. And when John Collier remembers this, his fantasies are as pefect as his murder stories.

"The Right Side" is such a story, and so is "Thus I Refute Beelzy." The latter is a magnificent fantasy—also a horror story—in which he who should, most certainly gets his proper come-uppance. Stories like "Ah, the University!," "Possession of Angela Bradshaw," and "Night! Youth! Paris! and the Moon!," fall into a different category and, since there's nothing to trip up the wit, are marvelously funny and absurd. In short, I, for one, wish John Collier would forget his preoccupation with the Devil, who's really a dull and unpleasant fellow, and too much around at present, anyway, with a lot of his lesser demons, and concentrate on murder long or short. Long, I hope, and lots of it.

Struthers Burt, "Lineal Descendant of Saki," *Saturday Review*, 5 February 1944, p. 15

BASIL DAVENPORT   ⟨. . .⟩ it is hard to say what th⟨e⟩ quality ⟨of Collier's stories⟩ is. It cannot be the eerie, although jinns, fiends, conversational gorillas, and Beelzebub himself figure prominently in many of the stories (and the eeriest of all, perhaps, is about the people who live all night in the big department stores). Some of the best of them, tales of murder revealed by an accident that was in the nature of things, or murders in the future, pointed out equally by the inexorable logic of the nature of things, have nothing haunted about them. It is not quite the macabre, though Mr. Collier can certainly get more fun than any living man out of a scene where a helpless young man is disemboweled before his own eyes (it *is* funny, and I *told* you John Collier was a hard man to convey); for there is nothing macabre in the straightforward spiritual brutality of the murder in "Wet Saturday." ⟨. . .⟩

Once or twice tenderness nearly or quite breaks in, and most vividly in the most unrealistic stories. There is a really idyllic feeling about the love of the night-watchman and the youngest of the people who haunt the dark department stores. But in general Mr. Collier remains the master of an irony so perfectly balanced that his horror is hardly ever quite free of humor, nor his humor of horror.

Basil Davenport, "Unlike Other Tales," *Saturday Review*, 22 December 1951, p. 16

ANTHONY BURGESS   People who read Irving Wallace and Irving Stone and the other Irvings may not be expected to read Collier, but scholars who write about Edith Wharton and E. M. Forster may also be expected to neglect him. Take it further: histories of Anglo-American fiction rarely, even at their most comprehensive, find room for him, but the same may be said of other imaginative writers who share some of his qualities—Saki, for instance, and Mervyn Peake, and the royal physician who wrote the anonymous comic masterpiece *Augustus Carp Esq.* (what a treat is coming to Americans when some publisher decides to reprint it). To write tales about hell under the floorboards, the devil as a film producer, men kept in bottles, a man who marries a chimpanzee is a sure way to miss the attentions of the "serious" chronicler of fiction. The puritanism of the scholarly tradition leads Oxford dons to produce detective stories pseudony-mously but to refuse to write "seriously" about the form (T. S. Eliot always promised to produce a considered thesis on the *genre*, but—because of shame or decorum or lack of time or something—the promise was not fulfilled). It also exhibits *pudeur* in the presence of fantasy, especially when it has no evident didactic purpose. *Gulliver's Travels* is all right, but the works of Carroll and Lear are for the depth psychologist rather than the literary historian.

John Collier is essentially a fantasist, but not of the romantic order that purveys Gothick, both paleo- and neo-, and science fiction. He makes literature out of the intrusion of fantasy, or quiet horror, into a real world closely observed, not out of the creation of a parallel world (windy, bosky, and machicolated; steely and computerized; hobbitish). ⟨. . .⟩

⟨. . .⟩ There is what is sometimes called *wickedness* in Collier—a quality different from salacity. There is also the logic of the metaphysical conceit ⟨. . .⟩, which does not balk, as the cartoon fantasy does, at the inescapable conclusion, though it leaves everything to the imagination. The Collierian melodic line deliberately seduces us into accepting reality through the agency of a "double take." It happens, for instance, at the end of the story called "Bottle Party," where the hero is glassed and corked and put on sale:

> In the end, some sailors happened to drift into the shop, and, hearing this bottle contained the most beautiful girl in the world, they bought it up by general subscription of the fo'c'sle. When they unstoppered him at sea, and found it was only poor Frank, their disappointment knew no bounds, and they used him with the utmost barbarity.

That final word covers a great deal, but Collier the scriptman, the visual conceptor, undoubtedly has a number of specific images in mind. Or just one.

Anthony Burgess, "Introduction," *The John Collier Reader* (New York: Alfred A. Knopf, 1972), pp. xii–xiv

---

TOM MILNE   ⟨In 1933⟩ Collier wrote a sort of declaration of faith: 'I cannot see much good in the world or much likelihood of good. There seems to me a definite bias in human nature towards ill, towards the immediate convenience, the ugly, the cheap . . . I rub my hands and say "Hurry up, you foulers of a good world, and destroy yourselves faster." ' The cynical disenchantment expressed here informs most of Collier's writing, but governs only the more conventional short stories, including the two selected by Hitchcock: diabolical murder plots conceived by resentful husbands and spiteful wives who observe the utmost social aplomb in the niceties of their strategy, and who are suavely brought to book by neat O. Henry twists, whether internal (both husband and wife execute the same successful plan simultaneously in 'Over Insurance') or external (the dead and buried wife in 'Back for Christmas' had previously arranged repairs to the cellar as a surprise for her husband). Mildred Natwick, blithely chirruping 'What seems to be the trouble, Captain?' as she stumbles upon Edmund Gwenn dragging a corpse about by the heels in *The Trouble with Harry*, is so quintessentially a Collier character that it is surprising as well as sad that Hitchcock—not to say Hollywood—never made more use of Collier as scriptwriter or source.

But Collier, of course, could be much subtler and more disorientating. The magnificent 'Are You Too Late or Was I Too Early?', conceived entirely as a subjective narrative, is the haunting love story of a man for the mysterious ghostly woman who appears, tantalisingly, in his flat as a Crusoe footprint, a breath dimming the mirror, a scented breeze in passing, until an overheard telephone conversation takes us through another looking-glass: 'I heard, in a full opening of the sense, the delicate intake of her breath, the very sound of the parting of her lips. She was about to speak again. Each syllable was as clear as a bell. She said, "Oh, it's perfect. It's so quiet for Harry's work. Guess how we were lucky enough to get it! The previous tenant was found dead in his chair, and they actually say it's haunted." '

The nightmares of the imagination discovered by Poe are never very far away in Collier's stories, where a sculptor seeking success as a ventriloquist creates a dummy so lifelike that it assumes his life ('Spring Fever'); a lovelorn young man conceives the notion of having himself stuffed and placed in his beloved's presence as an eternal reproach ('Squirrels Have Bright Eyes'); a stuffy father ordering his small son to banish an imaginary playmate called Mr. Beelzy is himself mysteriously consumed ('Thus I Refute Beelzy'). In these stories, however, Collier invariably sets out from reality: from the psychological inadequacies and emotional disturbances that lead to strange fancies. The Devil, for instance, might be said to have taken a hand at the end of 'Thus I Refute Beelzy'; more particularly, however, the child has simply turned at last on the father determined to mould him into a replica of his pedestrian self. ⟨. . .⟩

Despite the profusion of devils in his work, Hell, for Collier, is essentially of our own making. Yet even as he excoriates the world for its follies, Collier is clearly increasingly preoccupied by—and sympathetic to—the human predicament expressed by his collection of lonely castaways yearning for a little romance, a little tenderness and a little understanding. Oddly, but again not inappropriately, the man who hungered for the world to destroy itself more rapidly, and spent his days killing harmless beasts and birds, covertly expresses his new concern by way of the amazing collection of animals who proliferate in his stories, sometimes as mute (or not so mute) witnesses to human destructiveness, but more often as surrogates for the unrealised aspirations.

    Tom Milne, "The Elusive John Collier," *Sight and Sound* 45, No. 2 (Spring 1976): 107–8

BEN P. INDICK   Generally, when Collier employs Guignol, with its attendant murder and horror, he leavens it with ironic humor at the expense of some unfortunate if deserving wretch (and sometimes some undeserving ones as well). Such a denouement may include dismay, agony and even dismemberment; the humor is in the narrative style which tells us that the fate was, after all, well-earned, a mock lesson and a wry comment on the workings of Fate. The doctor in "Back for Christmas" who has laboriously chopped his annoying wife into pieces and buried her in neat parcels in the cellar leaves home for a presumed vacation, only to learn that his late wife had arranged to have a new cellar built in his absence. In "Green Thoughts" a horticulturist is literally absorbed, physically, by his unusual new orchid. When his avaricious nephew sees his uncle's face within the flower, and then discovers that the uncle's intention had been to cut him from his will, he snatches up a scissors . . . ⟨. . .⟩

    His Guignol, however, on occasion, retains the verve and shock without the relieving laughter, most classically in "The Touch of Nutmeg Makes It." A story of a particularly repellent murder, the work of an apparent madman, it is all the more peculiar that a sensitive, mild-mannered man has been accused of so heinous a crime. It is logical that no jury could accept him as a murderer, and he is acquitted; however, a subsequent trivial incident demonstrates more about the man than any amount of circumstantial evidence might. In "Special Delivery" a man falls in love with a department store mannequin; there is no humor as the story follows his stealing the doll to his eventual death at the hands of hooligans. Yet there is a disquieting fascination in his hopeless love, with its terrible fate as he is kicked to death and thrown with the mannequin into a chalk pit. "His head lay limp on her neck; her stiff arm was arched over him. In the autumn, when the overhang crumbled down on them, it pressed him close to her forever."

Ben P. Indick, "Sardonic Fantasists: John Collier" (1982), *Discovering Modern Horror II*, ed. Darrell Schweitzer (Mercer Island, WA: Starmont House, 1988), pp. 123–24

BETTY RICHARDSON   Like E. M. Forster, John Collier did not believe in belief. He was sympathetic toward the human desire for an earthly paradise, for he was born into a world of Victorian values and studied the works of the Victorian visionaries, but he realized that the desire for a lost Eden is no more than a poignant dream. He was profoundly skeptical of the twentieth-century dogmas and ideologies that promise to make this dream come true, just as he was skeptical of traditional theology that sought to restrict human behavior and cripple human aspiration for the sake of a paradise to come.

Collier's world view was that of a modern who accepts the Bergsonian concept of the world as process, flux, and change. To believe that some permanent order can be imposed on this universe is, at best, an act of self-deception. At worst, it is an excuse for authoritarian control of others and camouflage for those who want to manipulate others. Whether those who seek power for these reasons are Christian proselytizers or merely individual physicians or industrialists, Collier abhorred their ambition and attacked them. But, because he was a man possessed of a great love for life, a great hunger for experience, and a great capacity for enjoying all the riches of the earth, including the rich variety of human illusions and personalities, he attacked them with Rabelaisian laughter. ⟨. . .⟩

Collier's vision might well be one of despair and pessimism, but it is not, even though he is profoundly aware of man's mortality, of the desperation of thinking men and of the stultifying boredom and frustration of small men caught up in capitalistic machinery in which they are used as objects. What Collier stresses through his writing is the realization of the transience of all things, and he insists on stripping down the trappings of the world to bare essentials—time, sex, death, creativity. Granted awareness of these essentials, then a good life is possible, a life reminiscent both of a kind of existentialism and of those values that Collier inherited from his Victorian education and Edwardian boyhood—tolerance, loyalty, respect, dignity, affection, and, above all, pity.

But this good life is possible only to the man who is willing to remain an individualist, an outsider, roles that Collier accepted both in his life and in his writing. He belonged to no man and to no party, and he maintained his personal integrity and the integrity of his craftsmanship despite the temptations to which he occasionally and admittedly succumbed.

Betty Richardson, *John Collier* (Boston: Twayne, 1983), pp. 106, 108

JOHN J. KESSEL   Demons, witches, genies, and magic appear frequently in Collier's short fiction. Stories like "Fallen Star," "Bottle Party," "Pictures in the Fire," "The Devil George and Rosie," and "Halfway to Hell" are frankly presented as divertissements, but some of the snap of *His Monkey Wife* surfaces in others that use these materials to more serious effect. "Thus I Refute Beelzy" presents the persecution of a boy, Small Simon, by his father, Big Simon, in the name of "learning from experience." One day the father returns home early from his office and discovers Small Simon playing with his imaginary friend, Mr. Beelzy. Big Simon insists, in proper psychoanalytical terms, that the boy give up this fantasy before he turns to a real lie. Collier, in a few pages, deftly sketches in the tyranny of the father, the mother's ineffectuality, their neighbor's embarrassment, and the boy's desperate defense, culminating in Big Simon taking his son upstairs to beat the fantasy out of him. For once there are no authorial intrusions: the story consists almost entirely of dialogue and ends on the horrific note of Beelzy's refutation of the father. "It was on the second-floor landing that they found the shoe, with the man's foot still in it, much like the last morsel of a mouse which sometimes falls unnoticed from the side of the jaws of the cat."

The plot of this story, complete to the supernatural reversal at the end, is similar to those of Collier's more whimsical tales, but the domestic drama that leads up to this conclusion raises it beyond the merely clever. This story is more powerful than "Fallen Star" because it starts from a situation closer to reality. Any aware reader is going to expect the departure into fantasy in the end, where father gets his comeuppance, but what is unexpected is its disproportionate savagery and the matter-of-fact way in which Collier leads us from the comic psychological brutality of dad (whose attacks are veiled, as are most attacks in the civilized family) to the grim supernatural brutality of Small Simon's protector (whose attack is graphically physical, unveiled to us in the gruesome final line of the story). We begin the story reading light comedy and conclude in grand guignol. No authorial comment is necessary or offered, as the tale moves from the whimsical to the minatory.

John J. Kessel, "John Collier," *Supernatural Fiction Writers*, ed. E. F. Bleiler (New York: Charles Scribner's Sons, 1985), Vol. 2, p. 580

▨ *Bibliography*

His Monkey Wife; or, Married to a Chimp. 1930.

No Traveller Returns. 1931.

The Scandal and Credulities of John Aubrey. 1931.

Gemini. 1931.

An Epistle to a Friend. 1932.

Green Thoughts. 1932.

Just the Other Day: An Informal History of Great Britain Since the War (with Iain Lang). 1932.

Tom's a-Cold. 1933, 1933 (as *Full Circle*).

Defy the Foul Fiend; or, The Misadventures of the Heart. 1934.

The Devil and All. 1934.

Variation on a Theme. 1935.

Witch's Money. 1940.

Presenting Moonshine. 1941.

Wet Saturday. 1941.

The Touch of Nutmeg. 1943.

Fancies and Goodnights. 1951.

Pictures in the Fire. 1958.

The John Collier Reader. 1972, 1975 (as *The Best of John Collier*; abridged).

Milton's Paradise Lost: A Screenplay for Cinema of the Mind. 1973.

⊞ ⊞ ⊞

L. Sprague de Camp
b. 1907
Fletcher Pratt
1897–1956

MURRAY FLETCHER PRATT was born on April 25, 1897, in Buffalo, New York, the son of a farmer. As a youth, he held a variety of jobs including librarian and flyweight prizefighter before attending Hobart College. When family financial problems forced him to leave school, he found work on newspapers in New York and Pennsylvania. Burned out of his New York apartment in the early 1920s, Pratt and his second wife Inga used the insurance money to move to France, where he studied languages at the Sorbonne. Upon his return to the United States, he began writing and translating science fiction stories for the pulp magazines and established a reputation as a writer of popular history and nonfiction books.

Lyon Sprague de Camp was born on November 27, 1907, in New York City, the oldest of three sons born to Lyon de Camp, a sawmill owner, and Beatrice Sprague. His early education was divided between Trinity School in New York and a North Carolina military institute, the Snyder School. Eventually, he earned a degree in aeronautical engineering from the California Institute of Technology in 1930, and a master's in engineering and economics in 1933 from Stevens Institute of Technology in Hoboken, New Jersey. He taught courses in patents for inventors until 1937, when his first book, *Inventions and Their Management*, was published. That same year, he sold his first story to *Astounding Stories*, the magazine where he would become known as one of the most erudite and imaginative writers of science fiction's "Golden Age."

Pratt was introduced to De Camp in 1939, and he suggested that they collaborate on a story that would combine de Camp's wry sense of humor with Pratt's interest in language and mythology. The result was "The Roaring Trumpet," the first of the magical misadventures of Harold Shea, in which

Shea, a bumbling and egotistical experimental psychologist, accidentally transports himself to the world of the Norse Eddas, where he discovers that magic, rather than science, is that world's governing logic. The story appeared in the May 1940 issue of John W. Campbell's *Unknown*, where de Camp was already known for his amusing alternate histories, and it became the epitome of the magazine's brand of literate adult fantasy. The second Harold Shea story, "The Mathematics of Magic" (1940), took Shea to the world of Spenser's *The Faerie Queene*, where Shea learns to master magic like science. It was combined with "The Roaring Trumpet" for book publication as *The Incomplete Enchanter* (1941).

Shea's adventures continued in the world of Ariosto's *Orlando Furioso* in *The Castle of Iron* (serialized 1941; book publication 1950), and almost ended in fellow *Unknown* writer L. Ron Hubbard's "The Case of the Friendly Corpse" (1941), where his annihilation brought complaints from readers. De Camp and Pratt eventually resurrected Shea in two more adventures, "The Wall of Serpents" (1953) and "The Green Magician" (1954), which sent their antihero respectively to the worlds of the Finnish *Kalevala* and Irish mythology. In the meantime, they collaborated on *The Land of Unreason* (1942), a mingling of folk legend and political satire, and *The Carnelian Cube* (1948), a romp through "alternate heavens" made accessible by the possession of a magic talisman. In 1953, they collected a number of pun-filled tall tales told at a fictional watering hole as their final collaboration, *Tales from Gavagan's Bar*.

Although Pratt's later years were taken up mostly with writing popular history, he also produced the heroic fantasy *The Well of the Unicorn* (1948), the dream fantasy *The Blue Star* (1952), and several science fiction novels and anthologies before dying of complications of liver cancer on June 10, 1956. De Camp published alternate world fantasies in *Unknown*, including *The Undesired Princess* (1942) and *Solomon's Stone* (1942), and merged fantasy with science fiction in his futuristic Viagens Interplanetarias series, set in a future where Brazil has become the dominant world power, and his Krishna stories, set on planets where feudal governments hold sway. With Lin Carter and Bjorn Nyberg, he helped to organize and complete the saga of Robert E. Howard's Conan the Barbarian in a series of books published in the 1950s and 1960s. Among his recent works of fantasy are *The Honourable Barbarian* (1989), a continuation of his heroic Novarian saga set in the milieu he created in *The Goblin Tower* (1968), and *The Incorporated Knight* (1989) and its sequel *The Pixilated Peeress* (1991), written in collaboration with his wife Catherine Crook de Camp, whom he married in 1939. De Camp has written prolifically on ancient history, science, the craft of fiction writing, and numerous other topics, and is a recipient of the Nebula Grand Master Award from the Science Fiction Writers of America. In 1991 he resurrected Harold Shea one last time in the novella *Sir Harold and the Gnome King.*

▣ *Critical Extracts*

JOHN W. CAMPBELL   "The Mathematics of Magic" shows the results to be attained by a sound scientist, working with a knowledge of mathematics, logic, and the scientific method, stranded in a world where magic works. It takes the scientific method to make a real enchanter. The local yokels have some good tricks, but a pair of scientists at work analyzing magic into a system of law and order—with a highly elastic decimal point!— can really stir up something. Harold Shea, errant psychologist with an escape mechanism, really gets results in the world of Spenser's *Faerie Queene!*

John W. Campbell, "Of Things Beyond," *Unknown* 3, No. 5 (July 1940): 6

L. RON HUBBARD   ⟨I saw⟩ a man dressed in funny-looking clothes and when he saw me, he wanted to know who I was. I told him and asked him who he was and he said his name was—let's see, what did he say his name was? Hair—Harole She or Shay. Harold Shay, that was it. He said he was a magician from another world.

Well I was just about to show the dean this double wand so I said this would be a good time to try it out and see if it really worked. I said I'd make the snake and then he could rear up a monster and we'd see which one won. Well, he seemed kind of upset when I threw down the wand and it began to grow and he yelled some kind of chant that sounded like mathematics and the snake just kept on growing. I expected to see his monster any minute because he said he was a magician from another world and I figured he must be pretty good. But by golly, the snake just grew up and then grabbed him and ate him up before I could do anything about it.

> L. Ron Hubbard, "The Case of the Friendly Corpse," *Unknown* 5, No. 2 (August 1941): 31

BASIL DAVENPORT   When one adds that some of the adventures ⟨in *The Incomplete Enchanter*⟩ surprisingly manage to be genuinely exciting—after all, the giants of Jotunheim (who walk like Bowery toughs) are just as credible a menace as Dr. Fu Manchu—that should give some idea of this most unusual book. It has its faults, of course. There should be either more metaphysics or less; any reader worth entertaining should be willing to grant a possible world almost as a postulate, with a minimum of theory; but with so much explanation as there is here, one is inclined to ask the further questions of where the mind of Spenser is supposed to come in, and why Shea should vanish into another world by concentrating on propositions of logic which appear to be true of this one. And though he would be a bold man who would maintain that any given episode is not to be found in the proliferating forest of the *Faery Queene*, surely the Da Derga has strayed in there from the Irish epic cycle, and ought to be explained. Also, the book is uneven; the fun sometimes flags, and is sometimes forced. But the burlesque at its best, as in the treatment of Britomart, the lady athlete, is both genuinely amusing, and even as burlesque can be, convincing; this is at least a possible Britomart, as this is a possible world. It is a world, and a book, with its own wild logic, with some fighting and a lot of fun; and you never met anything exactly like it in your life.

> Basil Davenport, "Worlds in Time," *Saturday Review of Literature*, 4 October 1941, p. 19

IRIS BARRY   Of course, *The Incomplete Enchanter* is utterly preposterous, but the authors imply that they do not expect to be believed, only hope to be enjoyed. This, I think, may fairly be predicted. There is a heap of humanity and humor in the gods, trolls, enchanters whom our heroes encounter, while the puzzling circumstances they find themselves in are recounted with straightforward energy and abandon. Oddly enough, one of the pleasantest scenes in the book finds the two contemporary humans ardently engaged in a cockroach race while they languish in the unpleasant dungeon from which Snogg eventually releases them. It is perhaps this mingling of known habits and reactions with the remotest of backgrounds that makes the narrative lively. And there is a most un-Christian pleasure, too, in learning how the two psychologists manage to plumb the thoughts and desires of their fabulous friends of the long-ago past. They prove to be singularly like our own though dressed up in unfamiliar, impressive and obsolete guise.

> Iris Barry, [Review of *The Incomplete Enchanter*], *New York Herald Tribune Books*, 12 October 1941, p. 8

FREDERIK POHL   Archaeologist Arthur Cleveland Finch, digging for Hittite artifacts in Armenia, comes across a cube of carnelian stone which transports him to three worlds of his dreams. All three seem to center around the state of Kentucky, and the time seems to be the Twentieth Century—but in the first the government is of, for and by a gang of super-wardheelers who hold the populace in subjection; in the second, the state is divided into feudal—and feuding—baronies, complete with lavender armored limousines; and the third presents the picture of a sort of permanent fancy-dress ball, where everyone takes part in reconstruction of famous historical events. The trouble, in the last case, is that the games are played for keeps; and the Archaeologist Finch discovers himself cast as a slave doomed to execution.

The team of de Camp and Pratt has produced some of the funniest fantasies ever to see print. *The Carnelian Cube*, almost alone among fantasy books, has never been published in magazine form—but one wonders how the magazines missed it.

> Frederik Pohl, "The Science Fictioneer," *Super Science Stories* 5, No. 1 (January 1949): 92

A. LANGLEY SEARLES   Readers who remember these two authors' previous collaborations—*The Incomplete Enchanter* and *The Land of Unreason*—will approach this third one with a good deal of anticipation.

They are sure to be entertained and often amused by it, and probably a little disappointed, too, for *The Carnelian Cube* does not duplicate the high standards of its predecessors. But then, what fantasy novel does these days?

There are three separate episodes in the book, every one in a different dream-world, and archeologist Arthur Cleveland Finch gets himself into plenty of adventurous trouble in each. It all begins on an expedition in Asia Minor when he encounters a carnelian cube engraved with cryptic Etruscan characters. This cube, he discovers, is a "dreamstone," and if the owner sleeps with it under his pillow he will be taken to heaven.

The first "heaven" he lands in is an interesting feudal hierarchy where people are named according to their occupations. Finch Arthur Poet finds himself in progressively hotter water, and escapes into heaven number two just one jump ahead of the forces of law and order.

The second world likewise has a feudal set-up, but it proves to be anarchistic than anything else, what with Kentucky colonels and their retainers feuding furiously all over the Kentucky landscape. There are no end of goofily unusual characters here, but it is a familiar seductive siren whose ardent pursuit of Finch causes him to use the carnelian cube yet a third time.

I suspect the final locale is intended as a semi-satire on modern scientific methods; but totally aside from that it is probably the most intriguing of all three, ending the novel on a pleasant note. I, for one, wish Messrs. de Camp and Pratt would put their imaginations together more often.

A. Langley Searles, [Review of *The Carnelian Cube*], *Fantastic Novels* 4, No. 1 (May 1950): 116

SAM MERWIN   Continuing the adventures of hapless Harold Shea and the devious Professor Reed Chambers ⟨sic⟩ inaugurated recently in book form in *The Incomplete Enchanter* (Prime Press, Philadelphia), when Shea became first involved in the world of the Norse gods and then in that of the *Faerie Queen*, when he brought back the fair Belphebe to wife.

In this even daffier sequel Professor Chambers, in an effort to prevent his snow-maiden light-of-love from melting in the first hot spell, has conveyed not only his ice-born Lady Florimel and himself but Belphebe into the troubadoric magic land of the Chanson of Roland.

Shea, in prosaic Ohio of this world, promptly finds himself about to be charged with murder, kidnaping and sundry other capital offenses when Chambers, in need of help, whisks him, along with a screwball fellow psychologist, a cop and one other adjacent character, into a Mohammedan heaven—a sort of way station.

Shea and his screwball pal manage to join Chambers, who is operating more or less happily in the enchanted castle of the Moorish wizard Atlantes, and Shea at once learns that his beloved Belphebe has become inextricably and schizophrenically involved with a local maiden of somewhat similar name and personality.

From then on in the ratrace is as merry and fantastic as the most devout de Camp–Pratt fans could wish. We don't intend to spoil it in these columns and will content outselves with a most hearty recommend. Should be enjoyed by all those who love cats, love dogs and detest toast buttered only in the middle.

> Sam Merwin, [Review of *The Castle of Iron*], *Thrilling Wonder Stories* 37, No. 2 (December 1950): 159–60

ANTHONY BOUCHER and J. FRANCIS McCOMAS   At last the superlative magazine series by L. Sprague de Camp and Fletcher Pratt, recounting Harold Shea's experiences with the mathematics of magic in alternate universes, is all in print in a completely revised and expanded form. *The Incomplete Enchanter* (universes of Norse Gods and of the Faerie Queene) has been reissued by Prime; and Gnome has brought out for the first time the fuller version of *The Castle of Iron* (universe of Orlando Furioso). The last is in plot much the weaker of the two; but the whole series marks a high-point in the application of sternest intellectual logic to screwball fantasy.

> Anthony Boucher and J. Francis McComas, "Recommended Reading," *Magazine of Fantasy and Science Fiction* 1, No. 5 (December 1950): 104

FLETCHER PRATT   With the first issues of *Weird Tales* in 1923 and of *Amazing Stories* in 1926, it was discovered that a class of reader existed who was careless of the thematic material or the outcome of the story as long as it dealt with other times, other spaces of the world of wonder. That is, these readers were more interested in the background against which a story took place than in the story itself. In the early days of science fiction and fantasy as a consciously adopted form this produced some frightfully bad writing—long passages of undigested description, stories that were little more than catalogs of the strange monsters found in distant planets and the marvelous inventions of the remote future. It was responsible for the "pseudoscience" tag that many people still attach to imaginative fiction and for the fact that it could only make its beginning among the highly uncritical readership that follows the pulps. It accounts for the other fact that most science fiction and fantasy is still comparatively weak in characterization and even in emotional content. The primary response sought by the author and furnished by the reader, when the story is a success, is an intellectual pleasure. Usually it is the pleasure of discovering that in a shrinking world there are still horizons.

It is worth re-emphasizing that this habit on the part of science fiction–fantasy readers and the characters of the readers themselves, not only allows the writers to deal with some fairly ponderous material, but demands that they do it in a readable way. One of the most curious characteristics of this entire field of literature is this combination of careful thinking in the background with a lightness of exposition that almost amounts to levity.

> Fletcher Pratt, "Introduction: The Nature of Imaginative Literature," *Worlds of Wonder*, ed. Fletcher Pratt (New York: Twayne, 1951), pp. 18–19

DAMON KNIGHT   *Tales from Gavagan's Bar*, by de Camp and Fletcher Pratt, contains the respectable total of twenty-three stories, all dealing with supernatural goings-on at Gavagan's. This is a long way to stretch a gag; I think a little too far. Some of the tales, like "Elephas Frumenti," "The Green Thumb" and "Caveat Emptor," are purely wonderful; others like "The Love Nest," with its totally improbable exit line, are good stories that give the impression they didn't want to come into Gavagan's in the first place.

> Damon Knight, [Review of *Tales from Gavagan's Bar*], *Science Fiction Adventures* 2, No. 3 (May 1954): 124

P. SCHUYLER MILLER   The closest thing to these tales from Gavagan's—rhymes with "a pagan's"—are the occasional commentaries by Lord Dunsany's widely traveled friend Jorkens (I am unhappy to say that I have never learned what happened on the occasions when *Jorkens Had a Large Whiskey*). But those were the misadventures of one man, and these are things which have happened to people as different as an automobile salesman ("Corpus Delectable"), a drummer in toys ("Beats of Bourbon"), an attorney ("The Black Ball"), and a woman married to a were-dachsel ("Here, Putzi!"). My own favorite is still the classic "Elephas Frumenti."

P. Schuyler Miller, "The Reference Library," *Astounding Science Fiction* 53, No. 6 (August 1954): 148

ALFRED BESTER   Although *Fantasy & Science Fiction* (the magazine, not the field) has inherited the mantle of the fabulous *Unknown*, we all have a warm spot in our hearts for that great trail-breaker and welcome each re-print from its pages. Latest is *The Incomplete Enchanter* by L. Sprague de Camp and Fletcher Pratt.

The authors waste no time getting down to their fantastick business. They hocus-pocus Harold Shea, a XXth century psychologist, back to the para worlds of Norse mythology and Spenser's *Faery Queen,* and involve him in adventures that follow the pattern of *The Connecticut Yankee.* They lean heavily on anachronistic dialogue for laughs, but the book holds up amazingly well after twenty years.

Alfred Bester, [Review of *The Incomplete Enchanter*], *Magazine of Fantasy and Science Fiction* 19, No. 4 (October 1960): 94

FLOYD C. GALE   De Camp and Pratt were far and away the finest team of fantasy collaborators. In their present misadventures, Shea and his Faerie wife, Belphebe, become involved in the Finnish land of Kalevala and the Ireland of the hero, Cuchulainn.

If de Camp's and Pratt's heroes and villains alike are usually ineffectual and usually likeable, their stories are always chuckle-filled delights.

Floyd C. Gale, [Review of *Wall of Serpents*], *Galaxy* 20, No. 2 (December 1961): 145

LIN CARTER   This combination of wacky logic and scientific analysis ⟨in "The Roaring Trumpet" and "The Mathematics of Magic"⟩ delighted the readers to no end; they ate up both yarns with relish and hungrily howled for more. Pratt and de Camp obliged six issues later with a novel called *The Castle of Iron*, which ran in the April 1941 *Unknown*. The story opened with yet another display of what this incomparable team could do with rational, realistic thinking as against the sloppy romanticism common to pulp writers. In the usual run of pulp adventure yarns, hero and heroine return from their magical adventures and that's that. But Pratt and de Camp opened the novel with a grueling scene in which the cops are interrogating poor Harold under the broiling lights. Not unnaturally, they think he has done away with his boss, disposing of the body somewhere. After all, he and Chalmers were in the lab together . . . and only Harold came out of it, with a girl, probably his accomplice in the murder.

Of course, Harold doesn't have much luck persuading them that Chalmers has accepted a job as chief magician, settled down to married life with a lovely lady made out of snow, and has relocated to Fairyland! In fact, the only thing he can think to do is to try to get back to the universe of the *Faerie Queene*. But everything goes wrong: by accident he takes one of the cops along, and they end up universes away in another literary cosmos, that of the Xanadu of Coleridge's poem, "Kubla Khan." Another hop brings all the characters together in a universe singularly close to that of Spenser's poem, to wit the universe of Ariosto's *Orlando Furioso*, from which Spenser borrowed rather heavily for his style and many of his ideas.

The team continued to delight the readership of *Unknown* with some of the most sprightly, entertaining, witty fantasies ever written, fantasies in which romantic adventure took a back seat to rational plotting and interesting characterization. In novels like *The Land of Unreason* and *The Carnelian Cube*, as well as two further Harold Shea stories—in which the syllogismobile journeys into the realm of the *Kalevala*, and at last to the world of Irish myth—they were far and away the most admired and popular of the writers for *Unknown*.

Lin Carter, *Imaginary Worlds: The Art of Fantasy* (New York: Ballantine Books, 1973), pp. 79–80

L. SPRAGUE DE CAMP   For obvious reasons, I cannot objectively assess the virtues and faults of these novels. I will only say that they were certainly heroic fantasy, or swordplay-and-sorcery fiction, long before these terms were invented. While Robert E. Howard is justly hailed as the main American pioneer in this genre, neither Pratt nor I, when we started the Shea stories, had ever read a Conan story or heard enough about Howard to recognize his name. By coincidence, our colleague Lester del Rey had the idea of a parallel story laid in a parallel world of Scandinavian myth at just about the time we did. Alas for Lester! we got our manuscript in first.

Our method of collaboration was to meet in Pratt's apartment and hammer out the plot by discussion, of which I took shorthand notes. Observing the utility of Pratt's knowledge of shorthand from his journalistic days, I taught myself Gregg and have found it valuable ever since.

When I had taken home the notes, I wrote a rough draft. Pratt then wrote the final draft, which I edited. In a few cases in our later Gavagan's Bar stories, we reversed the procedure, Pratt doing the first draft and I the second. This did not work out so well. In such collaborations, I think, it is generally better for the junior member to do the rough draft, since the senior member, as a result of experience, is likely to have more skill at polishing and condensation.

A fan magazine once asserted that, in the Harold Shea stories, de Camp furnished the imaginative element and Pratt the controlling logic. Actually, it was the other way round. Pratt had a livelier and more creative imagination than I, but I had a keener sense of critical logic. In any case, I learned much of what I think I know about the writer's craft in the course of these collaborations. Pratt's influence on me in this matter was second only to ⟨John W.⟩ Campbell's.

L. Sprague de Camp, "Parallel Worlds: Fletcher Pratt," *Literary Swordsmen and Sorcerers: The Makers of Heroic Fantasy* (Sauk City, WI: Arkham House, 1976), pp. 182–83

BRIAN STABLEFORD   The method by which de Camp and Pratt worked was first to decide on a plot; then de Camp would do a first draft and Pratt a final one. All of their early writing must have been done very quickly (de Camp wrote one other novella and two novels for *Unknown* in the same period, plus numerous short pieces for *Unknown* and *Astounding*); it is not really surprising that the authors sometimes seem to be failing to make the most of their premises. Only in the first two novellas, where the whole business was so new and exciting, did they muster the verve and vitality to make everything flow smoothly and perfectly; the three novels became steadily more mechanical as they materialized.

The three long stories that de Camp wrote on his own for *Unknown* during the period of his collaborations with Pratt are much the same kind of work. "The Wheels of If" (1940) is a lively story of alternate possibilities. *The Undesired Princess* (1942; in book form, 1951) takes yet another not very heroic hero in a fairy-tale world painted in primary colors where statements are taken altogether too literally. Though *Solomon's Stone* (1942; in book form, 1957) seems to have been written in the same frenetic rush, it is perhaps the best of the three. Prosper Nash, an accountant whose body is borrowed by a demon, finds himself on the astral plane, which is inhabited by the dream creations of men in the real world. He finds that his fantasy self is a dashing cavalier, and in that form he must steal the eponymous talisman from an enchanter if he is to stand a chance of recovering his own body.

All these stories demonstrate that de Camp—with or without Pratt's help—was rather limited in his plotting strategy. Either he thrusts a hero into an awkward situation where the story is kept rolling simply by recounting the hero's attempts to stay alive or, more often, he provides the hero with a motive for searching out and securing an object of some kind. Because of these limitations his longer stories—including the longer collaborations with Pratt—are nothing but a series of exotic encounters strung together like beads in a necklace. The strand usually has some gems but other beads seem to be there only to fill the gaps. In general de Camp seemed to be careless in connecting up the episodes of his longer stories and ended up arbitrarily switching from one briefly sketched situation to another.

Brian Stableford, "L. Sprague de Camp and Fletcher Pratt," *Supernatural Fiction Writers*, ed. Everett F. Bleiler (New York: Charles Scribner's Sons, 1985), Vol. 2, p. 927

DAVID DRAKE   These are fast-paced adventure novellas in which fairly ordinary folk from the present-day transport themselves into myth-worlds populated by monsters and villains, wizards and heroes—including some characters who mix several of the categories.

And that's important too, because the characters behave refreshingly like people instead of fitting neatly into one or another stereotype. Heroes can be hot-tempered, stupid and arrogant. Villainous wizards may turn out to be intelligent, success-oriented fellows, so similar to modern academics that it can be a little difficult to pick sides in the struggle between good and evil. A modern man doesn't become a mythic hero simply because he's dropped into a heroic myth—but he may be able to learn some of the attributes of heroism that remain valid in his world as well.

The rigor of the stories appears in two fashions: the authors display expert knowledge of the myths which form the framework for the novellas; *and* they display expert knowledge of the real conditions of the worlds on which the myths are based.

> David Drake, "Introduction," *The Complete Compleat Enchanter* (New York: Baen Books, 1989), p. 2

STEFAN DZIEMIANOWICZ   The May ⟨1940⟩ issue ⟨of *Unknown*⟩ stands as a landmark for bringing together the formidable talents of L. Sprague de Camp and Fletcher Pratt in *The Roaring Trumpet*, the first of the Harold Shea novels. Shea is a vain experimental psychologist who, along with several colleagues, discovers a perfectly logical and rational way of stepping from his own world into the alternate worlds of myth and literature. In *The Roaring Trumpet,* he accidentally plunks himself down in the Fimbulwinter of the Norse Eddas, on the eve of Ragnarok. Unlike *Lest Darkness Fall,* in which de Camp had shown that 20th century technology would be possible, if difficult, in sixth century Rome, this novel proposed that science would have no effect in lands where magic is the rule. Shea discovers to his dismay that, in the imagined worlds, guns will not fire, cigarette lighters will not light and stainless steel rusts because the principles behind them were known neither to the races who created the legends nor the writers who wove the legends into narratives. Only when Shea masters "the mathematics of magic" (the title of the second Harold Shea novel) does he achieve some control over his environment—with predictably hilarious results.

The Harold Shea stories are perfect examples of the type of unconventional fantasy one could find in *Unknown*. Where so much weird fiction dealt with creatures who enter our world from outside, de Camp and Pratt inverted the idea, having human characters project themselves into worlds of fantasy and magic. Just as *Lest Darkness Fall* had been a variation on both the gadget and time travel stories of science ficton, the Harold Shea stories were fantasy equivalents of a familiar science fiction theme, the voyage to an alien world—in this case, though, the space ship is replaced by "the syllogismobile," science by "the mathematics of magic" and gadgets by magic spells.

> Stefan Dziemianowicz, *The Annotated Guide to* Unknown *and* Unknown Worlds (Mercer Island, WA: Starmont House, 1991), pp. 29–30

◈ *Bibliography*

The Incomplete Enchanter. 1941.

Land of Unreason. 1942.

The Carnelian Cube. 1948.

The Castle of Iron. 1950.

Tales from Gavagan's Bar. 1953, 1978.

Wall of Serpents. 1960.

The Complete Enchanter: The Magical Adventures of Harold Shea. 1975, 1989
    (as *The Compleat Complete Enchanter*).

E. R. Eddison
1882–1945

ERIC RUCKER EDDISON was born in Yorkshire, England, on November 24, 1882, and was educated at Eton and Trinity College, Oxford. From an early age he had an interest in Norse mythology, and he studied Icelandic in order to read the Norse sagas. At Oxford, he acquired a solid background in the classics and mastered Greek, Latin, and French. In 1906, the year after he graduated, he began work as a civil servant with the British Board of Trade, a job he would hold until 1937. In 1909 he married Winifred Grace Henderson, with whom he had one daughter, Jean.

Although Eddison had an aptitude for writing and was a patron of the arts, his literary inclinations were not realized until his first book, *Poems, Letters, and Memories of Philip Sidney Nairn,* was published in 1916. The full measure of his talents became known when his first novel, *The Worm Ouroboros,* appeared in 1922. The epic tale of an average man who is transported magically to the planet Mercury inhabited by warring factions comprised of nobles and sorcerers, it is told in a deliberately archaic style that mixed allusions to classical mythology and Elizabethan drama to evoke a spirit of romance. Lauded by James Branch Cabell, James Stephens, and other of Eddison's contemporaries, the book found only a small readership until 1926, when an American edition coincided with the publication of *Styrbiorn the Strong,* a historical novel of the Vikings.

Between 1926 and 1935 Eddison continued in his civil servant position, rising to the level of deputy comptroller general of overseas trade and assuming a membership on the Council for Art and Industry. His only literary effort during this period, a translation of *Egil's Saga,* appeared in 1930. Then, in 1935, he published *Mistress of Mistresses,* a semisequel to *The Worm Ouroboros* and the first book in what would become known as his masterwork of heroic fantasy, the Zimiamvian trilogy. *Mistress* establishes the topography of Zimiamvia, a feudal world of three kingdoms recently united by King Mezentius, whose death threatens them with dissolution and war. The second Zimiamvian novel, *A Fish Dinner in Memison* (1941), is a prequel to *Mistress*, but nonetheless builds upon concepts introduced in the first novel, most importantly the idea that male and female characters on Zimiamvia and Earth are imperfect avatars of the divinities Zeus and Aphrodite. As a foreword to the novel, Eddison included a lengthy letter that outlined the philosophical foundations of his writing and emphasized the straightforward, nonallegorical orientation of his romances. The vast scope of these novels and the vivid realization of their imaginary realms brought Eddison to the attention of fantasists C. S. Lewis, J. R. R. Tolkien, and Charles Williams, all of whom he met in the early 1940s.

Eddison retired from the civil service in 1937 with the honored titles of Companion of St. Michael and St. George and Companion of the Order of the Bath. He was at work on the third novel in the trilogy when he died on August 18, 1945. In 1958 Eddison's widow published the novel's finished chapters and his synopses for the remainder of the book under the title *The Mezentian Gate*.

▨ *Critical Extracts*

EDWIN CLARK   This romance ⟨*The Worm Ouroboros*⟩ has the gaudiness and flair of the Elizabethans. It has the exuberance of great appetites and vigorous living. It transcends all ordinary life. It burns with the wonder and awe of excess. Such Elizabethans as Marlowe, Webster and Greene, had they collaborated upon a prose narrative, as they did in playmaking, might have written a romance with such elemental havoc and physical force. The scope of the book is truly epical—to distinguish that much abused word. Yet it will be recalled that Homer nods. So does Eddison. His epical happenings lapse from time to time from his furies and surging energy to bombast. The battles before Troy have been known to weary in recounting. The series of battles in the fore part of this narrative give a like return. The windy and lengthy speeches between the captains on both sides lack interest and check the advance of the narrative overmuch. Surely the interest and compactness of form would have been considerably benefitted by careful and prudent cutting. This new writer is stylistic in the grand and heroic manner that evokes beauty and vigorous life, yet it seems to us that without injury to his verbal charm or loss of beauty in his passage of atmosphere saturated with glamour of nature, he could have removed much that would quicken the action of his narration to a more attractive pace. Eddison is a poet, his sensitiveness finely depicting contrasts of living forces. And *The Worm Ouroboros* is the product of a first-class imagination that has yet to be fully mastered by art.

> Edwin Clark, "Mythology à la Mode," *New York Times Book Review*, 6 June 1926, p. 20

KENNETH BURKE   Most novelists of this age place their emphasis elsewhere, trying primarily to reveal aspects of human psychology, or dealing with the phenomena of social transvaluation, and so on, whereas Mr. Eddison's chief intention ⟨in *The Worm Ouroboros*⟩ is to exemplify rhetorical or literary virtues. Fantasy, or romance, is the natural outlet for such a "pure" interest. (I use the adjective in its chemical and philosophical sense, not as a moral attribute.) Fantasy is the natural result when an author lacks utilitarian interests, or "gravitational pull." For if the usual writer occasionally produces beauty in the process of trying to convince his reader of something else, the "pure" writer consistently produces fantasy in the process of trying to convince his reader of beauty. In other aspects of art the subject is the end, beauty is the means—in fantasy beauty is the end, the subject is the means. Thus, in turning to romance or fantasy Mr. Eddison could be said at least to orientate himself by the use of a compass which points resolutely toward beauty—and the constancy of his concern could readily be identified with the attainment of his purpose. I should presume to caution against this confusion, asking that we say less about the book's beauty and more about its constant outstretching of the arms toward beauty. Nor need this be taken as an adverse criticism, but as an observation, rather, since of itself it specifies the type rather than attempts at rating within the type.

> Kenneth Burke, "Romance in Vacuo," *New York Herald Tribune Books*, 4 July 1926, p. 3

UNSIGNED   This ⟨*Styrbiorn the Strong*⟩ is not, of course, a book for everybody. But those who read books for their quality rather than their theme, will see in it something fine and different. A thrilling book, in the sense that Dumas is thrilling, it is not. There is plenty of bloodshed in it, plenty of heroism and excitement; but its essential appeal is the appeal of poetry. Mr. Eddison has given it the spirit of the sagas, aware that their strength and vigor are infinitely more satisfying than any tricks of writing aimed to complicate or mystify. His story has about it the very breath of the old North—blond giants, and mighty horses, and the sea. The story, however, is given something of modern compactness, and Mr. Eddison's method and style are altogether praiseworthy. We can be grateful for his skill in altering the story where it needed alteration, and for his restraint in not touching it where it needed to be left alone. We can be grateful also for the vitality and beauty he has given the style of the book, yet for the good sense which led him for the most part to retain its simple, old-fashioned air. It is all in all a thoroughly satisfying achievement which offers a second side of the man who wrote *The Worm Ouroboros*.

Unsigned, "The Old Norsemen," *New York Times Book Review*, 19 September 1926, p. 16

BASIL DAVENPORT   Theophanies are notoriously dangerous, and Mr. Eddison's world ⟨in *Mistress of Mistresses*⟩, which is huge enough to hold all other elements in a self-contained harmony, is too keen and harsh, and even brutal for the occasionally misty enchantments by which one figure melts into another.

Beyond that, we may object to the book from our point of view, but not from its own. It is undeniably ornate; but then it belongs to a taste which positively prefers to call sighs "Windy suspirations of forc'd breath." It does not clearly explain itself; and neither does the other world that we now live in. If a man can make a planet that exists in its own right, he may be allowed to make it please himself, and we may be glad to be allowed the run of it. It is to be feared that *Mistress of Mistresses* will not appeal to many readers in this age, which is neither an age of poetry, nor like the eighteenth century an Age of Prose rightly regarded as an achievement, but an age merely of the makeshift prose of M. Jourdain. But for readers who wish a tale as shadowy and as vivid as old romances, for readers who give more than lip-service to the romantic and the heroic, for readers who for its own sake are interested in the romantic, here is a book.

Basil Davenport, "The Heavenly Aphrodite," *Saturday Review of Literature*, 10 August 1935, p. 6

JAMES STEPHENS   In some sense Mr. Eddison can be thought of as the most difficult writer of our day, for, behind and beyond all that which we cannot avoid or refuse—the switching as from a past to something that may be a future—he is writing with a mind fixed upon ideas which we may call ancient, but which are, in effect, eternal—aristocracy, that is, and courage, and a "hell of a cheek". It must seem lunatic to say of any man that always, as a guide of his inspiration, is an idea of the Infinite. Even so, when the proper question is asked, wherein does Mr. Eddison differ from his fellows? that is one answer which may be advanced. Here he does differ, and that so greatly that he may seem a pretty lonely writer.

There is something, exceedingly rare in English fiction, although everywhere to be found in English poetry—this may be called the aristocratic attitude, and accent. The aristocrat can be brutal as ever gangster was, but, and in whatever brutality, he preserves a bearing, a grace, a charm, which our fiction, in general, does not care, or dare, to attempt.

Good breeding and devastating brutality have never been strangers to each other. You may get in the pages of, say, *The Mahabharata*—the most aristocratic work in all literature—more sheer brutality than all our gangster fictionists put together could dream of. So, in these pages, there are villainies, and violence, and slaughterings that are, to one reader, simply devilish. But they are devilish with an accent—as Milton's devil is; for it is instantly observable in him, the most English personage of our record, and the finest of our "gentlemen", that he was educated at Cambridge. So the colossal gentlemen of Mr. Eddison have, perhaps, the Oxford accent. They are certainly not accented as of Balham, or Hoboken.

All Mr. Eddison's personages are of a "breeding" which, be it hellish or heavenish, never lets its fathers down and never lets its underlings up. So, again, he is a different writer, and a difficult.

James Stephens, "Introduction" (1941), *A Fish Dinner in Memison* (New York: Ballantine Books, 1968), pp. xi–xii

C. S. LEWIS   You may like or dislike ⟨Eddison's⟩ invented worlds (I myself like that of *The Worm Ouroboros* and strongly dislike that of *Mistress of Mistresses*) but there is here no quarrel between the theme and the articulation of the story. Every episode, every speech, helps to incarnate what the author is imagining. You could spare none of them. It takes the whole story to build up the strange blend of renaissance luxury and northern hardness. The secret here is largely the style, and especially the style of the dialogue. These proud, reckless, amorous people create themselves and the whole atmosphere of their world chiefly by talking.

> C. S. Lewis, "On Stories," *Essays Presented to Charles Williams* (London: Oxford University Press, 1947), p. 104

G. ROSTREVOR HAMILTON   I give all my admiration to Fiorinda's beauty of person, exquisitely robed or in voluptuous naked splendour. I admire her as a lofty, dangerous and unscrupulous woman, or as a goddess of like character, and, as such, she has her just pre-eminence in a country the nobility of which would be nothing without its savage and even brutal aspect. But I rebel when I am asked to recognize her as "*omnium rerum causa immanens:* the sufficient explanation of the world"; one, the service of whom is the only wisdom. And her boundless self-preoccupation is a travesty of that intellectual love with which, in the phrase of Spinoza, God loves His Own Self. *Mistress of Mistresses* and the *Fish Dinner* present high matter for the imagination, and the moral or religious censor would deserve to be prosecuted, should he break in and trespass on this ground. But when, as here and there, the high moral or religious claim is expressed or clearly implied, the censor cannot refuse the invitation to protest.

The truth is that Eddison fell deeply in love with his imagined world, from Fiorinda to the least blade of grass, and like a lover, he could see nothing amiss. He is completely serious and takes his stand on philosophy, reducing Truth, Beauty and Goodness to one ultimate value, Beauty: a thing you may only do, if in Beauty you include not only sensuous beauty of form and beauty of action but also—and not dependent on these—beauty of character, according to the highest conception of the Good. It is his failure to recognize this which I regard as the chief defect in Eddison's Utopia. And yet to bring it into the open is to risk a loss of perspective: for this fault has the same root as his virtue, so that one may almost say—*felix culpa.*

It was just because he saw with the eyes of a lover that he was able to present his world with so amazing a vitality.

G. Rostrevor Hamilton, "The Prose of E. R. Eddison," *English Studies* 2 (1949): 45–46

J. R. R. TOLKIEN   I read the works of Eddison, long after they appeared; and I once met him. I heard him in Mr. Lewis's room in Magdalen College read aloud some parts of his own works—from the *Mistress of Mistresses*, as far as I remember. He did it extremely well. I read his works with great enjoyment for their sheer literary merit. My opinion of them is almost the same as that expressed by Mr. Lewis on p. 104 of the *Essays Presented to Charles Williams*. Except that I disliked his characters (always excepting the Lord Gro) and despised what he appeared to admire more intensely than Mr. Lewis at any rate saw fit to say of himself. Eddison thought what I admire 'soft' (his word: one of complete condemnation, I gathered); I thought that, corrupted by an evil and indeed silly 'philosophy', he was coming to admire, more and more, arrogance and cruelty. Incidentally, I thought his nomenclature slipshod and often inept. In spite of all of which, I still think of him as the greatest and most convincing writer of 'invented worlds' that I have read. But he was certainly not an 'influence'.

J. R. R. Tolkien, Letter to Caroline Everett (24 June 1957), *Letters of J. R. R. Tolkien,* ed. Humphrey Carpenter and Christopher Tolkien (London: George Allen & Unwin, 1981), p. 258

E. R. EDDISON   *The Mezentian Gate*, last in order of composition, is by the very fact first in order of ripeness. It in no respect supersedes or amends the earlier books, but does I think illuminate them. *Mistress of Mistresses*, leaving unexplored the relations between that other world and our present here and now, led to the writing of the *Fish Dinner;* which book in turn, at its climax, raised the question whether what took place at that singular supper party may not have had yet vaster and more cosmic reactions, quite overshadowing those affecting the fate of this planet. I was besides, by then, fallen in love with Zimiamvia and my persons; and love has a searching curiosity which can never be wholly satisfied (and well that it cannot, or mankind might die of boredom). Also I wanted to find out how it came that the great King, while still at the height of his powers, met his death in Sestola; and why, so leaving the Three Kingdoms, he left them in a mess. These riddles begot *The Meʒentian Gate*.

Without current distraction, political, social and economic, this story (in common with its predecessors) is as utterly unconcerned as it is with the Stock Exchange procedure, the technicalities of aerodynamics, or the Theory of Vectors. Nor is it an allegory. Allegory, if its persons have life, is a prostitution of their personalities, forcing them for an end other than their own. If they have not life, it is but a dressing up of argument in a puppetry of frigid make-believe. To me, the persons *are* the argument. And for the argument I am not fool enough to claim responsibility; for, stripped to its essentials, it is a great eternal commonplace, beside which, I am sometimes apt to think, nothing else really matters.

> E. R. Eddison, "Letter of Introduction," *The Meʒentian Gate* (1958; rpt. New York: Ballantine Books, 1969), pp. xiii–xiv

ORVILLE PRESCOTT   What are the reasons for considering this flawed masterpiece ⟨*The Worm Ouroboros*⟩ (so noble in concept and so mighty in scope and yet marred with a few irksome failings) worthy of the attention of serious students of literature? First of all, there is the lordly narrative sweep of it, the pure essence of story-telling for its own sake such as has become increasingly rare in our introspective modern world. Second is the splendor of the prose, the roll and swagger and reverberating rhythms and the sheer gorgeousness of much of its deliberate artifice. And third is the blessed sense of vicarious participation in a simpler, more primitive world where wonders still abound and glory is still a word untarnished by the cynical tongues of small-minded men.

> Orville Prescott, "Introduction" (1962), *The Worm Ouroboros* by E. R. Eddison (New York: Ballantine Books, 1967), p. xiv

FRITZ LEIBER   *The Worm* has no single, logical rationale, either fantasy or science fiction. It is instead a composite. But since Eddison has taste and good judgment, his composite has style, inner consistency, and the ring of truth. Despite its leisurely telling, the story maintains a varied suspense and teems with inventions: sweating sorceries, moving mythic themes, wondrous landscapes, strong clashes of character, a sand sea with tides, flying serpents, hippogriff rides, swashing sword-fights, an evil king who when he dies is always revived in another body, mantichores that put all the great apes of fiction to shame, dire comets, and many other "rare and remarcable occurants and observacions."

It is aristocratic melodrama, which pits not so much good against evil, as warlike and ambitious princes who are honorable against their opposite numbers who are *dis*honorable in varying degrees; but both sorts live for action "that shall embroil and astonish the world"—which makes me think of Ferdinand's dying lines in *The Duchess ⟨of Malfi⟩*: "I shall vault credit and affect high pleasures beyond death."

Fritz Leiber, [Review of *The Worm Ouroboros*], *Fantastic Science Fiction* 18, No. 4 (April 1969): 142–43

URSULA K. LE GUIN   The archaic manner is indeed a perfect distancer, but you have to do it perfectly. It's a high wire: one slip spoils all. The man who did it perfectly was, of course, Eddison. He really did write Elizabethan prose in the 1930s. His style is totally artificial, but it is never faked. If you love language for its own sake he is irresistible. Many, with reason, find him somewhat crabbed and most damnedly long; but he is the real thing, and just to reaffirm that strange, remote reality I am placing a longer quotation from him here. This is from *The Worm Ouroboros*. A dead king is being carried, in secrecy, at night, down to the beach.

> The lords of Witchland took and the men at arms bare-the-goods, and the King went in the midst on his bier of spear-shafts. So went they picking their way in the moonless night round the palace and down the winding path that led to the bed of the combe, and so by the stream westward toward the sea. Here they deemed it safe to light a torch to show them the way. Desolate and bleak showed the sides of the combe in the windblown flare; and the flare was thrown back from the royal jewels of the crown of Witchland, and from the armoured buskins on the King's feet showing stark with toes pointing upward from below his bear-skin mantle, and from the armour and the weapons of them that bare him and walked beside him, and from the black cold surface of the little river hurrying forever over its bed of boulders to the sea.

> The path was rugged and stony, and they fared slowly, lest they
> should stumble and drop the King.

That prose, in spite or because of its archaisms, is good prose: exact, clear, powerful. Visually it is precise and vivid; musically—that is, in the sound of the words, the movement of the syntax, and the rhythm of the sentences—it is subtle and very strong. Nothing in it is faked or blurred; it is all seen, heard, felt. That style was his true style, his own voice; that was how Eddison, an artist, spoke.

> Ursula K. Le Guin, "From Elfland to Poughkeepsie" (1973), *The Language of the Night: Essays on Fantasy and Science Fiction*, rev. ed. (New York: HarperCollins, 1992), pp. 85–86

HELMUT W. PESCH   At least in one respect, *The Mezentian Gate* is the most skillful of Eddison's works because it integrates philosophy and action. It has been said that while the *Worm* is Homeric, the Zimiamvian novels are Machiavellian, not so much because the world of Zimiamvia resembles renaissance Italy but because the element of intrigue is so predominant in the story itself. What has irritated G. Rostrevor Hamilton and infuriated ⟨L. Sprague⟩ de Camp is that the characters do not behave like gods. They are capable of cruelty and cunning and deem themselves superior to other people. Philosophically, this may even be justified. Viewed in social terms, it is nevertheless highly suspect. It ought to be noted again, though, that these characters are not just one-dimensional figures representing abstract values. Eddison's aforementioned dislike of allegory is firmly based on the notion that there are no general principles except as embodied in the particular, and that no single manifestation is sufficient to denote them. The characters in his novels have their individual characteristics, reflecting, no doubt, to some extent the author's own cultural prejudices.

But even if there is no strict allegory, there is a certain quasi-allegorical, philosophical layer which appears superimposed on the political intrigue. In the *Worm*, heroic action is an aim in itself, but in *Mistress*, the political action is interspersed with philosophical discussions, mainly situated in isolated places like the timeless gardens of the philosopher magician Doctor Vandermast, who, having aged beyond the desires of the flesh, is almost the image of Death itself. In *Fish Dinner* the action is more or less subordinate to the philosophical preoccupations. Only in *The Mezentian Gate* do both intrigue and philosophical desire interact, leading to a common aim—the death of King Mezentius.

Death is the central theme of Eddison's final work. It has already been a subject of discussion in the earlier novels, but only under the aspect of transition, as a gate to a fuller, more conscious life. As such, it is discussed by the first-person narrator of the "Overture" to *Mistress*, who has some features in common with Doctor Vandermast. In *Fish Dinner* the author has Lessingham say, "Perhaps if people knew, beyond quibble or doubt, what was through the Door the world would be depopulated?" What is through the Door is a Death, so easy, so familiar and dreadless, to a believer. But a curious problem remains unresolved: Why does Lessingham have to wait another fifty years before he may join his beloved once more in another world? What purpose is there to cogitation that has no aim? In the "Praeludium"—and it ought to be noted that Eddison chooses his titles with care: this is no "opening" or "induction"—the central aspect of death is that of negation. Here, in our world, the thought of "leaving one's love alone" is indeed the ultimate terror, even if death—either as a forgetting or a new beginning—holds no fear.

To Mezentius, death is at first only a temporary forgetting, a starting anew with a blank page, as he and Zeus have done again and again. But it cannot "redeem this all-knowing knowing," the time-transcending knowledge enclosing all existence first revealed to Mezentius in the Fish Dinner episode. It is basically the same problem we have already encountered at the end of *The Worm Ouroboros*: the question of awareness in reenaction, which can now no longer be ignored.

Helmut W. Pesch, "The Sign of the Worm: Images of Death and Immortality in the Fiction of E. R. Eddison," *Death and the Serpent: Immortality in Science Fiction and Fantasy*, ed. Carl B. Yoke and Donald Hassler (Westport, CT: Greenwood Press, 1985), pp. 98–99

VERLYN FLEIGER   A galloping horse, a portrait in oils, a click of castanets; these are clues to the simultaneous occurrence of separate but intrinsically identical events linking the two worlds—Earth and Zimiamvia—of *A Fish Dinner*. Seemingly unimportant events in one world become significant as they echo or mirror events in the other, though at times the mirror appears to be held at a slant. Carl Jung calls this synchronicity, wherein causally unrelated but coincidental events give meaning to one another. It is a function of time in which two schemes intersect and interact, even when, as in A *Fish Dinner*, the schemes themselves are of different worlds.

Whatever the scheme, time in both worlds is governed by love. First, because it is lovers' time, seeming to run swift or slow according as lovers are together or apart. Second, because, as we will see, it is time literally created for Love in its feminine personification, time controlled by Her, from Her perspective, experienced by Her men. It is time both austere and erotic, strict and yielding, reminiscent of the contradiction inherent in those naive china figurines which used to grace drawing-room mantelpieces: demure but entirely naked young ladies with clocks in their stomachs, reminding observers that it is love that makes the world go round.

This saying, trite as it sounds, is the idea behind the *Fish Dinner*, but under Eddison's hands the triteness falls away to reveal a concept ambiguous in its presentation and disturbing in its ramifications.

A *Fish Dinner* begins with one love affair, parallels that with a second, and frames both with a third. All of them connect, and all of them (as we come to know by the end of the book) are the same love. The first lovers are Edward and Mary Lessingham, whose time of love is all on Earth, (or so it seems), but who are counterpoint to their Zimiamvian selves: Barganax and Fiorinda and King Mezentius and Duchess Amalie. All six lovers are aspects of one another, parts of what Eddison describes in his unpublished notes as "duality in unity (Zeus & Aphrodite: Masc. & Feminine: Love & the Object of Love: Power & Beauty)."

This interweaving of personae, this unity in multiplicity set in Eddison's larger than life world, conveyed in his immense prose, confers sublimity on the trite saying, taking time and love away from the naked china lady and giving them back to the Gods. Where other authors take love as their theme, Eddison weaves it into his thesis. His contention is simple in concept, complex and various in the mutual but dissimilar needs of Lover and Beloved: it is a magic circle in which Love cannot exist without that Love. It is a kind of Worm Ouroboros. In that energy all is engendered; from that dynamic all proceeds.

Not until the end of the book are we permitted to see and appreciate Eddison's design in all its fullness and complexity. Not till this is it made clear that surrounding and containing all secondary partnerings is the formal and formative relationship of Mezentius and Fiorinda, who never touch, but who are the ultimate Lover and Beloved in whom and for whom all Creation exists. Eddison's particular genius is to project this interplay of God and Goddess onto their lesser selves, separated aspects through whom the supreme Self and Co-Self can know and delight in one another.

But to reduce this to a thesis is to do violence to Eddison's imagination. He has written a novel, not a dissertation. Thesis is implied, never stated, and so clothed in the sensuous interaction of lovers that argument dissolves into poetry.

> Verlyn Fleiger, "The Ouroboros Principle: Time and Love in Zimiamvia," *Mythlore* 15, No. 4 (Summer 1989): 43–44

WILLIAM M. SCHUYLER, JR.   Like virtually every Englishman of his class and time, Eddison had a classical education. It was perhaps a more lasting influence on him than it was on many of those who shared his background. His solutions to the problems of purpose and of injustice in a world created by divinity are built on the framework erected by Descartes, Hume, Kant, and Schopenhauer. To this company ⟨. . .⟩ we must add Spinoza. Despite his admiration for the sagas and their heroes, he turned to Greece when it came time to shape his philosophy of human nature: his later books are peppered with Latin and Greek. However, his interpretations of the modern philosophical tradition and the classical legacy are idiosyncratic.

He takes as his foundation the proposition that only consciousness of the present moment can be known to be real. (Descartes was right about where we must begin.) Reason can take us no further. (Hume's objections to Descartes' rationalism are sound.) Yet there must be something further which cannot be known by logic (as Kant maintains). This can be reached only by the poet's vision (else Schopenhauer's truth would be unavoidable). What the poet seeks is ultimate value, that which is desired as an end in itself and not as a means to something else. One ultimate value seems to be sufficient.

For Eddison, following in the steps of such thinkers as Shaftesbury, that value is Beauty: all others, including Good, derive from it. However, one and many, universal and particular, abstract and concrete; each member of every pair is dependent on the other. Moreover, if value is the ground of existence, then "ought" implies "is": whatever exists must be what ought to exist ("Letter").

There is, then, a multitude of beautiful things, and everything which exists is somehow beautiful. This seems contrary to our experience and must somehow be placed in perspective so that it falls in line with theory. There is no need for the world to be as it is (or we could discover the necessity by reason). Therefore it must be that someone or something wanted it like this, and the best motive that Eddison can think of for that is that it is amusing, although it is certainly not we who are amused.

Who, then, is amused? The foundation of any value, including Beauty, is that it is desirable. In accord with Eddison's principle of complementary pairs, there must be one that desires and one that is desired. The complementary (not opposing) principles of his dualism are personified as Zeus and Aphrodite. The reason for choosing Zeus is that the father of gods is suitable for a creator, the critical role he fills in Eddison's fantasies. And who better than Aphrodite to personify Beauty and the object of desire? It is they who are in some way amused by this world as they, not we, see it.

The problem facing anyone who postulates a creator is why a perfect, self-sufficient being would have bothered to create the universe. Eddison's dualism provides a solution for this puzzle. All the worlds are created for love, as homages to Aphrodite.

William M. Schuyler, Jr., "E. R. Eddison's Metaphysics of the Hero," *New York Review of Science Fiction* 3, No. 7 (March 1991): 13–14

▨ *Bibliography*

Poems, Letters, and Memories of Philip Sidney Nairn (editor). 1916.

The Worm Ouroboros: A Romance. 1922.

Styrbiorn the Strong. 1926.

Egil's Saga: Done into English out of the Icelandic. 1930.

Mistress of Mistresses: A Vision of Zimiamvia. 1935.

A Fish Dinner in Memison. 1941.

The Mezentian Gate. 1958.

Zimiamvia ⟨*Mistress of Mistresses, A Fish Dinner in Memison, The Mezentian Gate*⟩. 1992.

Robert E. Howard
1906–1936

ROBERT ERVIN HOWARD, the only child of Dr. Isaac Mordecai Howard and Hester Jane Ervin Howard, was born on January 24, 1906, in Peaster, Texas. He spent most of his life in Cross Plains, a part of the post oaks region of Texas, and grew up familiar with the region's frontier legends and folklore. Bookish and introverted as a child, Howard endured bullying until high school, when he transformed himself into a formidable physical figure through bodybuilding. Howard enrolled in Howard Payne College in 1924 but left shortly after selling "Spear and Fang" and two other stories to the pulp magazine *Weird Tales,* thereby embarking on a career as a writer. However, he was unable to support himself completely by writing until 1929, and he took on a variety of jobs to make ends meet.

Howard tried his hand at a number of different story types—western, sports, adventure, detective, love stories—but it was in the weird fiction magazines that he would carve out a name for himself. The August 1928 issue of *Weird Tales* carried his novella "Red Shadows," which introduced the series character Solomon Kane, a seventeenth-century Puritan vigilante who proved the first of a succession of swashbuckling heroes who would dominate Howard's writing. The following year *Weird Tales* published "The Shadow Kingdom," the first of several tales of King Kull of the ancient land of Valusia who, like Kane, was fashioned out of both the heroic frontier legends and Howard's interest in ancient history. In 1932 Howard rewrote a Kull story he could not sell as "The Phoenix on the Sword," renaming the main character Conan the Cimmerian, a warrior of the prehistoric Hyborian Age whose barbaric comportment distinguished him from the noble savages that hitherto had dominated adventure fiction. A mouthpiece for Howard's social philosophies concerning the failures of civilization, Conan became the hero of a score of stories written between 1930 and 1936, and one of the most popular characters to emerge from the pulp magazines. Conan's exploits inaugurated the fantasy subgenre of "sword-and-sorcery," a blend of heroic action adventure and supernatural fiction, and earned Howard a reputation as one of the bloodiest writers for the pulps.

In 1930 Howard began corresponding with fellow *Weird Tales* author H. P. Lovecraft, who affectionately dubbed him "Two-Gun Bob" in his letters. Their mutual interests in history and social philosophy forged a fast friendship that was integral to Howard's intellectual development. Howard would ultimately contribute a handful of stories to the shared universe of horror fiction created by Lovecraft, Clark Ashton Smith, August Derleth, and others, known today as the Cthulhu Mythos. During the depression, Howard wrote prodigious amounts of fiction and verse for a variety of magazines to offset the shrinking of his literary markets and earn a living that would allow him to provide for his ailing mother. Deeply affected by his mother's lapse into an irreversible coma, Howard took his own life on June 11, 1936, with a gunshot wound to the head.

Although Howard never saw any of his fiction collected in book form, his growing literary reputation led to the posthumous publication of nearly every scrap of his writing. Starting with the efforts of L. Sprague de Camp in the 1950s to edit and systematize the Conan stories, and flesh out Howard's chronology for the series with his completions of Howard's literary fragments, "Howardiana" became a cottage industry that created its own branch of fantasy fandom and culminated in de Camp's official biography, *Dark Valley Destiny* (1983), and two film adaptations of the Conan saga in the 1980s. Howard's early autobiographical novel, *Post Oaks and Sand Roughs*, appeared in 1990.

Critical Extracts

ROBERT E. HOWARD   For the world as a whole, civilization even in decaying form, is undoubtedly better for people as a whole. I have no idyllic view of barbarism—as near as I can learn it's a grim, bloody, ferocious and loveless condition. I have no patience with the depiction of the barbarian of any race as a stately, god-like child of Nature, endowed with strange wisdom and speaking in measured and sonorous phrases. Bah! My conception of a barbarian is very different. He had neither stability nor undue dignity. He was ferocious, brutal and frequently squalid. He was haunted by dim and shadowy fears; he committed horrible crimes for strange monstrous reasons. As a race he hardly ever exhibited the steadfast courage often shown by civilized men. He was childish and terrible in his wrath, bloody and treacherous. As an individual he lived under the shadow of the war-chief and the shaman, each of whom might bring him to a bloody end because of a whim, a dream, a leaf floating on the wind. His religion was generally one of dooms and shadows, his gods were awful and abominable. They bade him mutilate himself or slaughter his children, and he obeyed because of fears too primordial for any civilized man to comprehend. His life was often a bondage of tabus, sharp sword-edges, between which he walked shuddering. He had no mental freedom, as civilized man understands it, and very little personal freedom, being bound to his clan, his tribe, his chief. Dreams and shadows haunted and maddened him. Simplicity of the primitive? To my mind the barbarian's problems were as complex in their way as modern man's—possibly more so. He moved through life motivated by whims, his or another's. In war he was unstable; the blowing of a leaf might send him plunging in an hysteria of blood-lust against terrific odds, or cause him to flee in blind panic when another stroke could have won the battle. But he was lithe and strong as a panther, and the full joy of strenuous physical exertion was his. The day and the night were his book, wherein he read of all things that run or walk or crawl or fly. Trees and grass and moss-covered rocks and birds and beasts and clouds were alive to him, and partook of his kinship. The wind blew his hair and he looked with naked eyes into the sun. Often he starved, but when he feasted, it was with a mighty gusto, and the juices of food and strong drink were stinging wine to his palate. Oh, I know I can never make myself clear; I've never seen anyone who had any sympathy whatever with my point of view, nor do I want any. I'm not ashamed of it. I would not choose to plunge into such a life now; it would be the sheerest of hells to me, unfitted as I am for such an existence. But I do say that if I had the choice of another existence, to be born into it and raised in it, knowing no other, I'd choose such an existence as I've just sought to depict. There's no question of the relative merits of barbarism and civilization here involved. It's just my own personal opinion and choice.

Robert E. Howard, Letter to H. P. Lovecraft (2 November 1932), *Selected Letters 1931–1936*, ed. Glenn Lord, Rusty Burke, S. T. Joshi, and Steve Behrends (West Warwick, RI: Necronomicon Press, 1991), p. 35

ROBERT BLOCH   I am awfully tired of poor old Conan the Cluck, who for the past fifteen issues has every month slain a new wizard, tackled a new monster, come to a violent and sudden end that was averted (incredibly enough!) in just the nick of time, and won a new girl-friend, each of whose penchant for nudism won her a place of honor, either on the cover or on the inner illustration. Such has been Conan's history, and from the realms of the Kushites to the lands of Aquilonia, from the shores of the Shemites to the palaces of Dyme-Novelle-Bolonia, I cry: 'Enough of this brute and his iron-thewed sword thrusts—may he be sent to Valhalla to cut out paper dolls.'

Robert Bloch, "The Eyrie," *Weird Tales* 24, No. 5 (November 1934): 651

H. P. LOVECRAFT   The character and attainments of Mr. Howard were wholly unique. He was, above everything else, a lover of the simpler, older world of barbarian and pioneer days, when courage and strength took the place of subtlety and stratagem, and when a hardy, fearless race battled and bled, and asked no quarter from hostile nature. All his stories reflect this philosophy, and derive from it a vitality found in few of his contemporaries. No one could write more convincingly of violence and gore than he, and his battle passages reveal an instinctive aptitude for military tactics which would have brought him distinction in times of war. His real gifts were even higher than the readers of his published works would suspect, and, had he lived, would have helped him to make his mark in serious literature with some folk epic of his beloved Southwest.

It is hard to describe precisely what made Mr. Howard's stories stand out so sharply; but the real secret is that he himself is in every one of them, whether they were ostensibly commercial or not. He was greater than any profit-making policy he could adopt—for even when he outwardly made concessions to Mammon-guided editors and commercial critics, he had an internal force and sincerity which broke through the surface and put the imprint of his personality on everything he wrote. Seldom, if ever, did he set down a lifeless stock character or situation and leave it as such. Before he concluded with it, it always took on some tinge of vitality and reality in spite of popular editorial policy—always drew something from his own experience and knowledge of life instead of from the sterile herbarium of desiccated pulpish standbys. Not only did he excel in pictures of strife and slaughter, but he was almost alone in his ability to create real emotions of spectral fear and dread suspense. No author—even in the humblest fields—can truly excel unless he takes his work very seriously; and Mr. Howard did just that even in cases where he consciously thought he did not. That such a genuine artist should perish while hundreds of insincere hacks continue to concoct spurious ghosts and vampires and space-ships and occult detectives is indeed a sorry piece of cosmic irony!

> H. P. Lovecraft, "In Memoriam: Robert Ervin Howard," *Fantasy Magazine* No. 28 (September 1936): 30–31

FRITZ LEIBER   The landscape, plan, diagram, or microcosm of each of Howard's earlier stories is as simple, limited, and complete as that of a boy's daydream, a hewn-out stage setting that can be held in the mind while the story progresses. It has no more parts than a good diagram. There is no worry at all how it intersects the real world. It is an inner world for a boy's solemn adventuring. In most fantasy there are only traces of this boyish stage in the development of the dream world (Eddison naming his rival nations in *The Worm* Demons, Witches, Pixies, Goblins, Imps, and Ghouls) but in Howard (especially to my mind in the King Kull and Solomon Kane stories) it is dominant.

Most of us, I imagine, create in childhood starkly simple landscapes for adventuring. I spent a lot of time on a rope bridge over a dark chasm; often there was a tiger at one end and a lion at the other. But it took Howard's unique talent and intensity to make powerful genuine stories directly out of these materials with almost no disguise at all.

Broad strokes, stark landscapes, near-clichés of power—like I said.

I'm not belittling Howard when I denominate his writing as boyish. I'm thinking of his freshness, sincerity, and exuberance as much as anything else, and there is an undeniably boyish element in all swordplay-and-sorcery fiction, even the most sophisticated or wickedly decadent. When the author of *Vathek* came of age, or into his great inheritance, his comment was something like "Now my friends will expect me to behave like a man. How much they are deceived, for I intend to remain a child always!" This was the same Beckford who when a great tower he was having built on his estate collapsed, instantly reacted, "Ah, if only I'd been there to see it fall!"

⟨. . .⟩

Nor am I saying that Howard used clichés on the order of stony silence, iron will, morbid curiosity seekers, and rapier-like wit—but rather the near-clichés of the horror story, such as words like strange, weird, and eerie. (If something is strange, a good writer ought to be able to spot wherein the strangeness lies, and surely his description will be more effective if he can.) Howard generally didn't over-use those particular words, but he leaned heavily on such cousin-words as grim, black, dark, and ghostly.

> Fritz Leiber, "Robert E. Howard's Style" (1961), *Fafhrd & Me: A Collection of Essays* (Newark, NJ: Wildside Press, 1990), p. 47

ROBERT WEINBERG   "Red Shadows" was the first Kane story and, in many ways, the best. It presented the closest look at Kane and all that he represented. It was a fast-paced adventure story with a strong sense of atmosphere and just the right touch of the weird. It was evidently written for *Argosy* or *Adventure* but did not sell and finally made it to *Weird Tales*. It did suffer from several faults which would haunt the entire series. Most prominent was the dreadful use of coincidence to forward the plot. There was no attempt at any complication in the plot. Nor are any of the characters other than Kane anything more than cardboard. The villains are typical stereotypes and are a shade too evil.

Balancing out these faults were Howard's gift for storytelling, along with some fine writing and notable description. ⟨. . .⟩

Throughout the entire series much is made of Kane's cold fury. He is a relentless fighter, one who never seems to tire, and while not a flashy fencer, one of the deadliest swordsmen alive. This picture of the man is skillfully developed by Howard more through understatement than anything else. Kane sounded deadly because of what he did not say more than from what he did say. The grim menace of his promise, "Men shall die for this," perfectly presents the deadly determination of Solomon Kane.

"Red Shadows" also had Howard at his descriptive best, telling of the menacing lure of the jungle. The African sequence of the novelette was notable for its atmosphere. A feeling of dark lurking menace hangs over the entire section of the story, making the land a place of mystery and dark death. The spirit of the jungle, the soul of Africa, the thrum, thrum, thrum of jungle drums seems to echo in the print. The Black God of the natives is made menacingly real and the picture of hidden menace is perfectly maintained.

Robert Weinberg, *The Annotated Guide to Robert E. Howard's Sword & Sorcery* (Mercer Island, WA: Starmont House, 1976), pp. 7–8

GEORGE KNIGHT   Most commentators on Robert E. Howard's writing typically group it with the work of William Morris, Lord Dunsany, and J. R. R. Tolkien—writers with whom Howard has very little in common. Because his most popular creations are his fantasy tales, Howard is put into the category of "fantasy writer," yet to me the most interesting aspect of his fiction is not the fantasy but the realism—a realism springing from Howard's class, environment, beliefs, and the age in which he wrote. It is Howard's impulse toward realism that makes him unique in fantastic literature and one of the most important American writers to contribute to the form.

Howard wrote at a time when civilization was in upheaval. World War I, the Russian Revolution, the Great Depression, the rise of fascism in Europe and gangsterism in the United States—these factors greatly affected his vision of civilization crumbling before the tides of barbarism. Civilization as it had been known to Western culture—the era of the far-flung British Empire, of America's Manifest Destiny—was changing rapidly, and as far as the forces of established order were concerned, it was changing for the worse. 〈. . .〉

In the cheap wood-pulp magazines popular fiction was changing, becoming more violent, more realistic, told in terse, newspaper-like language. In *Black Mask* magazine Dashiell Hammett and others took the immensely popular classic murder mystery and Americanized it, brought it up-to-date. 〈. . .〉 Howard, in the pulp pages of *Weird Tales*, did much the same thing for the fantasy story—he broke it away from the lush stylists like Hodgson, Dunsany, and Eddison and wrote in direct language. He eschewed the arty toying about with elves, enchanted princesses, and magical dragons and cut loose with stories about thick-armed warriors, harem girls, and flesh-eating apes. He was not catering to the reader of James Branch Cabell, Dunsany, or Morris any more than Hammett was catering to the reader of the most popular American mystery writer of the day, S. S. Van Dine. Though Howard showed traditional tastes in his poetry, and took a slam at jazz in his privately circulated newsletter *The Golden Caliph,* his accomplishment in his best fiction is very modern. Howard and Hammett were each creating a distinct genre for their audience, the American pulp magazine reader.

George Knight, "Robert E. Howard: Hard-Boiled Heroic Fantasist," *The Dark Barbarian: The Writings of Robert E. Howard—A Critical Anthology,* ed. Don Herron (Westport, CT: Greenwood Press, 1984), pp. 117–18

DON HERRON   Of course before Howard, Edgar Rice Burroughs in Tarzan and Rudyard Kipling in the earlier Mowgli, of *The Jungle Books,* created *barbarian* figures. When Lord Greystoke shed the trappings of civilization to roam Africa in loincloth and knife as Tarzan of the Apes, a more barbaric image would be difficult to create. Mowgli, raised by wolves, trained by bear, panther, and snake, is equally stripped of the costumes and conventions of civilization in Kipling's tales. These figures certainly set a precedent for Howard's Conan the Cimmerian, but Howard carried the matter further, into a distinct literary type. The fact that he usurped the swordplay of Dumas and a good measure of supernatural horror from Lovecraft added to the distinction.

Yet the overriding difference is in mood and philosophy. Burroughs' Tarzan is a respectable pillar of civilization as an English Lord, and preserves the twentieth-century American sense of the *status quo* even when adventuring naked in time-lost cities and primeval forests. The thrust of the Mowgli stories is the jungle giving way before civilization's inroads, and the man-child leaving the forest and his bestial comrades to live as man, not as an animal. In Howard, the unquiet surge of barbarism ever threatens to sweep the works of civlization under, the *status quo* is at best shaky—even when Howard's barbarians use their swords to put themselves on the thrones of the ruling class.

The Howardian mood and philosophy is not simply barbaric, it is a *dark barbarism,* a pessimistic view that holds the accomplishments of society of little account in the face of mankind's darker nature. The famous lines at the end of the Conan story "Beyond the Black River" epigrammatize this philosophy:

> Barbarism is the natural state of mankind. Civilization is
> unnatural. It is a whim of circumstance. And barbarism must
> always ultimately triumph.

Beyond the Black River the barbarians wait their chance to rush in. The fact that the river is "Black" is aptly symbolic of Howard's underlying meaning. The words "black" and "dark" appear often in fantasy titles, perhaps more because they represent Howard's *content* than for any lack of inventiveness on his part.

This dark and brooding attitude was at the core of Howard's creative impulse. His artistic leanings toward the poetic and the romantic, his compulsion for violence, his interests in history, myth and adventure all fell easily into this shadow of barbarism.

> Don Herron, "The Dark Barbarian," *The Dark Barbarian: The Writings of Robert E. Howard—A Critical Anthology*, ed. Don Herron (Westport, CT: Greenwood Press, 1984), pp. 150–51

MARC A. CERASINI and CHARLES HOFFMAN   Conan and most of Howard's other heroes are presented far more realistically than the characters of Howard's fellow pulp writers, such as Edgar Rice Burroughs and Lester Dent. One of the ways in which Howard tempered the fabulous vision of his fantasies with a stiff dose of reality was to stress the humanity of his protagonists. Howard's heroes are always formidable, but never invincible. They can and do get hurt as a result of their dangerous exploits. Solomon Kane gets the worst of his duel with Le Loup in "Red Shadows." Kull is cut nearly to ribbons in both "The Shadow Kingdom" and "By This Axe I Rule!" Conan is no exception; he suffers great wounds in many of his adventures, which in reality are the prices a hero usually pays for an action-filled life.

Another way in which Howard's protagonists differ from the general run of popular culture heroes is that they are motivated by impulses more complex than the simplistic good guy/bad guy morality that most "genre" writers adhere to. The Shadow and Solomon Kane both fight for good against evil. However, while The Shadow's motivations are never made clear, Solomon Kane is driven by impulses that Howard renders recognizable and plausible to the reader. Howard's ability to fully realize subtle aspects of characterization was especially evident with Conan. Indeed, each of the characters we have examined displays characterization far more sophisticated than that usually found in popular fiction. Bran Mak Morn's obsession with preserving his race and culture, Solomon Kane's religious fanaticism, and Kull's philosophical brooding are all clearly and concisely presented by

Howard in the body of each short work. Because he worked within the limits of the short story, Howard was compelled to be spare. Nevertheless, his characterization is convincing, and Conan is another step forward in Howard's crafting of believable characters. That Howard considered Conan to be his "most realistic" character was undoubtedly because Conan possesses a more "normal" personality than his previous characters: that is, Conan's personality is more readily understandable to the average reader. Like most men, Conan is motivated by self-gratification, a healthy sex drive, a desire for wealth, and a hunger for experience. Conan is spoken of as being "fond of women and strong drink." Howard also mentions Conan's "gigantic melancholies and gigantic mirth." If the latter statement suggests a manic-depressive nature, Conan nonetheless possesses a greater capacity for pleasure than Bran Mak Morn, Solomon Kane, and Kull put together. Though Conan is referred to as being frequently sullen and moody, he is usually only *spoken of* in this manner. The aspect of Conan we are most often shown, however, is one of vitality and humor. Conan is an extrovert, not a religious fanatic. He is no slave to obsession or morbid introspection. Devoid of neuroses and inhibitions, Conan is free of what Blake called "the mind forg'd manacles." Howard would consider these "manacles" to be the trappings and conventions of civilization.

At the core of Conan's personality is the unmistakable purity of what Dryden called "the noble savage." The cult of the noble savage, at least in modern times, originated with the Swiss philosopher Jean Jacques Rousseau, who considered man in his natural state to be free of vice. ⟨. . .⟩ Howard took a more sophisticated view. Though not necessarily noble, Howard's savages are possessed of many qualities lacking in civilized men. All the attributes of actual barbarians are present in Conan. He is stronger and fleeter than someone raised in a civilized environment. Having been bred in the wilderness, he is inured to discomfort and hardship, even pain. His senses are keener than those of civilized men, and his reflexes are set on a hair-trigger. All of these qualities, says Howard, give Conan an edge in any situation or conflict.

Marc A. Cerasini and Charles Hoffman, *Robert E. Howard* (Mercer Island, WA: Starmont House, 1987), pp. 61–62

RUSTY BURKE   By 1930, Howard had become confirmed enough in his Irishness, steeped enough in the history and lore of the subject, to begin writing fiction in this vein. The first story to emerge from this new *persona* is "The Dark Man": Bran Mak Morn, the Pictish chieftain who was one of Howard's earliest creations, is in this story a legend of the remote past—a statue of him plays a central role in the plot. Replacing him as the featured character is a Celt—an Irish adventurer named Turlogh Dubh O'Brien. That Howard was enthusiastic about the new character is evident from the fact that he hopes to sell a series of stories about him. Only one other story of O'Brien sold, though: two months after the acceptance of "The Dark Man," Howard reports that Farnsworth Wright ⟨editor of *Weird Tales*⟩ bought "The Gods of Bal-Sagoth." Another story apparently failed to sell, and one unfinished fragment completes what we now have of the Turlogh Dubh O'Brien series.

At about the same time he sold "The Dark Man," Howard sold another story featuring a Celtic warrior. Cormac of Connacht, leader of a band of Irish who are settling the Scottish region of Dalriada, is not the best-known character in "Kings of the Night," but is central to the story, which is actually seen as if through his eyes. Most commentaries on this tale focus only on the meeting of two of Howard's more popular heroes, Bran Mak Morn and Kull. But there are in fact three Kings of the Night. When the Pictish shaman Gonar says "All things that ever were, are, or ever will be, transpire now," he could well have been referring to the kings: Kull of the past, Bran of the present, and Cormac of the future. Bran wins his battle with Rome in the story, but as Howard well knew, the future of Scotland belonged to the Gaels. Robert Weinberg, in his commentary on this story, says "Strangely enough, the tale is seen through the eyes of Cormac . . ." This is not so strange when we see this story in its proper context. ⟨. . .⟩

Only three further purely Celtic stories are documented after 1930: "Spears of Clontarf," a story concerning the battle in which the High King Brian Boru broke the power of the Vikings in Ireland, was rejected by the Clayton Publications in mid-1931; a revised version of this story, "The Grey God Passes," which gave it a more supernatural focus, was rejected by *Weird Tales* later in the year. "The Cairn on the Headland," which used Clontarf as the background for a modern horror tale, was accepted in early 1932. And "The People of the Dark," accepted at about the same time, featured a black-haired Gael of Eireann named Conan who encounters a race of underground dwellers either influenced by the Little People of Welsh fantasist Arthur Machen, or derived from the same sources. This story really ends Howard's purely Celtic period, and presages the advent, only a few weeks later, of the character generally considered Howard's greatest creation, Conan of Cimmeria.

Rusty Burke, "The Active Voice: Robert E. Howard's Personae," *Dark Man* No. 3 (April 1993): 24–25

▨ *Bibliography*

A Gent from Bear Creek. 1937.

The Hyborian Age. 1938.

Skull-Face and Others. [Ed. August Derleth.] 1946.

Conan the Conqueror. 1950.

The Sword of Conan. 1952.

King Conan. 1953.

The Coming of Conan. 1953.

The Challenge from Beyond (with C. L. Moore, A. Merritt, H. P. Lovecraft, and Frank Belknap Long). 1954.

Conan the Barbarian. 1954.

Tales of Conan. 1955.

Always Comes Evening. 1957, 1977.

The Dark Man and Others. 1963.

Almuric. 1964.

The Pride of Bear Creek. 1966.

Conan the Adventurer (with L. Sprague de Camp). 1966.

Conan the Warrior. Ed. L. Sprague de Camp. 1967.

Conan the Usurper (with L. Sprague de Camp). 1967.

King Kull (with Lin Carter). Ed. Glenn Lord. 1967.

Conan (with L. Sprague de Camp and Lin Carter). 1968.

Wolfshead. Ed. Glenn Lord. 1968.

Etchings in Ivory. 1968.

Red Shadows. 1968.

Conan the Avenger (with Björn Nyberg and L. Sprague de Camp). 1968.

Conan the Freebooter (with L. Sprague de Camp). 1968.

Conan the Wanderer (with L. Sprague de Camp and Lin Carter). 1968.

Conan of Cimmeria (with L. Sprague de Camp and Lin Carter). 1969.

Bran Mak Morn. 1969.

The Moon of Skulls. 1969.

Singers in the Shadows. 1970.
The Hand of Kane. 1970.
Solomon Kane. 1971.
The Red Blades of Black Cathay (with Tevis Clyde Smith). 1971.
Black Dawn. 1972.
The Road to Rome. 1972.
Echoes from an Iron Harp. 1972.
Marchers of Valhalla. 1972.
The Sowers of the Thunder. 1973.
A Song of the Naked Lands. 1973.
The Vultures. 1973.
The Incredible Adventures of Dennis Dorgan. 1974.
Tigers of the Sea. 1974.
Worms of the Earth. 1974.
The Tower of the Elephant. 1975.
The Vultures of Whapeton. 1975.
Black Vulmea's Vengeance and Other Tales of Pirates. 1976.
The Book of Robert E. Howard. 1976.
The Iron Man and Other Tales of the Ring. 1976.
The Grim Land and Others. 1976.
Rogues in the House. 1976.
The Second Book of Robert E. Howard. 1976.
Swords of Shahrazar. 1976.
Night Images. 1976.
The Hour of the Dragon. 1977.
Son of the White Wolf. 1977.
Three-Bladed Doom. 1977.
The Lost Valley of Iskander. 1977.
Sword Woman. 1977.
Red Nails. 1977.
The People of the Black Circle. 1977.
Black Canaan. 1978.
Kull. 1978.
Queen of the Black Coast. 1978.
Marchers of Valhalla. 1978.
The Last Ride. 1978.
Black Colossus. 1979.
Mayhem on Bear Creek. 1979.

The Road of Azrael. 1979.

The Howard Collector. Ed. Glenn Lord. 1979.

The Gods of Bal-Sagoth. 1979.

Hawks of Outremer. 1979.

Lord of the Dead. 1981.

The Ghost Ocean. 1982.

Bran Mak Morn: A Play, and Others. 1983.

The She Devil. 1983.

Robert E. Howard's Kull. 1985.

The Adventures of Lal Singh. Ed. Robert M. Price. 1985.

The Pool of the Black One. 1986.

Cthulhu: The Mythos and Kindred Horrors. Ed. David Drake. 1987.

Robert E. Howard's World of Heroes. Ed. Mike Ashley. 1989.

Selected Letters. Ed. Glenn Lord, Rusty Burke, S. T. Joshi, and Steve Behrends.
        1989–91. 2 vols.

Post Oaks and Sand Roughs. 1990.

Robert E. Howard's Fight Magazine. Ed. Robert M. Price. 1990– . 8 issues
        (projected).

Fritz Leiber
1910–1992

FRITZ REUTER LEIBER, JR., was born in Chicago on December 24, 1910, the son of distinguished Shakespearean actor and theatrical manager Fritz Leiber and Virginia Bronson Leiber. Exposure to members of his mother and father's acting troupe introduced the young Leiber to a variety of interests, including reading, chess, and the stage. Leiber spent most of his childhood in Chicago, eventually enrolling in the University of Chicago, from which he graduated with a B.A. in 1932.

Upon graduating, Leiber served as an Episcopal minister but a crisis of conscience over his lack of religious faith sent him back to graduate school. After a brief but unsuccessful stint on the stage, Leiber returned once again to school, where he met Jonquil Stephens. The two were married in 1936 and moved to Hollywood to live with Leiber's parents while Fritz embarked on an abortive career in film. Their only son, Justin, was born in 1938. Over the next few decades, Leiber held a succession of jobs in publishing.

While at college, Leiber was introduced to the work of weird fiction writer H. P. Lovecraft, whom he would later cite as one of the most important influences on his writing. He corresponded with Lovecraft a short time before the latter's death in 1937 and sent his early efforts at fiction writing for Lovecraft's criticism. Also while in college, Leiber met Harry Otto Fischer, who shared many of Leiber's interests. In their correspondence, the two playfully imagined themselves as heroic fantasy characters named Fafhrd (Leiber) and the Gray Mouser (Fischer), who became the subjects of several stories by Leiber.

Leiber submitted several stories for publication to *Weird Tales* in the late 1930s, eventually selling his horror story "The Automatic Pistol" in 1938 (not published until 1940). To John W. Campbell's fantasy magazine *Unknown*, he sent the tales of Fafhrd and the Mouser that had been rejected by *Weird Tales*. Campbell would publish five of these, starting with "Two Sought Adventure" in the August 1939 issue. The Fafhrd and Mouser stories, with their squabbling antihero characters and sly humor, were immediately recognized as alternatives to the stereotypical blood-and-thunder type of heroic fantasy that hitherto had dominated the pulp fantasy magazines. Leiber also made a mark with his horror fiction, updating the tropes of Gothic horror for modern urban settings inhabited by psychologically complex characters in stories such as "Smoke Ghost" and his first novel, *Conjure Wife* (serialized 1941; revised for book publication 1953; filmed as *Weird Woman* in 1948 and *Burn, Witch, Burn* in 1963). The latter, a rational treatment of the persistence of witchcraft in the modern world, became one of the most influential horror novels of the twentieth century.

When *Unknown* folded in 1943, Leiber concentrated on writing science fiction, producing the novels *Gather, Darkness!* and *Destiny Times Three* for *Astounding Science Fiction*. His first book, the collection *Night's Black Agents*, was published in 1947. "You're All Alone" (final revision as *The Sinful Ones*, 1986), a short fantasy novel about alienation in the modern world, as well as stories Leiber wrote for the burgeoning science fiction market of the 1950s, blurred the boundaries of science fiction, fantasy, and horror through their imaginative expression of America's postwar angst. Recovering from the first of several bouts with alcoholism in the 1960s, Leiber began extending the saga of Fafhrd and the Mouser in the pages of *Fantastic* and paperback story collections, where the growth of the characters increasingly came to reflect his own developing understanding of himself.

Over the last twenty-five years of his life Leiber amassed numerous awards for his writing, including seven Hugos, four Nebulas, and the World Fantasy Award for his novel *Our Lady of Darkness* (1977), a tale of urban paranoia set in his adopted town of San Francisco. He became the only writer to win lifetime achievement awards in the fantasy, horror, and science fiction fields. Although hobbled by health problems throughout the 1980s, Leiber continued to write, producing the lengthy and insightful autobiographical essay "Not Much Disorder and Not So Early Sex" for his collection *The Ghost Light* (1984) and a final collection of Fafhrd and Mouser stories, *The Knight and Knave of Swords* (1988). He died from complications of a series of strokes on September 5, 1992.

⬛ *Critical Extracts*

ROBERT BLOCH   Mr. Leiber ⟨in *Night's Black Agents*⟩ has given us a clue as to his concept of blackness by arbitrarily dividing the tales in his collection into two sections, with one tale of transition. His story-groupings are labeled *Modern Horrors* and *Ancient Adventures*. In the first section we find the memorable "Smoke Ghost"—dweller in a world of "dirty sunsets" and "blackish snow"—an inky phantom leaving smudges, black footprints, and grime in its wraithlike wake, a horror that materializes as a shadow suffusing flesh with a smoky hue. Darkness, to Leiber, is an omnipresent blight in the modern world, a compound of industrial smudge hovering like a monstrous pall over a mechanized civilization and giving birth to horrors typical of the new Dark Ages. It is obvious that to Leiber our civilization presents a very dark picture indeed.

"The Man Who Never Grew Young," an ingenious tale of transition, exemplifies his recoil from today's reality. But distance lends enchantment. And in the two tales which conclude his book—"The Sunken Land" and the masterful, hitherto unpublished novel, "Adept's Gambit"—one finds darkness assuming a classic glamour. It is a black cloak, worn by swashbuckling adventurers, a black hood veiling the features of warlocks and wizards—black magicians. In modern times the night-sky is an embodiment of evil; but in the blackness of prehistoric dawn, Leiber sees the "self-consistent stars."

> Robert Bloch, "Through a Glass Darkly," *Arkham Sampler* 1, No. 1 (Winter 1948): 85

FRITZ LEIBER   We've grown fond of these old fears, haven't we? So tender with our monsters! Because they are almost the only hint of what imagination can attain beyond the star-high walls that ring this plain. And they've grown weak, you know. Look here—'t was not a silver bullet killed the werewolf.

But come now, sit and rest—may be your only chance between the recent planet-maiming war and some atomic doom that's just ahead. Find each a friendly boulder. Eat and drink. Lick your old wounds. Set one to play the flute—some dreamy, solemn strain to make our ears forget the querulous, muttering voices of the plain. And deeply rest—things will not seem so bad when we have rested.

How do I know? By what authority do I speak to you? By none. I'm nothing. Just someone whom you've paid to dream for you. A kind of twilight skald.

You say, Dark Eyes and Weary Smile, we're going nowhere? That our small band is out of touch with life? Our path only a circling retreat, a flight to childish, superstitious dreams? What then, I ask you, are those peaks ahead, that black, forbidding rampart in the sky? Oh, an illusion, is it? The plainsmen say the mountains are not real and you, Dark Eyes, believe them? Well, just wait! When the cold blasts that brim the passes chill your bones, when your lungs strain to gulp the icy air, when the jagged pinnacles cut and bruise your feet—then tell me it's illusion.

You in that rusty cuirass, what said you? They laugh at us and jeer at *Fantasy?* Well, let them. When haven't men going somewhere been laughed at? Stiffen your backs, scoff at the scoffers, pay them sneer with sneer. Best, burnish your armor till it reflects back an image of their stunted, monstrous selves, set against those mountains they insist aren't there, and they run off in headlong stumbling flight, their insane laughter echoing in their ears.

Oh, but your doubts go deeper, Grim Face, eh? You think that everything that thrills's been done, that there's no more true eeriness in life, but just a wearisome atomic round, and that the future—if only a tag end—belongs to some pragmatic plodding breed who never heard Pan pipe or feared the darkness that's between the stars? That is to laugh! Pass me the wine-skin. And yet that's just how I feel part of the time.

But how untrue! When each new fact, like an old witch, has as familiar some new mystery, when each conquered realm opens a new wilder, wider frontier, when man's about to leap to the planets . . .

No! The fault's in us. Open your eyes, close your ears to the drug-murmurous voices of the plains, polish the windows of your mind, and you will see wonders undreamed of, innumerable—and I don't mean bright gadgetry to prick desires and empty pocketbooks. Wonder as great as in archaic times made gleaming eyes by rocks like these at Stonehenge and in the darkling woods where satyrs danced.

Fritz Leiber, "Fantasy on the March," *Arkham Sampler* 1, No. 2 (Spring 1948): 43–44

MARSHALL McLUHAN   In a story called "The Girl with the Hungry Eyes," by Fritz Leiber, an ad photographer gives a job to a not too promising model. Soon, however, she is "plastered all over the country" because she has the hungriest eyes in the world. "Nothing vulgar, but just the same they're looking at you with a hunger that's all sex and something more than sex." Something similar may be said of the legs on a pedestal. Abstracted from the body that gives them their ordinary meaning, they become "something more than sex," a metaphysical enticement, a cerebral itch, an abstract torment. Mr. Leiber's girl hypnotizes the country with her hungry eyes and finally accepts the attentions of the photographer who barely escapes with his life. In this vampire, not of blood but of spirit, he finds "the horror behind the bright billboard . . . She's the eyes that lead you on and on and then show you death." She says to him: "I want you. I want your high spots. I want everything that's made you happy and everything that's hurt you bad. I want your first girl . . . I want that licking . . . I want Betty's legs . . . I want your mother's death . . . I want your wanting me. I want your life. Feed me, baby, feed me."

Marshall McLuhan, *The Mechanical Bride: Folklore of Industrial Man* (Boston: Beacon Press, 1951), p. 101

DAMON KNIGHT   *Conjure Wife*, by Fritz Leiber, is easily the most frightening and (necessarily) the most thoroughly convincing of all horror stories. Its premise is that witchcraft still flourishes, or at any rate survives, an open secret among women, a closed book to men. Under the rational overlay of 20th-century civilization this sickly growth, uncultivated, unsuspected, still manages to propagate itself:

> ". . . I don't do much. Like when my boyfriend was in the army, I did things to keep him from getting shot or hurt, and I've spelled him so that he'll keep away from other women. And I kin annernt with erl for sickness. Honest, I don't do much, ma'am. And it don't always work. And lots of things I can't get that way.
>
> ". . . Some I learned from Ma when I was a kid. And some from Mrs. Neidel—she gots spells against bullets from her grandmother who had a family in some European war way back. But most women won't tell you anything. And some spells I kind of figger out myself, and try different ways until they work."

Tansy Saylor, the wife of a promising young sociology professor at an ultra-conservative small American college, is, like most women, a witch.

She is also an intelligent, modern young woman, and when her husband happens to discover the evidence of her witchcraft (not his own easy advancement, which he ascribes to luck, but certain small packets of dried leaves, earth, metal, filings, &c.) he's able to convince her that her faith in magic is compounded of superstition and neurosis. She burns her charms; Norman Saylor's "luck" immediately turns sour. But this is not all—the Balance has been upset.

> The witches' warfare . . . was much like trench warfare or a battle between fortified lines—a state of siege. Just as reinforced concrete or armor plating nullified the shells, so countercharms and protection procedures rendered relatively futile the most violent onslaughts. But once the armor and concrete were gone, and the witch who had foresworn witchcraft was out in a kind of no man's land—
> For the realistic mind, there could be only one answer. Namely that the enemy had discovered a weapon more potent than battleships or aircraft, and was planning to ask for a peace that would turn out to be a trap. The only thing would be to strike instantly and hard, before the secret weapon could be brought into play.

Leiber develops the theme with the utmost dexterity, piling up alternate layers of the mundane and outré, until at the story's real climax, the shocker at the end of Chapter 14, I am not ashamed to say that I jumped an inch out of my seat. From that point onward the story is anticlimax, but anticlimax so skillfully managed that I am not really certain I touched the slip-cover again until after the last page. Leiber has never written anything better . . . which, perhaps, is all that needed to be said.

Damon Knight, "Campbell and His Decade," *In Search of Wonder* (Chicago: Advent, 1956), pp. 31, 33

FRANCIS LATHROP   What seems to make the Fafhrd-Mouser stories stand out is that the two heroes are cut down to a plausible size without loss of romance and a believed-in eerie, sorcerous atmosphere and with a welcome departure from formula. They are neither physical supermen of the caliber of Conan and John Carter, nor moral or metaphysical giants like Tolkien's Strider, etc., and Moorcock's Elric. They win out by one quarter brains, and at least fifty percent sheer luck. They have an engaging self-interest, blind spots and vices, a gallantry of sorts, and an ability to laugh at themselves—even if the Mouser occasionally finds the last quite galling. One's first impression may be that the Mouser is the darkly clever comedian and Fafhrd the somewhat stupid straight man, or Fafhrd the hero and the Mouser the comic relief, but a little reading reveals the self-infatuation underlying and sometimes tripping the Mouser's cunning, and also the amiable wisdom that now and then shows through Fafhrd's lazy complacency.

Francis Lathrop, [Review of Swords in the Mist, Swords against Wizardry, and The Swords of Lankhmar], Fantastic 19, No. 1 (October 1969): 129–30

TOM SHIPPEY   〈. . .〉 all the way through Conjure Wife draws power from its cool and rational tone, its everyday setting, while its central images— the cement dragon, the Prince Rupert drop, the shattering mirror—all carry a physical as well as a magical explanation. The book's penultimate paragraph, indeed, offers a rational explanation (that all women involved are psychotic) as an alternative to the fantastic one (that they are all witches), while the last words of all are Professor Saylor saying evasively "I don't really know". All this makes Conjure Wife fit one rather strict definition of fantasy, that it takes place just as long as one is uncertain about how to explain events. However, it also points out one way in which Conjure Wife does not fit the normal development of 'Frazerian' science fiction, for all its pioneering motifs and explanations.

That is, that most 'worlds where magic works' are alternate worlds, parallel worlds, future worlds, far-past worlds. Conjure Wife is one of the very few to be set in a recognisable present. It gains from this, of course, in realism; but loses, inevitably, a quality of romance. It has witches, and spells, and even the glimpsed presence of He Who Walks Behind; but there are no centaurs, or werewolves, or mermaids, or basilisks, or any of the other ancient images of fantasy. The only dragon in Conjure Wife is a cement one. Yet there is clearly an urge in many writers and readers to resurrect these images and use them again, partly no doubt as a result of 'escapism', but at least as much out of a kind of intellectual thrift: ideas compulsively attractive to mankind for so long, it is felt, are too good to throw away. Nevertheless this urge, powerful though it is, is met by an equally powerful current of scepticism. Twentieth-century readers, especially those with some scientific training or inclination, cannot even *pretend* to believe in anything that makes no sense, i.e., anything that has no rationalistic theory to cover it. Frazer and *The Golden Bough* provided a rationale for magic, as exploited by Leiber in *Conjure Wife*. But he dealt only with natural forces.

Tom Shippey, "*The Golden Bough* and the Incorporations of Magic in Science Fiction," *Foundation* No. 12 (March 1977): 123–24

JOHN CLUTE   Here is a mistake from Fritz Leiber, though it warms the heart. *Our Lady of Darkness* is a mistake of displacement. Whatever one reads of Leiber, in whatever genre he presents to us his skill and touch, the implied author (the author visible in the text, all we have a right to know) who speaks to one seems to exhale a kind of shy sacrificial gravitas, however garish or commercial the story he's telling happens to be. It somehow seems *brave* for an adult person like Fritz Leiber to expose himself without condescension or disguise to a readership comprised of people like us— young, claquish, aggressive, intrusive, we tend to demand complicity of our authors, and to punish those who turn a blank face, or (like Silverberg) a mask of anguish. Perhaps anguish comes too close to the foul rag and bone shop to be amenable to claims of complicity. And perhaps Leiber was after all right, in *Our Lady of Darkness*, to avoid telling the tale of anguish and mourning that lies palpably at the heart of its inspiration, and instead to displace that story into a routine tale of externalized haunting, even though injected with elements of an sf rationale, a good deal of social realism scarifyingly illuminating about life in California now (and in our future soon enough), and some interesting speculative musing about what the modern world city may be beginning to do to us.

But I don't believe it. I don't know (and have no right or inclination to speculate about) whether the real Fritz Leiber behind the sacrificial decency of the implied Fritz Leiber we read in his texts is or is not an anguished man; I do know that the implied author of *Our Lady of Darkness* sounds singularly ill-at-ease in his efforts to present us the story he does as though it were the real story. Thin ice does seem to bring out the jocosity in the best of us . . .

John Clute, [Review of *Our Lady of Darkness*], *Foundation* No. 14 (September 1978): 64–65

JEFF FRANE   In the vividly shocking climax of the novel ⟨*Conjure Wife*⟩, ⟨Norman⟩ succeeds in saving ⟨Tansy's⟩ life, but finds that she has lost her soul in the process. Through the anticlimactic scenes of the book, the two of them work together to recover it. Even now, Norman is not entirely convinced that what he has seen has really been magic. The more evidence that accumulates, the harder the rational portion of his mind resists. What he attempts to do then is rationalize the evidence to fit his own preconceptions. He attempts to convince himself—rather unsuccessfully—that the three other women are truly psychotic and that their control over Tansy's behavior is a result of her own neuroses and their psychoses. Therefore, he decides that his actions must play along with their obsessions if he is to rescue Tansy from her catatonic state. At those times when he does credit magic, he can only do so by thinking of it in terms of science, with the same concrete rules that govern the other sciences. He succeeds in developing a rationale to account for magic having been discredited as a science—that the laws of magic proceed through evolutionary changes which invalidate previous approaches and formulas. Through modern symbolic logic, he develops the essence of various spells so that he can recover Tansy's soul—or rescue her from her psychotic tormentors.

It is this struggle within Norman Saylor that creates the successful tensions within the novel. His dilemma is that of the reader, who throughout the story has suspended disbelief and accepted the proposition that magic does, in fact, exist. If Norman had willingly accepted the evidence of witchcraft that surrounded him (as is often true in contemporary tales of witchcraft), the reader's own skepticism would have been reinforced.

Jeff Frane, *Fritz Leiber* (Mercer Island, WA: Starmont House, 1980), p. 18

JUSTIN LEIBER   In his initial choice of supernatural horror and sword and sorcery genres, shy Fritz would seem to have found just what he needed to lose himself in. These are pulp, lowbrow genres—no pretension in that. They impose on those who write them a colorful and gaudy vocabulary and style; they also impose a special sort of atmosphere, landscape, and arcane lore. Excepting science fiction, they are alone among pulp forms in combining brawny, physical combat with the cut and thrust of intelligence.

Finally, these forms dictate clever, gimmicky plot construction and rapid action; even the emotional punch is much restricted. One can write recipes for these genres, and people do. It seems to follow that one reveals nothing about oneself in this type of writing except that one knows the recipe and can follow directions. Further, because these are both physical and minor genres, to write them reveals no pretensions to high art or fair fame. Rather, they generate a relatively small circle of initiates and playful semiprofessionals. Perhaps in this cozy circle Fritz found something of a replacement for "the company," his father's Shakespearian band.

Indeed, Shakespeare himself was both a "humble player" of a popular art and archmage of an arcane fellowship, and his plays continually reverberate with this. He was not only his characters in that they were people he might have been, but as Bergson suggests, Shakespeare also played these roles on stage. Shakespearian actors take particular relish in those "humble player" speeches which suggest that one is playing Shakespeare himself acting the part of a "humble player," who in turn is playing a particular role. Not only did Shakespeare create his actors and their ethos as the flip side of the onstage characters, but he made it easy for traditional Shakespearian actors to hallow deep within the conviction that "I am Shakespeare."

Perhaps Fritz should have been more wary. If the play, occasionally, is the thing to catch the conscience of the king, it is always ready to cast murky, indirect, and devastating reflections of the playwright. The Shakespearian actor does not run that risk of looking through a telescope at a strange and entrancing world only to find a terrifying reflection of the actor's self. The view that high art is confessional and consciously self-reflective suggests not only that it may be therapeutic but also that it is dangerous and painful.

Justin Leiber, "Fritz Leiber and Eyes," *Philosophers Look at Science Fiction*, ed. Nicholas D. Smith (Chicago: Nelson-Hall, 1982), pp. 179–80

TOM STAICAR   Leiber has repeatedly written about individualists because he is one. As an actor, the child of actor-parents, a pacifist who feared being drafted, a college teacher in a stifling atmosphere he hated, and as a writer who disliked the nine-to-five office routine, Leiber has always led what most Americans would consider an unusual existence.

The Sinful Ones explores this theme from several angles. For example, Jane has lived in secrecy, hunted by the group of awakened ones who jealously guard their nearly unique status. She has a cache of food and drink stored in the stacks of a large library, where she can hide. Elsewhere, she tries to observe the "rules" of life: blend in, don't be first or last in line, don't stand out, don't be early or late. Otherwise, you will be spotted as truly alive.

The bulk of the novel is taken up with chases and escapes by Jane and Carr. At all times the option remains open for them to blend in and to melt into the normal lives they once lived. As Jane tells Carr, "You're born with a feeling for the rhythm of life as the machine wants it. You automatically do and say what you're supposed to."

The sense of inertia in this machinelike world resembles the views about time expressed in Leiber's stories about time travel. Time has a strong inertia which tends to negate small changes in its pattern. According to Leiber, history reflects great events, such as major battles lost or won, and ignores the rest. In *The Sinful Ones*, one person's refusal to perform an action is usually ignored, and people go on much as they have, working around it.

Although Leiber seems rather disdainful about the mass of humanity in the novel, he shows that he does care about average people when Jane speculates, "I wonder if we haven't been wrong in some of our guesses. I wonder if perhaps there aren't more awakened people than we realize, living their lives in a trance, sticking to the pattern, but not just because they're nothing but machines, not just because their minds are black." Leiber sees some hope for people, so long as they examine their options in life.

Alienation is the basic theme here. The person who goes outside the norms of society becomes an outsider and an outcast. When other people observe this nonconformity, they become upset, suspicious, or distrustful. A child may be spurned by his schoolmates and an adult may be ignored by potential friends. Carr and Jane feel this ostracism keenly, and it alienates them. Leiber suggests that this alienation is an acceptable price to pay for being aware, awake, and truly alive.

Tom Staicar, *Fritz Leiber* (New York: Ungar, 1983), pp. 29–31

BRUCE BYFIELD   In *The Hero with a Thousand Faces*, ⟨Joseph⟩ Campbell suggests that many monsters encountered by the hero are versions of the father. In organizing the Fafhrd and Mouser stories, Leiber has given them father-figures in the form of Ningauble and Sheelba. In "The Frost Monstreme," they do not oppose their sorcerous mentors, but they do face near-equivalents in the invisible Oomforafor and the power magician

Khahkht. "Rime Isle" gives them even more powerful versions of the Father to oppose in Odin and Loki, who have strayed from our world into Newhon. All these figures, especially the two gods, whom the heroes resemble physically, seem to represent the heroes' past and their destructive impulses. Under Loki's influence, the Mouser leads a fleet against the sea-nomads, learning at the last moment that Loki plans to destroy the fleet in order to lure the nomads to destruction. Similarly, under Odin's influence, Fafhrd's berserkers, marching to the relief of a small town, are tempted to revert to their nature and die taking their enemies with them.

The heroes achieve victory only by resisting the gods' plans. At the last moment, the Mouser revises Loki's spell and limits its destructive power. Fafhrd, who deserts his responsibilities to rescue an adolescent girl from Oomforafor, is less lucky. He attempts the rescue, not because he is responsible for the girl, so much as because she is named Mara, like his first lover, whom he has felt guilty about ever since he abandoned her. Fafhrd rescues the girl, severing Oomforafor's hand, but his ally and ex-lover, Oomforafor's sister Hirriwi, tells him that she would have rescued the girl and prophesies that he will suffer "for deserting your men to chase this girl-chit". Rejoining his forces, Fafhrd recovers his sense of duty, refusing to let his forces wear the noose that is the sign of subjection to Odin. Vague apprehensions make him collect the nooses on the pretense that he needs them to brace his wrist for archery. His apprehensions prove well-founded when the Mouser's revised spell banishes Odin and Loki, who takes the nooses and his hand with them. Having needlessly mutilated Mara's abductor, Fafhrd suffers the same mutilation himself. Leiber passes quickly over this development in his interview with Jim Purviance, explaining only that he realized that his heroes had never been hurt, and that Fafhrd's adjustment to his handicap would give fresh story material. These motivations are valid, yet it is also true that Fafhrd's loss fits well with the idea expressed in *The Hero with a Thousand Faces* that suffering represents maturation achieved at a cost. In rejecting Odin in his morbid and destructive aspect, Fafhrd comes to resemble the god's aspect that is absent from "Rime Isle": Odin is a quester for wisdom who, as Campbell mentions, sacrificed an eye and crucified himself in pursuit of this goal. In metaphorical terms, Fafhrd overcomes his monstrous image of the Father and reaches maturation by imitating the Father. The Mouser's thwarting of Loki emulates Loki's own subversions, and, by defeating his Father-image, he also matures, although at a lower cost.

Bruce Byfield, *Witches of the Mind: A Critical Study of Fritz Leiber* (West Warwick, RI: Necronomicon Press, 1991), p. 61

▣ *Bibliography*

Night's Black Agents. 1947.

Gather, Darkness! 1950.

Conjure Wife. 1953.

The Green Millennium. 1953.

The Sinful Ones (with *Bulls, Blood, and Passion* by David Williams). 1953, 1972 (as *You're All Alone*), 1986 (as *The Sinful Ones*).

Destiny Times Three. 1957.

Two Sought Adventure: Exploits of Fafhrd and the Gray Mouser. 1957.

The Big Time (with *The Mind Spider and Other Stories*). 1961.

The Silver Eggheads. 1962.

Shadows with Eyes. 1962.

H. P. Lovecraft: A Symposium (with others). 1963.

The Wanderer. 1964.

A Pail of Air. 1964.

Ships to the Stars (with *The Million Year Hunt* by Kenneth Bulmer). 1964.

The Night of the Wolf. 1966.

Tarzan and the Valley of Gold. 1966.

The Secret Songs. 1968.

The Swords of Lankhmar. 1968.

Swords against Wizardry. 1968.

Swords in the Mist. 1968.

A Specter Is Haunting Texas. 1969.

The Demons of the Upper Air. 1969.

Night Monsters. 1969.

Swords and Deviltry. 1970.

Swords against Death. 1970.

The Best of Fritz Leiber. 1974.

The Book of Fritz Leiber. 1974.

The Second Book of Fritz Leiber. 1975.

The Worlds of Fritz Leiber. 1976.

Our Lady of Darkness. 1977.

Swords and Ice Magic. 1977.

Rime Isle. 1977.

The Change War. 1978.

Sonnets to Jonquil and All. 1978.

Bazaar of the Bizarre. 1978.

Heroes and Horrors. Ed. Stuart Schiff. 1978.

Ship of Shadows. 1979.

Ervool. 1980, 1982.

The World Fantasy Awards: Volume 2 (editor; with Stuart David Schiff). 1980.

The First World Fantasy Convention: Three Authors Remember (with Robert Bloch and T. E. D. Klein). 1980.

Riches and Power: A Story for Children. 1982.

The Mystery of the Japanese Clock. 1982.

Quicks around the Zodiac: A Farce. 1983.

The Ghost Light. 1984.

The Knight and Knave of Swords. 1988.

The Leiber Chronicles: Fifty Years of Fritz Leiber. Ed. Martin H. Greenberg. 1990.

Gummitch and Friends. 1992.

C. S. Lewis
1898–1963

CLIVE STAPLES LEWIS was born in Belfast, Ireland, on November 29, 1898. After the death of his mother in 1908 he saw little of his father and spent several miserable years at private schools in England. A private tutor prepared him for Oxford, but he joined the English army and went to France in November 1917. He was wounded at the Battle of Arras in 1918 and returned to England, the next year resuming his studies at University College, Oxford. He received his B.A. in 1922, taught philosophy for one term (1924–25) at University College, then spent the next thirty years as a tutor in English at Magdalen College, Oxford.

As a teenager Lewis had discarded the conventional Anglican religion of his parents and became for a time an atheist; but gradually he began converting to Anglo-Catholicism. His early religious struggles are poignantly etched in his autobiography, *Surprised by Joy* (1955). His conversion was complete by 1931, and after publishing a book of poems, *Spirits in Bondage* (1919) and a novel, *Dymer* (1926), under the pseudonym Clive Hamilton, Lewis began his prolific career as a Christian apologist, literary scholar, and fiction writer.

Of his Christian writings, *The Pilgrim's Regress* (1933) and *The Screwtape Letters* (1942) are the best-known. A series of radio broadcasts was collected as *Mere Christianity* (1952). *The Allegory of Love* (1936) was Lewis's first significant work of literary criticism, and he went on to write several other distinguished volumes, including *A Preface to* Paradise Lost (1942) and *English Literature in the Sixteenth Century, Excluding Drama* (1954), the latter for the prestigious Oxford History of English Literature series.

Around 1937 Lewis formed a loose group of friends called the Inklings to discuss literature and theology and to read their works in progress. This group included Lewis's longtime friend Owen Barfield, J. R. R. Tolkien (whom Lewis had first met in 1926), and later Charles Williams, who came to Oxford in 1939. A number of Lewis's works were developed from discussions with the Inklings.

Lewis's main contribution to science fiction rests in his trilogy of novels involving space travel, *Out of the Silent Planet* (1938), *Perelandra* (1943), and *That Hideous Strength* (1945). Some of his short stories also approach science fiction, especially those posthumously collected in *The Dark Tower and Other Stories* (1977), the title story of which is an unfinished novelette about time travel. Lewis has gained great renown as the author of a seven-volume series of fantasy novels for children, beginning with *The Lion, the Witch, and the Wardrobe* (1950) and continuing with *Prince Caspian* (1951), *The Voyage of the* Dawn Treader (1952), *The Silver Chair* (1953), *The Horse and His Boy* (1954), *The Magician's Nephew* (1955), and *The Last Battle* (1956). Both this series and the science fiction trilogy have been criticized as being excessively heavy-handed in their religious symbolism. Lewis also retold the myth of Cupid and Psyche in *Till We Have Faces* (1956).

In 1948 Lewis began corresponding with an American writer, Helen Joy Davidman Gresham. He met her for the first time in 1952, and in 1956, two years after her divorce from her estranged husband, he married her. She died in 1960, causing Lewis to write the anguished autobiography, *A Grief Observed* (1961). C. S. Lewis, who left Oxford in 1954 after nearly forty years there to become Professor of Medieval and Renaissance Literature at Magdalene College, Cambridge, died on November 22, 1963, on the same day as John F. Kennedy and Aldous Huxley.

▨ *Critical Extracts*

UNSIGNED   Like George MacDonald's *The Princess and the Goblin*, this story ⟨*The Lion, the Witch, and the Wardrobe*⟩ by a distinguished English writer has an underlying meaning in its theme. It tells of the struggle between good and evil in terms that make it a dramatic story. Good is personified in the great golden lion, Aslan; evil in the White Witch. The imaginative country that they inhabit is called Narnia, and the children in the story reach it through a wardrobe in an old English country house. Edmund, the youngest boy, is tempted to side with the White Witch, gets into her power, and is finally rescued by Aslan and the others. There is a tremendous battle between Aslan and the "good" forest people and the witch and her evil followers. The four children meet strange creatures in Narnia, some of them admirably characterized. Perhaps the most appealing are the two beavers who tell the children about Aslan and lead them to him. There is a homely wisdom and a humor in the beaver and his good wife that bring them into vivid contrast with the witch and even with the kingly Aslan.

Some of the word pictures are beautifully drawn. The witch has cast her spell of perpetual winter on the forest. When Aslan's power breaks it, Narnia is filled with the sound of running water and bird songs, with the scent and color of spring flowers. The story is illustrated with black-and-white drawings that effectively bring out the children, Aslan, and the wood creatures of Narnia. It is an exceptionally good new "fairy tale."

Unsigned, "Books for Young Readers: Insurance for a Merry Christmas," *Saturday Review*, 9 December 1950, p. 42

C. S. LEWIS   Some people seem to think that I began by asking myself how I could say something about Christianity to children; then fixed on the fairy tale as an instrument; then collected information about child-psychology and decided what age group I'd write for; then drew up a list of basic Christian truths and hammered out 'allegories' to embody them. This is all pure moonshine. I couldn't write in that way at all. Everything began with images; a faun carrying an umbrella, a queen on a sledge, a magnificent lion. At first there wasn't even anything Christian about them; that element pushed itself in of its own accord. It was part of the bubbling.

Then came the Form. As these images sorted themselves into events (i.e., became a story) they seemed to demand no love interest and no close psychology. But the Form which excludes these things is the fairy tale. And the moment I thought of that I fell in love with the Form itself: its brevity, its severe restraints on description, its flexible traditionalism, its inflexible hostility to all analysis, digression, reflections and 'gas'. I was now enamoured of it. Its very limitations of vocabulary became an attraction; as the hardness of the stone pleases the sculptor or the difficulty of the sonnet delights the sonneteer.

On that side (as Author) I wrote fairy tales because the Fairy Tale seemed the ideal Form for the stuff I had to say.

Then of course the Man in me began to have his turn. I thought I saw how stories of this kind could steal past a certain inhibition which had paralysed much of my own religion in childhood. Why did one find it so hard to feel as one was told one ought to feel about God or about the sufferings of Christ? I thought the chief reason was that one was told one ought to. An obligation to feel can freeze feelings. And reverence itself did harm. The whole subject was associated with lowered voices; almost as if it were something medical. But supposing that by casting all these things into an imaginary world, stripping them of their stained-glass and Sunday school associations, one could make them for the first time appear in their real potency? Could one not thus steal past those watchful dragons? I thought one could.

That was the Man's motive. But of course he could have done nothing if the Author had not been on the boil first.

C. S. Lewis, "Sometimes Fairy Stories May Say Best What's to Be Said" (1956), *Of Other Worlds: Essays and Stories,* ed. Walter Hooper (New York: Harcourt, Brace & World, 1967), pp. 36–37

CHAD WALSH   Some critics have asked whether the symbolic dimensions of the seven 〈Narnia〉 tales are handled in such a way as to make the stories more effective works of literature. Or rather, do Christian doctrines seem dragged in by their heels, converting the stories at their most theological moments into sugarcoated Sunday school instruction? Perhaps those best able to answer this question are the people who read Narnia as children. I have had the chance to talk with many of them, particularly as they move on into college and perhaps seek counsel on additional Lewis books they might read. I find two things: the first is that children almost always recognize a second level in the tales. This in no way obstructs or engulfs the primary level, which is simply a series of good stories. But they become alert to characters and events operating on two levels. This is rarely taken as the sly attempt of an older and pious man to sneak in religious propaganda. Children know from fairy tales and science fiction all about "willing suspension of disbelief." They enter into the game. They welcome Aslan as a special kind of talking animal and the focus of luminous meaning. Second, this acceptance of Aslan and the whole other level of the stories may or may not take an explicitly Christian form, depending on what sort of religious background the young reader has. The one who has been brought up as a Christian instantly recognizes Aslan as a kind of Christ for the talking animals and begins to see parallels with specific events in the life of Christ. The child lacking this background sees in Aslan something awe-some and compelling, however he may put it in words. It is interesting that often readers of both backgrounds single out the most theological events of the tales as the most effective episodes. This suggests that the firm theological themes running through the tales may be a literary asset rather than otherwise.

Another factor is at work here. If the Chronicles of Narnia were a straight allegory, in the manner of *The Pilgrim's Progress* (or *The Pilgrim's Regress*) the reader would expect every event to have a precise correspondence with some proclamation of Christian doctrine. In Narnia, life simply goes on. It has its occasional epiphanies and revelations, but it also has long stretches in which the characters have interesting but rarely definitive adventures. The realism and detail of these routine experiences help to make the high points stand out more sharply.

Chad Walsh, *The Literary Legacy of C. S. Lewis* (New York: Harcourt Brace Jovano-vich, 1979), pp. 131–32

MARGARET PATTERSON HANNAY   Lewis was perturbed by the simpering, wishy-washy way goodness was portrayed in most religious teaching, making children inevitably feel that it was much more glamorous to be bad. He agrees with the aesthetic tradition that art should teach by delighting, by making the reader enchanted with an ideal. Emotions should be evoked in order to develop the imagination, so that the person can conceive of a higher level of existence. "Imagination exists for the sake of wisdom or spiritual health—the rightness and richness of a man's total response to the world." The correct responses to life, although they may now be mocked as "bourgeois" and "conventional," are not innate; they must be carefully taught. Therefore, the older poetry, like that of Milton and Spenser, constantly insisted on certain themes—"Love is sweet, death bitter, virtue lovely, and children or gardens delightful." These writers were setting up models for each new generation to follow.

And this is what Lewis himself is doing. When he presents the heroism of Peter and the treachery of Edmund, what child would not rather be Peter than Edmund? When we see Lucy giving up her water ration for Eustace, after he has attempted to steal water from the crew, what child would not rather follow Lucy than Eustace? Again and again the children are confronted with situations when doing the right will be painful and difficult. Lucy is told she should have followed Aslan alone, even if the others were not willing to come; she must climb up to the magician's study to help the Dufflepuds no matter how frightened she is. Shasta must run to warn King Lune of Archenland, even though he is exhausted by his trip across the desert. Jill, Eustace, King Tirian, and Jewel must fight bravely, although all Narnia is being destroyed around them. And there are smaller decisions, too, which change the course of events. For example, Puddleglum stamps out the fire of the Emerald Witch, burning his feet, and so dissolves her enchantment.

These fairy tales react on the readers, making us understand and long for the Good. Most writers make the bad characters interesting, lively, and far more attractive than the good ones; Lewis does not, for he has a stern and splendid vision of goodness. We have been deceived, he says, by "that prosaic moralism which confines goodness to the region of Law and Duty, which never lets us feel in our face the sweet air blowing from 'the land of righteousness,' never reveals that elusive Form which if once seen must inevitably be desired with all but sensuous desire—the thing (in Sappho's phrase) 'more gold than gold.' "

Margaret Patterson Hannay, *C. S. Lewis* (New York: Ungar, 1981), pp. 59–60

THOMAS HOWARD   The tales of Narnia open up to us a certain kind of world. It is a world which has been made—made by Someone, beautifully made. Its fabric is shot through with glory. There is no peak, no valley, no sea or forest, but bears the weight of this glory, no law of the land that does not mirror the exact pattern of this glory, no spell or incantation or taboo that does not reach through the veil that protects the mundane and the obvious from the great glories and mysteries that press upon them. No creature—no faun, dryad, satyr, or winged horse—that does not bear about and exhibit in its own form some bit of the shape of that glory. And, alas, there is no evil that does not turn out to be fraud, parody, or counterfeit of that glory. In every case, the appeal of evil in Narnia springs from illusion and leads eventually to sterility, destruction, and anger.

Now, if that is the sort of world which the "fairy" chronicles of Narnia open up to us, it turns out to be a world identical in every significant point with the world that all myths and religions have told us we live in. Taken item for item, at least up to this point, Narnia turns out to be indistinguish-able from the world that the sages and seers and saints and druids and prophets have thought they saw. Indeed we could with no difficulty translate these items into the language of Jewish and Christian sacred texts. "It is a world which has been made—made by Someone" becomes Genesis 1. "No peak, no valley . . . but bears the weight of this glory," becomes Psalm 19. "No law of the land that does not mirror the exact pattern of that glory" becomes Psalm 119. The story of evil as fraud and illusion is told in Genesis. And so forth.

The point of all this is that if we find the chronicles of Narnia to be inconsequential in their subject matter, then the world pictured by all myths and religions is inconsequential.

Thomas Howard, C. S. Lewis: Man of Letters (Worthington, UK: Churchman, 1987), pp. 24–25

SUE MATHESON   To read the Chronicles of Narnia is to become involved in the process of self-transformation which the Lion represents; this, no doubt, accounts for the series' popularity. Professor Kirke's England and the twentieth century are prime examples of what Jung identifies as man "lost in the isolation of consciousness and its errors and sufferings." When the Lion created Narnia, he filled a gap in our social fabric. The Chronicles play a compensatory role, providing the reader with the healing experience of encountering what ⟨D. H.⟩ Lawrence calls "another kind of experience . . . truly imaginative." ⟨. . .⟩

Since the reading process of the Chronicles is a healing process, and the Lion is a healer as well as an Enchanter, the process of enchantment also extends to a function of the fantasist. True to Tolkien's definition, Lewis is a fantasist who creates the Chronicles of Narnia which he and the reader may enter and enjoy at will, but Aslan creates Narnia. He not only literally creates Narnia, but he also takes on the role of the *author* of the events which occur there. To Aravis he says, "Child . . . I am telling you your own story, not hers. No one is told any but their own." Aslan not only functions as selective narrator, he also explains events, providing expository lumps when necessary: to Shasta he says, "I was the lion who forced you to join Aravis, I was the cat who comforted you among the horses of the dead. I was the lion who drove the jackals from you while you slept. I was the lion who gave the Horses the strength of fear for the last mile so that you should reach King Lune in time."

In effect, Aslan is his own fantasist. Through the device of Story, he heals with his Magic, manifesting the reality of the psyche by using the process of the imagination. Story-telling is a part of the Mage's Enchantment. By creating a world of "arresting strangenesses" the Enchanter offers the reader another reality: in the case of Narnia, the subjective vision of child-hood. The constructor of his own fantasy world, Aslan is what Eliade defines as the zone of "absolute reality." In essence, he is the sacred center.

Aslan is that experience somewhere within us that Lawrence says "is the old experience of the Euphrates, Mesopotamia between rivers." Underlying the fantasy impulse, the primitive thirst for *being* which impelled primitive man to attempt to transform the profane into sacred time accounts for the intensity of response to the Lion. Fantasy is "a natural human activity" ⟨Tolkien⟩, and so is constructing according to archetype. On the profane level, the fantasist re-creates in *illo tempore* as best he can, because it is the point from which the creation of the fantasy world takes place. In the Chronicles of Narnia, the primordial image truly manifests itself, relegating the shamanistic function of the artist to a secondary concern, since the reader may encounter it in as direct a form as possible. The Lion's eruption into our conscious world is itself indicative of the process of Enchantment, because it heralds the replacement of the old, decayed Signature with the new and takes us back to that experience which not even twentieth century objectivism can destroy.

Sue Matheson, "C. S. Lewis and the Lion: Primitivism and Archetype in the Chronicles of Narnia," Mythlore No. 55 (Autumn 1988): 17–18

DAVID HOLBROOK   A title like that of Lewis's first fable for children offers a challenge—how do we connect a lion, a witch, and a wardrobe? It is the kind of challenge a preacher characteristically makes, and has done since the use of the *exemplum* in the Middle Ages. There is a tacit understanding between author and listener that these objects are offered as metaphors—just as objects in dreams and visions come as meta-phors. The mode belongs to a long tradition in which moral and spiritual aspects of "the journey of life" are examined in terms of a journey as in *The Plain Man's Pathway to Heaven* or *Pilgrim's Progress*. As a literary man, of course, Lewis knew many such allegories; and one can find in his fable writings elements from Spenser, medieval literature, the accounts of voyages of ancient saints (for example, Brendan) and so on.

⟨. . .⟩ Lewis himself tells us what the connection is between the wardrobe and the witch. As one of the illustrations in the Penguin edition makes clear, Digory takes the apple from the tree of life where a witch lurks to prevent him. He could only take this apple with the authority of the lion.

The Christian will see that as a test of obedience having to do with the forbidden fruit, Eden, and the Fall of Man. But who is the witch? If we put the Christianity in brackets and invoke psychoanalysis, we could argue that in going through the wardrobe the children are going through the mother's body as through the birth passage into another world, where the dead mother is to be found. She is there, in that world, and she has blighted it. The impulse to go into that world has to do with restoring her to life; but the problem is that since she is still the mother who rejected the child by dying, what happens if she is encountered, given new life, or brought back into this (real) world?

In exploring the possible meaning like this, I am also taking into account the meanings (as I see them) of George MacDonald's fantasies—fantasies that much influenced Lewis and that involve many processes of this kind. MacDonald, like Lewis, lost his mother as a young child; and all his work, I believe, is compelled by the quest for the dead mother. ⟨. . .⟩

But what then of Aslan? The answer perhaps is that the situation when the mother is lost the child's world is so dangerous that a substitute authority is needed to deal with reality. Lewis, like other individuals who suffered this trauma, was left with a profound hunger to find the mother in order to complete "being." The need is tremendous; and since it is an oral need, to love and be loved—hence, a fierce lion is an appropriate figure. Aslan doesn't eat anyone, but he growls and shows his teeth. He has claws and he lacerates and unpeels people. The oral element in Aslan's love must be seen in complex with other oral elements in Lewis's work—Aslan sings the world into being; Lewis himself feared to eat certain foods because they might arouse sexual feelings; sin is eating Turkish Delight; beatitude is eating heavenly food. Then there are creatures like the Harfangs and odd references as to "eating a baby." ⟨. . .⟩ Aslan's particular kind of minatory authority seems to me to come from another source, from the internalization of a figure *in loco parentis*.

The title of the first fable we examine virtually means, by my phenomeno-
logical analysis, "the strong (oral) authority I needed to invoke in my search
through the birth-passage into the world of death for my dead mother who,
I feared, might be a witch." The very fact that the fable is offered in terms
of such symbolism actually invites such an interpretation, and to interpret
is quite legitimate—as Lewis hinted he believed.

> David Holbrook, *The Skeleton in the Wardrobe: C. S. Lewis's Fantasies: A Phenomenolog-
> ical Study* (Lewisburg, PA: Bucknell University Press, 1991), pp. 27–30

COLIN MANLOVE   Appearing in the early 1950s, the Narnia
books represented a quite startling transformation of children's literature
after the relative doldrums of the 1940s. They helped begin a renaissance
in children's literature, and to some extent reassured librarians and school-
teachers, who had for too long to contend with the popularity of such
authors as W. E. Johns (of the "Biggles" books), or the multitudinous and
too-readily digested works of Enid Blyton, of the potency of the genre. More
specifically, together with the work of Tolkien, Lewis's books ushered in
the present popularity of the genre of fantasy.

The *Chronicles of Narnia* represented a return to the scope of children's
fantasy seen in the work of Charles Kingsley, George MacDonald, Rudyard
Kipling, and John Masefield. With their use of covert Christian themes and
their admission of profound topics of sacrifice, death and resurrection, the
nature of evil, the measure of faith, the divine creation and ending of a
world, and the quest for the divine, they bring into children's literature an
"adult" profundity of which it had long been felt incapable. Nor is this
done awkwardly. The living strength of the *Chronicles* is in the way that
such profundity is integrated with vivid characters and adventures, so that
it is possible to read the narrative without becoming aware of any further
significance, and likewise, when made aware of that significance, to be the
more deeply affected by it through the very surprise of its presence. Beyond
this, the *Chronicles* are profoundly *literary*, both in the way that (unlike
most other children's books) they draw naturally on the great cultural
tradition of Homer, Virgil, Dante, Spenser, Shakespeare, Milton, and Bun-
yan, and in the clarity and complexity of their style and form. Lewis maintained that he did not write specifically for children at all, but wrote in the
fairy-tale mode because, as the title of one of his essays has it, "Sometimes

Fairy Stories May Say Best What's to Be Said." Before Lewis, whether in William Thackeray's *The Rose and the Ring*, Lewis Carroll's "Alice" books, Mary Molesworth's *The Cuckoo Clock*, Kenneth Grahame's *The Golden Age* and *The Wind in the Willows*, Edith Nesbit's magic books, Sir James Barrie's *Peter Pan*, A. A. Milne's "Pooh" books, or Arthur Ransome's stories, the reader had been asked to enter a child's world; now the child's world was entering that of the adult reader. If there is any final ethic that is taught by Lewis's books out of this, it is that nothing is "mere." The apparently small—a fairy tale, a little world called Narnia, a group of contemporary children—can contain the very large (just as, in *The Last Battle*, a stable is seen as once having contained the entire world). Lewis deliberately startles us into awareness by the very abruptness with which his child characters become great heroic figures in Narnia. In essay after essay after essay he makes war against dismissive attitudes toward children's literature: " 'Juveniles,' indeed! Am I to patronize sleep because children sleep sound? Or honey because children like it?" After Lewis children's literature was not, and was not seen to be, quite so provincial again.

> Colin Manlove, *The Chronicles of Narnia: The Patterning of a Fantastic World* (New York: Twayne, 1993), pp. 8–9

❖ *Bibliography*

Spirits in Bondage: A Cycle of Lyrics. 1919.

Dymer. 1926.

The Pilgrim's Regress: An Allegorical Apology for Christianity, Reason and Romanticism. 1933.

The Allegory of Love: A Study in Medieval Tradition. 1936.

Out of the Silent Planet. 1938.

The Personal Heresy: A Controversy (with E. M. W. Tillyard). 1939.

Rehabilitations and Other Essays. 1939.

The Problem of Pain. 1940.

The Weight of Glory. 1942.

The Screwtape Letters. 1942, 1961 (with *Screwtape Proposes a Toast*).

A Preface to Paradise Lost. 1942.

Broadcast Talks ⟨*The Case for Christianity*⟩. 1942.

The Abolition of Man; or, Reflections on Education with Special Reference to the
    Teaching of English in the Upper Forms of Schools. 1943.
Christian Behaviour: A Further Series of Broadcast Talks. 1943.
Perelandra. 1943.
Beyond Personality: The Christian Idea of God. 1944.
The Great Divorce: A Dream. 1945.
That Hideous Strength: A Modern Fairy-Tale for Grown-Ups. 1945.
George MacDonald: An Anthology (editor). 1946.
Essays Presented to Charles Williams (editor). 1947.
Miracles: A Preliminary Study. 1947.
Vivisection. c. 1947.
Autumn. 1948.
Transposition and Other Addresses. 1949.
The Lion, the Witch, and the Wardrobe: A Story for Children. 1950.
The Literary Impact of the Authorised Version. 1950.
Prince Caspian: The Return to Narnia. 1951.
The Voyage of the Dawn Treader. 1952.
Mere Christianity. 1952.
The Silver Chair. 1953.
English Literature in the Sixteenth Century, Excluding Drama. 1954.
The Horse and His Boy. 1954.
De Descriptione Temporum: An Inaugural Lecture. 1955.
The Magician's Nephew. 1955.
Surprised by Joy: The Shape of My Early Life. 1955.
The Last Battle. 1956.
Till We Have Faces: A Myth Retold. 1956.
Reflections on the Psalms. 1958.
The Four Loves. 1960.
The World's Last Night and Other Essays. 1960.
Studies in Words. 1960.
An Experiment in Criticism. 1961.
A Grief Observed. 1961.
They Asked for a Paper: Papers and Addresses. 1962.
Beyond the Bright Blur. 1963.
Letters to Malcolm, Chiefly on Prayer. 1964.
The Discarded Image: An Introduction to Medieval and Renaissance Literature.
    1964.
Poems. Ed. Walter Hooper. 1964.

Screwtape Proposes a Toast and Other Pieces. 1965.

Of Other Worlds: Essays and Stories. Ed. Walter Hooper. 1966.

Studies in Medieval and Renaissance Literature. Ed. Walter Hooper. 1966.

Letters. Ed. W. H. Lewis. 1966, 1988 (ed. Walter Hooper).

Spenser's Images of Life. Ed. Alastair Fowler. 1967.

Christian Reflections. Ed. Walter Hooper. 1967.

Letters to an American Lady. Ed. Clyde S. Kilby. 1967.

Mark vs. Tristram: Correspondence between C. S. Lewis and Owen Barfield. Ed. Walter Hooper. 1967.

A Mind Awake: An Anthology of C. S. Lewis. Ed. Clyde S. Kilby. 1968.

Narrative Poems. Ed. Walter Hooper. 1969.

Selected Literary Essays. Ed. Walter Hooper. 1969.

God in the Dock: Essays on Theology and Ethics. Ed. Walter Hooper. 1970.

The Humanitarian Theory of Punishment. 1972.

The Dark Tower and Other Stories. Ed. Walter Hooper. 1977.

They Stand Together: The Letters of C. S. Lewis to Arthur Greeves 1914–1963. Ed. Walter Hooper. 1979.

A Cretaceous Perambulator (with Owen Barfield). Ed. Walter Hooper. 1983.

Boxen: The Imaginary World of the Young C. S. Lewis. Ed. Walter Hooper. 1985.

Letters to Children. Ed. Lyle W. Dorsett and Marjorie Lamp Mead. 1985.

The Latin Letters of C. S. Lewis to Don Giovanni Calabria of Verona and to Members of His Congregation 1947–1961. Ed. Martin Moynihan. 1987.

The Essential C. S. Lewis. Ed. Lyle W. Dorsett. 1988.

All My Road Before Me: The Diary of C. S. Lewis 1922–1927. Ed. Walter Hooper. 1991.

David Lindsay
1876–1945

DAVID LINDSAY was born on March 3, 1876, in Blackheath, outside of London. His Scottish father, Alexander Lindsay, deserted the family shortly after David was born, leaving his English wife, Bessy Bellamy Lindsay, to provide for herself and their three children. Lindsay attended the Lewisham Grammar School, where he proved an exceptional student and won a university scholarship; due to the family's precarious finances, however, Lindsay had to leave school at age sixteen to work as a clerk at the insurance firm of Price, Forbes in London. Although a diligent and successful clerk, Lindsay disliked his work immensely. He continued his education on his own, teaching himself German and studying the works of Schopenhauer and Nietzsche.

Lindsay's life underwent a radical change with the onset of World War I in 1914. He joined the Grenadier Guards (over the objections of his family, who wanted him to join the Scots Guards) and spent the war working as a clerk in London. During this time, he met Jacqueline Silver, whom he married in 1916—a union opposed by both their families, as she was twenty years his junior. They eventually had two daughters. When the war ended and Lindsay was released from service, he resigned his post at Price, Forbes and moved with his wife to Cornwall in 1919 to pursue a literary career.

In 1920 Lindsay published *A Voyage to Arcturus,* a philosophical fantasy about life on another planet that would become his best-known work. The book was not a success at the time of publication, receiving negative reviews and poor sales. Lindsay had trouble finding a publisher for his next book, *The Haunted Woman* (1922), a problem that would worsen as his career progressed. He published *Sphinx* in 1923 and followed with his only nonfantasy work, the historical novel *Adventures of Monsieur de Mailly,* in 1926 (published in the United States as *A Blade for Sale* in 1927). In 1929, monetary problems forced the Lindsays to move to Sussex, where they eventually ran a boarding-house in Brighton.

Lindsay's last published novel, *Devil's Tor* (1932), was a financial and critical failure and effectively ended his literary career. Lindsay became extremely depressed and neglectful of his health, which was compromised by an inherited blood disease. In 1945 the Lindsays' house in Brighton was hit by a German bomb; although the bomb failed to explode, it crashed through the bathroom ceiling as Lindsay was taking a bath, injuring him and worsening his mental condition. He finally developed a dental abscess, which he, ever suspicious of doctors, deliberately concealed until blood poisoning developed. He died on July 16, 1945, leaving a diary and two unpublished manuscripts, *The Violet Apple* and the unfinished *The Witch*, which were published in 1976.

Critical Extracts

UNSIGNED   However much one may resent such a book as *A Voyage to Arcturus*, one must pay tribute to the cleverness which enables Mr. David Lindsay to capture the elusive quality of the worst kind of nightmare. He does not content himself with giving us a vivid description of life as it conceivably might be on another planet; we are transported to remote regions of space in order that the riddle of human existence may be studied in true perspective; and the solution thence afforded is very much what one might expect a temporarily unbalanced mind to arrive at if an anaesthetic were potent for just one critical instant longer—which, mercifully, it never is. Mr. Lindsay's imagination is prolific rather than powerful, and he has not controlled it towards any coherent result. For instance, the hero of the adventure, Maskull, encounters on his journey in Arcturus a number of entities—human, superhuman, and diabolic—whose relation to him and to each other never becomes clear; nor can we find any connecting link between the startling and often gruesome episodes which mark his progress. There may be an intention of allegory in what appears to be simply the riot of morbid fancy; but we doubt whether many readers will be inclined to pursue the possible hidden meaning over a quagmire and through a noisome fog. For the book is, at any rate, consistent in respect of its uniform unwholesomeness; the keynote being struck in the opening chapter, which recalls Baudelaire, or Poe in his most grisly vein. It is, no doubt, a legitimate aim of the writer of fiction to make the flesh creep; scarcely, we think, to make the gorge rise.

Unsigned, [Review of A Voyage to Arcturus], Times Literary Supplement, 30 September 1920, p. 637

DAVID LINDSAY   You remark—'Poetry is generated by the clash of the male and female elements in the personality.' I go further and say that all the works of creative genius are the children of the union of the male and female elements, and that it is the female that produces them. Moreover, 'male' and 'female', in my opinion, are not to be understood metaphorically, but literally. The male body contains female atoms and combinations of atoms, and in genius the proportion of this female element is larger than in the generality of men. Hence your very true fact that 'the faces of men of genius have often a feminine appearance'—not *because* they are men of genius, but on account of their excess of female physical atoms, or whatever we may call them.

With regard to Carlyle's dictum that 'genius is an infinite capacity for taking pains'—in that case the world might be full of geniuses. Unfortunately, it *isn't*, and so another definition must be sought. My own (I do not say it is the final one!) is—'genius is the infinite capacity for striking into new paths'.

David Lindsay, Letter to E. H. Visiak (9 February 1922), "Letters to E. H. Visiak from David Lindsay and Victor Gollancz," ADAM International Review Nos. 346–48 (1971): 46–47

COLIN WILSON   ⟨. . .⟩ Lindsay was not a fully grown up man— that is to say, there were many unresolved contradictions in him. There is no telling what might have happened if *Arcturus* had achieved the success it deserved. Its basic thesis is a Buddhistic world-rejection. Lindsay wrote:

> One must regard the world not merely as the home of illusions, but as being *rotten* with illusion from top to bottom. . . . The most sacred and holy things ought not to be taken for granted, for if examined attentively, they will be found as hollow and empty as the rest. . . . Behind this sham world lies the real, tremendous and

awful Muspel-world, which knows neither will, nor Unity, nor
Individuals; that is to say, an inconceivable world.

The last sentence identifies Lindsay clearly as a mystic, or at least as some
extreme kind of Kantian philosopher who believes that all the 'necessary'
conditions of our world—space, time and so on—are somehow not at all
necessary.

But the deepest vein in Lindsay's nature was not of mysticism, but a kind
of Scots religious seriousness. He was a relative and an admirer of Carlyle,
and anyone who has read Carlyle will see the similarity of temperament.
Lindsay also reminds me of the mystic William Law, who declared himself
'a stranger to revelation', and whose *Serious Call to a Devout and Holy Life*
identifies religion with self-discipline and strong-mindedness. ⟨. . .⟩

One notes the awkward style of the novels, and it is clear that part of
Lindsay's problem as a writer was ⟨his⟩ immense shyness and constraint.
Arcturus swings into a powerful un-selfconscious stride after its stiff beginning. After this book, Lindsay was aware that he was writing for publication.
The 'reader over his shoulder' may explain the stiffness of the prose. It's a
pity he was not more like ⟨D. H.⟩ Lawrence, who was too sure of himself
to suffer from self-consciousness, and who is consequently never afraid to
write as he would talk. Among letters Lindsay wrote to ⟨E. H.⟩ Visiak,
I found a perceptive fragment from some unknown correspondent that
summarises the faults of Lindsay's style:

> With this [mystical] Lindsay I am in sympathy, and the other
> simply has to be endured for his sake. The Lindsay who writes
> about 'high life' in hotels is ignorant, pretentious and inherently
> vulgar. He is a hopeless victim of Mark Twain's 'nickel-plate
> style'; his characters never go, they proceed, they can't just get
> into a train, they must journey by first-class, they don't leave,
> they take departure, they don't say yes, they assent. In short, they
> are hopelessly underbred. They talk in a stilted, ceremonious style
> which I last remember to have met in a penny novelette I had
> borrowed from the maid. . . .

While this makes the point with pungency, it is not perhaps entirely fair.
⟨. . .⟩ one experiences the intuition that the novel was not his true medium.
What would have happened if Carlyle had tried to launch himself with a
novel instead of *Sartor Resartus* and *The French Revolution?* The interesting

thing is that the unique quality of Lindsay's mind still stamps itself upon his unworthy material, making it oddly memorable.

Colin Wilson, "Lindsay as Novelist and Mystic," *The Strange Genius of David Lindsay*
by J. B. Pick, Colin Wilson, and E. H. Visiak (London: John Baker, 1970), pp. 42–44

E. H. VISIAK   Lindsay's imperturbable composure was but the surface-layer of a great deep. He was radically unhappy, dissatisfied, hungry for recognition in the literary world. Withal, he was extremely sensitive, extremely impressionable. When, one day, I remarked that I ranked *A Voyage to Arcturus* in genius with Kafka's *The Castle*, he blushed.

Beneath it all, however, he was a mystic, and here he tried to express it by the word, *dark*, which involved, as I have said, some kind of mystical intuition. I felt it was the key-word to his imagination ⟨. . .⟩

Of this, I was afforded, as it happened, a remarkable illustration, even a demonstration. It occurred during my stay at Ferring, while we were out for a walk, one night, in the countryside. Suddenly I was brought to a stand, arrested by the *very* strange aspect of the moon. It was at the full, bright, white, yet having a transparent, vacuous appearance, as if it itself was an orifice in space.

'Oh, just look at the moon!' I exclaimed.

He was already looking up at it. 'White,' he murmured. 'White, *empty*.' His face looked wild and tragic, and he cried with startling emphasis, 'I ought *never* to have been born in this world!'

I was amazed, but I said mechanically, 'In what world, then, ought you to have been born?'

'In *no* world!'

He went on urgently as if he were under a stress, a great urgent desire to express himself, to make me understand. I cannot recall his actual words, but they were spasmodic, disjointed, intensely passionate endeavours to express a yearning, an ideal, an antithesis, the unearthly, unimaginable contrast to normal experience, sense sensation; the absolute negation of mundane conditions: an unthinkable and, to me, appalling state of arctic or extra-arctic abstraction. To himself, it was something pure, essential, ineffable—the Muspel, or 'Divine Light' or his *Arcturus* in its positive aspect, as inexpressible. I suppose, it would correspond to the Buddhistic *Nirvana*, with the great paradox, 'It is not this, and it is not that.'

E. H. Visiak, "Lindsay as I Knew Him," *The Strange Genius of David Lindsay* by J. B. Pick, Colin Wilson, and E. H. Visiak (London: John Baker, 1970), pp. 100–101

J. B. PICK   ⟨*The Violet Apple*⟩ can be interpreted in several ways. In one it is an allegory of love and marriage—the original bewildering attraction, and sense of joint destiny and kinship; the blind, idealistic passion; the lapse into prosaic domesticity; the slow return to deepest fullness.

In another sense it is a parable of death and resurrection: the death of self-pride, swallowed in the experience of sublimity and communion, and resurrection in simplicity and truth. In a sense closely akin to this it is an image and parable of the life-criterion of 'attaining to the sublime and performing the common task'. Before the apple, illusion and ignorance; the apple, an experience of sublimity; after the apple, an acceptance of the common task, and eventually a dedication to work which will recreate through the common task an experience of the sublime. All this is achieved with a very remarkable simplicity and economy of means. The book has a kind of beauty that does not depend upon the words themselves but upon its very essence.

Its theme transcends that of *Devil's Tor* which, with a sublimity so laboured as to be falsified from pure perception, charts the fated achievement of a marriage whose sole aim is the production of a superhuman saviour. In *The Violet Apple* the sublime relationship is its own justification. This books draws down the sublime into a reality which all can recognise and by its very simplicity grows conviction like a tree.

J. B. Pick, "The Unpublished Novels: *The Violet Apple* and *The Witch*," *The Strange Genius of David Lindsay* by J. B. Pick, Colin Wilson, and E. H. Visiak (London: John Baker, 1970), p. 157

ERIC S. RABKIN   David Lindsay's *A Voyage to Arcturus* (1920), a powerful and confusing work set largely on a distant planet, obviously springs from the world of science fiction. One purist's definition of that genre calls for the exercise of utterly logical—scientific, if you will—extrapolation. Yet even in a paradigmatic science fiction novel like Wells' *The Time Machine* (1895), the future setting is justified, made *science* fiction, by the fantastic device of the time machine itself. All science fiction is to some extent fantastic. Yet the extent to which science fiction can use the startling and assumption-reversing devices of the fantastic is much greater than Wells made clear. ⟨. . .⟩

The story begins when two Englishmen, Maskull and Nightspore, come to a séance intended to thrill jaded sensibilities. An apparition indeed appears. As the guests watch, a man rushes into the room and strangles the apparition, which dies with a hideous grin. The man, Krag, turns out to know Nightspore and offers to take him and his friend to Arcturus in search of Surtur, apparently some type of demi-god. Lindsay follows the effective hocus-pocus of the séance with the strange science Maskull soon encounters at Starkness, the abandoned Scottish observatory from which Krag proposes to leave. There Maskull finds a tower which he hasn't the strength to climb, for as he goes up, its gravity increases geometrically: gravity as inverse electromagnetic phenomenon. Of course, there is no extraliterary justification for this kind of gravity, but once introduced, it functions "scientifically," extrapolatively, with mathematical precision—until Krag arrives. He administers a ritual arm wound to Maskull and this magic suddenly allows Maskull to walk up the stairs with ease. The narrative attitude toward science here is ambiguous. What after all should we make of our science if it functions in the same realm as magic? By writing science fiction as fantasy, Lindsay makes science fiction a tool for questioning the ostensible precision of science itself. ⟨. . .⟩

The bulk of the novel is Maskull's journey across Tormance, each episode employing a new locale, new characters, and new modes of perception. Within each environment, we find an inner logic such as we would expect in more extrapolative science fiction. ⟨. . .⟩

The science fiction is pushed far toward fantasy by the utter conflict between the logic within each episode and the discontinuous perceptual changes that accompany each of the frequent and unexpected changes of locale. Just as Alice enters a new world each time she jumps over a brook in *Through the Looking Glass* (1872), so Maskull enters a new world each time he continues on his journey. That each locale obeys its own science fictional logic extrapolated from its own repertoire of fantastic assumptions does not prevent the overall effect of the book to be, as with Lewis Carroll's work, that of a thorough fantasy. ⟨. . .⟩

Lindsay was as well aware of his science fiction forebears as he was of his mythic sources. ⟨. . .⟩ But in the mad rush from episode to episode, and in the utterly unjustified leaps from physiology to physiology, from sense to sense, and from mythology to mythology, Lindsay has also created a fantasy that shows toward perception, that first fundamental of science, the same deep ambivalence that Mary Shelley felt toward refined science alone. In treating science as a question of perception, Lindsay begins to create a framework for questions that need not concern science alone. When we finally see the journey as a moral odyssey, and feel the despair of its painful message of uncertainty, then Lindsay has succeeded in entering the great flux of Western religious debate. He has exploited fantasy to extend the range of science fiction into ultimately serious myth.

Eric S. Rabkin, "Conflation of Genres and Myths in David Lindsay's *A Voyage to Arcturus*," *Journal of Narrative Technique* 7, No. 2 (Spring 1977): 149–52, 155

BERNARD SELLIN   *The Witch* reveals no drastic change in Lindsay's ideology. There is visible, on the contrary, the continuity of an ideology already partially revealed previously. Lindsay, however, by the richness of his explanations, his association of elements hitherto separated, and his care to go to the root of matters, has produced a book of enormous interest to anyone studying his ideology. Perhaps the most striking feature, when one considers his writing, extending over some twenty years, is the homogeneous nature of the whole output. There can be no doubt that *The Witch* will be of value to anyone trying to interpret the labyrinth of symbols in *A Voyage to Arcturus*. The essential basis of *The Witch* is already contained in Lindsay's first novel, with man as the prisoner of the tangible world, the quest for spirituality, the beneficial effect of pain and sacrifice, music as a message from the hereafter and as a technique of expression, and the need to suffer in order to be able to reach a superior level of consciousness. The distinction between 'spirit' and 'self', as present in *The Witch*, is analogous to the separation of the 'green sparks' and the 'whirls' in *A Voyage to Arcturus*. Muspel has become 'The Unself', whilst Krag has taken the form of a woman in Urda. The pessimistic outlook inspired by Schopenhauer is varied slightly, even to the extent of being coloured with Christian mythology in *The Violet Apple*.

One notable absentee, however, from *The Haunted Woman* onwards, is Crystalman. Although the windfall of one solitary novel, he will undoubtedly remain Lindsay's most memorable character. Even though the values that he personified continue to be denounced with no less virulence than before, Crystalman himself appears no more in the form of such an autonomous character and unifying symbol. Lindsay's imaginative power, on the contrary, moved toward his antithesis in the Divinity embodied sometimes in the Great Mother and sometimes in Urda, or the vital principle. Along with Crystalman, there also disappeared the conception of an evil God, the incarnation of a primitive Divinity, reigning over the visible world. The idea by which the Creator allowed himself to be contaminated by Evil is still present in *Devil's Tor*. In *The Witch*, there is no longer any question of it. Evil is inherent in life. The delusions of man merely serve to increase his unhappiness.

Bernard Sellin, "*The Violet Apple* and *The Witch*," *The Life and Works of David Lindsay*, tr. Kenneth Gunnell (New York: Cambridge University Press, 1981), pp. 229–30

HAROLD BLOOM   Yeats, in the note he added to Lady Gregory's *Cuchulain of Muirthemme*, in 1903, spoke of that traditional element in romance when "nobody described anything as we understood description" because all was figurative: "One was always losing oneself in the unknown, and rushing to the limits of the world." This is certainly the world of Tormance ⟨in *A Voyage to Arcturus*⟩, where every antagonist to Maskull's Promethean quest is only another pleasure, another rejected otherness that ensnares Maskull briefly, intensely, and to no purpose. A narrative that is nothing but a remorseless drive to death, beyond the pleasure/pain principle, can proceed only by a systematic assault upon the reader's sensibilities, because the reader *is* the antagonist, whose motive for reading at least begins in pleasure, and desires to end in pleasure. Lindsay audaciously sets as many obstacles for the reader to break through as his master Carlyle did, but the reader who persists will be rewarded, albeit somewhat belatedly. ⟨. . .⟩

⟨. . .⟩ there is not the slightest doubt but that Maskull is doom-eager, in the mode of Shelley's Poet in *Alastor*, or of Ovid's Narcissus. He is also astonishingly violent, and awesomely capable of enduring the really unbearable climates, regions and beings of the accursed world of Tormance. The typical inhabitant of Tormance is summed up in the description of one particular ogre as someone "who passed his whole existence in tormenting, murdering, and absorbing others, for the sake of his own delight." Since Maskull is hardly interested in his own delight, but only in his own possible sublimity, a very curious narrative principle goes to work as soon as Maskull starts walking due North upon Tormance. It is that singular kind of nightmare some of us dream obsessively, in which you encounter a series of terrifying faces, and only gradually do you come to realize that these faces *are terrified*, and that *you* are the cause of the terror. Maskull himself is at once the most remarkable and most frightening consciousness upon Tormance, and Maskull after all is technically a lost traveller, cut off in space and time. His truest precursor ⟨. . .⟩ may be Browning's Childe Roland, who is himself far darker than the dark tower he searches out.

Lindsay's narrative thus has the shape of a destructive fire seeking for a kindlier flame, but finding nothing because it burns up everything in its path. As we discover only in the book's last scene, after Maskull is dead, there is no Muspel or divine flame anyway, because Nightspore's true encounter with the Sublime, beyond death, results in his beautiful realization "that Muspel consisted of himself and the stone tower on which he was sitting. . . ." By then, the exhausted reader has transferred his identification from Maskull to Nightspore, from Prometheus-Narcissus to what Blake called "the real Man the imagination." It is the progressive exhaustion of the reader, through violence and through identification with Maskull, which is the true plot of Lindsay's narrative ⟨. . .⟩

That exhaustion, and the textual violence provoking it, are the uncanny or Sublime splendor of Lindsay's book, and place the book, I would argue, at the very center of modern fantasy, in contrast to the works of the Neochristian Inklings which despite all their popularity are quite peripheral. Tolkien, Lewis and Williams actually flatter the reader's Narcissism, while morally softening the reader's Prometheanism. Lindsay strenuously assaults the reader's Narcissism, while both hardening the reader's Prometheanism and yet reminding the reader that Narcissism and Prometheanism verge upon an identity. Inkling fantasy is soft stuff, because it pretends that it benefits from a benign transmission both of romance tradition and of Christian doctrine. Lindsay's savage masterpiece compels the reader to question both the sources of fantasy, *within the reader*, and the benignity of the handing-on of tradition. Fantasy is shown by Lindsay to be a mode in which freedom is won, if at all, by a fearful agon with tradition, and at the price of the worst kind of psychic over-determination, which is the sado-masochistic turning of aggressivity against the self.

> Harold Bloom, "*Clinamen*: Towards a Theory of Fantasy," *Bridges to Fantasy*, ed. George E. Slusser, Eric S. Rabkin, and Robert Scholes (Carbondale: Southern Illinois University Press, 1982), pp. 13–15

DOUGLAS A. MACKEY   Is the world as we know it but a halluci-nation implanted in our minds by an evil aspect of God, a false God, who suffers under his own limitations of fate?

The answer of David Lindsay in *A Voyage to Arcturus* (1920) is clearly affirmative. Lindsay's demiurge is called Crystalman. He steals the green sparks of vital spiritual fire of Muspel, domain of Surtur, the true God, and "crystallizes" them into living forms. When Lindsay's hero Maskull tours the planet Tormance, he confronts an amazing series of individuals, each with different sensory organs such as third eyes or tentacles sprouting from the chest—and correspondingly differing philosophies and theologies. The woman Joiwind, a beautiful and unselfish child of nature, identifies the Creator (Crystalman) as God and accepts the state of nature as good; despite her virtue, she has made an intellectual error, as Maskull later realizes. On Tormance, truth and beauty are not the same. Beauty and pleasure constitute the net of Crystalman which ensnares the sparks of Muspel light. ⟨. . .⟩

⟨. . .⟩ The radical gnostic sensibility separates appearance from reality. When the gnostic tries to purify the pneuma of the influence of material existence, he does so out of conviction that this existence has no more reality than a hallucination.

Who is the true God in gnosticism? According to William Irwin Thompson, "Hebrew mythology, cast in the mirror of Gnosticism, comes out reversed: Jahweh is the Devil, and the serpent in the garden is the Saviour." In *A Voyage to Arcturus*, the true God, Surtur, appears under the incarnation of the ugly, unpleasant Krag, considered by most on Tormance as the Devil. But a passion for truth will always be considered evil where the real Devil (Crystalman) masquerades successfully as God. Krag is only appreciated for what he is at the end of the novel. Maskull dies and releases Nightspore, his pneumatic spark, who ascends the tower of Muspel. There he gains a vision of Crystalman as a shadowy body who feeds on Muspel fire, trapping it in life forms that are driven to strive painfully for pleasure. "He comprehended at last how the whole world of will was doomed to feel anguish in order that one Being might feel joy." Nightspore realizes that the entire created cosmos is Crystalman's, and Muspel is nowhere else but in himself, in the spark of green Muspel light that is his very being. In a sense Krag has saved him by guiding him; in another way, he has earned his own enlightenment by questing (as Maskull) for truth amidst a bewildering variety of types of error. Jacques LaCarriere make a relevant comment in *The Gnostics*:

> The soul is not immortal by nature, it can only become so if man feeds and sustains this privileged fire which he carries within him. Otherwise, ineluctably, he will return to nothingness. . . . Man is called upon, in this struggle against the generalized oppressiveness of the real, *to create a soul for himself*, or if you prefer, to nourish, fortify, and enrich the luminous spark he carries in his innermost being.

Krag does not fight Nightspore's battle for him. Gnosis is an active process. It is earned, not bestowed. In Elaine Pagel's words, "The gnostic understands Christ's message not as offering a set of answers, but as encouragement to engage in a process of searching." When Gangnet (Crystalman in disguise) bestows a mystical ecstasy of self-annihilation upon Maskull, it proves to be delusory. The kind of pleasure that seems to promise transcendence of self is the subtlest of Crystalman's deceits. Gnostic transcendence is self-possessed, accepting not abnegation before God but rather identification and merging.

Douglas A. Mackey, "Science Fiction and Gnosticism," *Missouri Review* 7, No. 2 (1984): 113–15

Bibliography

A Voyage to Arcturus. 1920.
The Haunted Woman. 1922.
Sphinx. 1923.
Adventures of Monsieur de Mailly ⟨*A Blade for Sale*⟩. 1926.
Devil's Tor. 1932.
The Violet Apple and The Witch. Ed. J. B. Pick. 1976.

A. Merritt
1884–1943

ABRAHAM MERRITT was born on January 20, 1884, to a Quaker family living in Beverly, New Jersey. He attended school in nearby Philadelphia but was forced to drop out of high school and later withdraw from taking law classes at the University of Pennsylvania owing to his family's financial difficulties. In 1902 he obtained work as a cub reporter with the *Philadelphia Inquirer*, a job that exposed him to a wide range of human experiences and, for a year, exiled him from the United States to prevent his testifying in court on criminal evidence he had uncovered. Merritt spent the year mostly in Mexico and Central America, exploring Mayan ruins and cultivating interests in anthropology, archaeology, and history that he would later put to use in his fiction.

After rising to the position of city editor a year after his return to the United States, Merritt took a position as assistant editor of the Hearst syndicate's *American Weekly* in New York in 1912. In 1917 Merritt's first story, "Through the Dragon Glass," was published in the popular general fiction magazine, *All-Story Weekly*. An adventure tale leavened with fantasy and Oriental mystery, its exotic flourishes set the tone for all Merritt's stories. The following year he wrote a novella, "The Moon Pool," about a malignant entity lurking in the ruins of Micronesia that abducts unwary travelers into another dimension. Reader acclaim was so tremendous that Merritt was persuaded to write a novel-length sequel, "The Conquest of the Moon Pool," which developed ideas introduced in the novella into a lost-race epic with science fiction overtones set in a subterranean world beneath the Caroline Islands. Merritt extensively revised the two stories for hardcover publication under the title *The Moon Pool* in 1919.

Merritt's second novel, *The Metal Monster* (serialized 1920; published as a book 1946), an ambitious attempt to use the lost-race fantasy as a vehicle for speculations on the origins of life, met with a lukewarm reception. Crestfallen, Merritt withdrew from fiction writing until 1923, when positive response to his novella "The Face in the Abyss" (later incorporated into its novella-length sequel, "The Snake Mother," in 1931) induced him to return. With *The Ship of Ishtar* (1926) and *Dwellers in the Mirage* (1932) Merritt perfected his trademark type of story in which a heroic character's removal to an exotic fantasy land experiencing internecine war—and the romantic love he experiences while there—forces him to confront and resolve conflicting impulses of good and evil within himself before he can help others to overcome their adversaries. With these novels, Merritt achieved a popularity among his reading public second only to that of Edgar Rice Burroughs.

In 1928 Merritt published *Seven Footprints to Satan*, a suspense novel with supernatural elements. He pursued this splicing of the mystery and horror genres in his last two novels, *Burn, Witch, Burn!* (1933) and its sequel *Creep, Shadow!* (1934). In 1937 Merritt became editor of the *American Weekly* and his career as a fiction writer effectively ended, except for a revision of *The Metal Monster* in 1941 for *Famous Fantastic Mysteries*, a pulp magazine comprised mostly of reprints where his work experienced a revival in the 1940s. Merritt died suddenly of a heart attack while on a business expedition to Florida on August 21, 1943. Between 1946 and 1947 Hannes Bok, one of several fantasy and science fiction writers strongly influenced by Merritt's writing, finished two stories left incomplete at Merritt's death, "The Fox Woman" and "The Black Wheel." A collection of Merritt's short fiction and uncompleted story fragments, *The Fox Woman and Other Stories*, was published posthumously in 1949.

▧ *Critical Extracts*

UNSIGNED   Fantasy, romance, adventure; something of mystery, something of the supernatural; a weaving together of ancient legends, older by far than any historical records, with the scientific knowledge of the present day; and side by side with these, yet far above and mastering them, the power of human love and willing self-sacrifice, the whole held together by a shimmering, glittering web of imagination—such, in so far as words of ours can briefly describe it, is this fascinating romance of *The Moon Pool*. In certain ways, it is nearer akin to such tales as those of *She* and *When the World Shook* than to any others of which we can think at the moment, but it is very far indeed from being a mere echo or imitation of Sir Rider Haggard. And if it is, indeed, as would appear from the title page, a first novel, then it marks the debut of a writer possessed of a very unusual, perhaps one might call it, extraordinary richness of imagination. The book is very long; adventure follows adventure and marvel marvel; but the author's energy and fertility of imaginative resource never seem to lessen, up to the climax when in all its splendor of evil, radiant beauty, the "Shining One" sweeps forward to conquer the stronghold of the "Three."

Unsigned, [Review of The Moon Pool], New York Times Book Review, 23 November 1919, p. 674

VINCENT STARRETT   Mr. Merritt ⟨in *Seven Footprints to Satan*⟩ has a better tale to tell than Mr. Priestley ⟨in *The Old Dark House*⟩, and does not begin to tell it as well as the English critic does his story of the Welsh hills. It is, none the less, a better piece of imagining, being in point of fact one of the maddest yarns placed upon paper—quite "cuckoo," as somebody said. Written by Mr. Priestley, Mr. Merritt's tale might have taken on plausibility that would have made it great. However, it was not written by Mr. Priestley, and the result again is disappointment. *Seven Footprints to Satan* is a dime novel selling at $2, and its creatures are the two-dimensional creatures of dime novels; not one is memorable. The dialogue is banal and atrocious. Yet Mr. Merritt has an idea that was a good one, and the book contains some ingenious situations. It will be read by thousands of those no doubt fortunate persons who care not at all for style or distinction in a story as long as it moves rapidly, as long as all sinister forces succumb at length to the absurd hero, as long as ultimately that ridiculous creature gets the girl. For my own part, I am concerned for Mr. Merritt's health. When he feels another such book coming over him, I think he should take a couple of allonals and try to get some sleep. The allonals failing, he might try some veronal, and failing that arsenic in large quantities.

Vincent Starrett, "Several Kinds of Detective Thrillers," New York World, 22 April 1928, p. 11

WILL CUPPY   What this department wants to know, among other things, is this: If Sir H. Rider Haggard's name is a household word, beloved by the populace, taught in our colleges and so on, why not A. Merritt's. (Of course, it is, to some extent, but we mean still more so.) We are rather vague about the details of Allan Quatermain and the Lady known as She, but they gave us a very special kick, and you'll find the same voltage in the works of this Mr. Merritt, the which we urge you to try at your earliest convenience.

Mr. Merritt has oodles of originality, and is doubtless a trifle fed up with being compared to Sir Rider; none the less, it is his destiny for the moment, and he must lie in it. If you've perused *The Face in the Abyss*, *The Moon Pool* and *Seven Footprints to Satan*, you're aware of this author's talent for fantastic imagery, his slick maneuvering of illusion and reality, his surprising fertility in strange invention and his all-round scrivening powers. If not, get busy.

Just to give you a hint, Leif Langdon, a gigantic young American of Viking forebears, accompanied by Jim Eagles, an educated Cherokee (they were chums at Dartmouth), hits for the Alaskan wilderness and comes to the Valley of the Mirage, inhabited by the little people, who are held in thrall by the Ayjir, a full-sized tribe ruled by Lur the Sorceress, Yodin the High Priest and Tibur the Laugher. Moreover, there's a lovely heroine, Evalie, and it all has lots to do with Leif's earlier adventures in the Gobi Desert, where the leaders of the Uighurs had recognized him as Dwayanu the Deliverer, who's to bring back their ancient glories.

Ensuing events are all we have promised. What say to deadly flowers and leeches the size of walruses, and heathen rites, the devil's cauldron, the Lake of Ghosts, the Great Kraken itself, the Ordeal of Khalk'ru and true love? The catch is that Mr. Merritt never reaches that much-too-much stage where the mouth-filling marvels degenerate into mere wind and silliness. The boy has real writing power and is therefore required adventure reading.

Will Cuppy, [Review of *Dwellers in the Mirage*], *New York Herald Tribune Books*, 12 June 1932, p. 7

WILLIAM C. WEBER   Mr. Merritt is hardly a new name in the domain of death and terror—more than a decade ago he wrote *The Moon Pool*, a Rider-Haggardish affair that has not grown old with the passage of years. But *Burn, Witch, Burn* is without doubt the grisliest piece of writing that has come from his pen, and since *The Moon Pool*, the most worthy of a large and terror-stricken audience. A sinister Italian lady is able to endow certain costume dolls she constructs, in a peculiarly horrible manner, with the power of motion. She bends the dolls to her will and with needle-sharp poniards 'round their necks they venture out by night and kill as she bids them. It will chill the blood of the hardiest mystery hound. This reader saw strange little figures scuttling into dark corners the night he read it. Try it yourself—and wake up screaming.

> William C. Weber, "Murder Will Out," *Saturday Review of Literature*, 25 February 1933, p. 457

H. P. LOVECRAFT   Merritt is a stout, sandy, grey-eyed man of about 45 or 50—extremely pleasant and genial, and a brilliant and well-informed conversationalist on all subjects. He is associate editor of Hearst's *American Weekly*, but all his main interests center in his weird writing. He agrees with me that the original "Moon Pool" novelette in the *All-Story* is his best work. Just now he is doing a sequel to *Burn, Witch, Burn* (which I haven't read but which he says he'll send me), whose locale will be the fabulous sunken city of Ys, off the coast of Brittany. It will bring in the comparatively little known legendry of *shadow-magic*. Merritt has a wide acquaintance among mystical enthusiasts, and is a close friend of old Nicholas Roerich, the Russian painter whose weird Tibetan landscapes I have so long admired. I was extremely glad to meet Merritt in person, for I have admired his work for 15 years. He has certain defects—caused by catering to a popular audience—but for all that he is the most poignant and distinctive fantaisiste now contributing to the pulps. As I mentioned some time ago—when you lent me the *Mirage* instalment—he has a peculiar power of working up an atmosphere and investing a region with an aura of unholy dread. I think I've read everything of his except *The Metal Monster* and *Burn, Witch, Burn*—and thanks to him these two deficiencies will probaly be remedied before long.

> H. P. Lovecraft, Letter to Robert H. Barlow (13 January 1934), *Selected Letters 1932–1934*, ed. August Derleth and James Turner (Sauk City, WI: Arkham House, 1976), pp. 341–42

A. MERRITT   You ask me to define fantasy. That is quite a job, I fear. Nor have I yet found any all-encompassing formula to satisfy me of what it is—although I am quite sure of what it is *not*.

Some say that it is the art of making the unreal seem real, but I think this is a highly vulnerable definition. If I succeed in making the unreal real to the reader, does not then the unreal cease to be unreal; become reality?

And what is unreal?

I think that true fantasy must have two basic elements. One is the spirit that makes poetry. And the second is the rhythm of true mathematics.

By true mathematics I do not mean the spirit of the abacus, or of the counting house, but the linked sequences, the clarity, the inevitableness of those higher mathematics which can crystallize the idea, for example, of relativity.

> A. Merritt, "What Is Fantasy?" (1941), cited in Sam Moskowitz, A. Merritt: Reflections in the Moon Pool (Philadelphia: Oswald Train, 1985), p. 361

JAMES BLISH   There is evidence that the intoned style of the fantasies was a mannerism with Merritt, as opposed, for example, to that of H. P. Lovecraft, who told everything in about the same tone of voice. When Merritt wanted to write a story in which the fantasy elements were of relatively minor importance, or were to be explained away, his prose lost many of its kinks. This is apparent, for instance, in *Seven Footprints to Satan*. This is the style which ⟨Sam⟩ Moskowitz called "restrained, almost journalistic in tone." Brian Aldiss has teased Moskowitz for the characteristic infelicity of this formulation, but there is a certain amount of justice hidden in it; compared to the style of the fantasies, that of *Satan* shows much less effort to be "poetic," and is more closely reportorial, which probably is what Moskowitz meant. It is certainly an improvement upon that of Merritt's contemporary Sax Rohmer, upon whose Dr Fu-Manchu *Satan* was apparently modeled.

Merritt seldom showed that much restraint, however. "The Moon Pool" (1919) is almost unreadable now—stuffy, empty and dated; and its sequel, "Conquest of the Moon Pool," is no better. Their magic, whatever it may have been forty-five years ago, has vanished with time. The style of both is windy and cliché-ridden, as well as being ungrammatical with great frequency. The scientific rationale—again, regardless of how convincing it may have seemed in 1919, when terms like magnetism and radioactivity were apparently being allowed to mean anything an author found it convenient, like Humpty Dumpty, to say that they meant—has been turned by time into nonsense. The characters are stock: a fey Irish-American, a pedantic professor, a Scandinavian sailor who invokes Norse gods, the perennial Russian spy, and so on. (In successive rewrites, of which Merritt did many, his Russian villains often got changed into Germans, and then back into Russians again in a determined effort to keep the clichés current.)

The major trouble with *The Moon Pool*, however, lies elsewhere; other fantasies have survived faults as serious, in the sense that it is still possible to read them without one's eyes glazing over by page 68. The difference is that Merritt's novel is not about anything; it has no central idea to draw its events together. Unlike the similarly wooden fantasies of Haggard, or the similarly overwritten fantasies of C. A. Smith, *The Moon Pool* appears to be purely a private work, written out of Merritt's dream life and using images which may have pith and system for him—though even that concession is difficult to defend in the face of the deadness of the novel—but which the reader cannot share. Indeed, the only attempt Merritt made to give the reader access to them was to cram them into a completely predictable plot with cardboard inhabitants.

Why, then, has this crude performance been so highly touted for so many years? Nostalgia may provide one answer; and the book does contain a certain amount of misty sensuality, some derring-do, and a number of faraway places with strange-sounding names. It is also the perfect demonstration that these three standard ingredients of romantic fantasy cannot produce a good book all by themselves.

James Blish (as William Atheling, Jr.), "Exit Euphues: The Monstrosities of Merritt" (1957), *More Issues at Hand* (Chicago: Advent, 1970), pp. 80–82

P. SCHUYLER MILLER   Merritt grew up in and wrote for a generation that was enamored of words. It delighted in large and varied vocabularies; it liked the *sound* of words; and its poetry was of the Tennyson, Wordsworth, Scott variety that was built on these things. It was also a generation to which far parts were, almost by definition, romantic and colorful. The East was the *mystic* East, and just about everything in it had to be wonderful. In fact, just about anything unknown was wonderful.

The essence of all A. Merritt's writing is in his use of these qualities. He fills his scenes with the gaudiest of colors, the most flamboyant of oriental-seeming music; his people are strange and exotic; his places are in this world yet out of it, in the unexplored corners where anything may be. He piles allusion on allusion, drawing them out of strange sounding mythology—and the better-educated sector of his readers knew quite a lot about mythology in those days, and knew what he was talking about. (The authenticity of these allusions isn't essential, of course; Dunsany and Lovecraft made theirs up out of whole cloth).

Our generation, on the other hand, has seen the far parts of the world—usually under military auspices—and found them dull, dirty, uncomfortable, and full of foreigners. The romance of unknown places is pretty well gone, except in science fiction. We have also lost our taste for words. Like Rudolph Flesch, we want our words and our sentences short and simple. We want them to refer directly to us, or to things we know. We want the realism of today's successful novelists, and the bare-bone cacophony of modern poetry. In fact, *Saturday Review*'s John Ciardi covered the change pretty well when he said that *real* poetry is based on economy of words. The stuff we find in Merritt—and Tennyson—is not poetry but rhetoric, and we've no time for it in 1957.

If you accept this evaluation of what is good writing for today, Merritt is ruled out practically by definition. He used whole phrases and clauses where others, even in his own day, used single adjectives. He strung picture on picture, all painted with broad strokes of a dripping brush. I think ⟨Virgil⟩ Finlay could do a complete Merritt novel in a series of fantastic full-color tableaux and lose very little of the story: the successive scenes are almost like frames in a Technicolor, wide-screen spectacle.

This is why I like Merritt's short stories better than his novels. You get one terrific scene—the Face hovering in the abyss—the slug-people drifting in the pit—the Dweller racing down the moon-path—and that's it. By the same token the novels were better as eight part serials than as three-parters, and better in three chunks than taken at one sitting. How much plantation cake can you eat at one time?

As he went on Merritt put more and more human action and motivation into his books, and his "e" (communicative energy) -index goes up accordingly. *The Face in the Abyss* is crammed with fascinating people and creatures, but in *The Metal Monster* very little really happens to the harassed characters: they just stand and look at a series of set pieces in which the metal creatures go through their calisthenics. The concept of metallic life was terrific for the time, and the scenes themselves were crammed with sound and color, but Norhala is no Snake Mother—she's not even Anita Ekberg.

I hate to believe that we have lost the love of words and the ability to enjoy their lavish use in painting fantastic pictures. This is why I still like Burroughs' Mars—the lush "Green Kingdom" in Elizabeth Maddux's book—Conan and Northwest Smith and the Gray Mouser. And the best of Merritt.

P. Schuyler Miller, "The Reference Library," *Astounding Science Fiction* 60, No. 5 (January 1958): 142–43

SAM MOSKOWITZ   From the vantage point of the somewhat more sophisticated modern reader, "The Conquest of the Moon Pool" reveals glaring flaws. In contrast to "The Moon Pool" there are sequences that show obvious signs of haste. The movement of events follows the standard pattern of thrillers of an earlier period. The characters of the Moon Pool stories are stereotypes: Larry O'Keefe, the Irishman; Olaf, the Scandinavian; Von Hertzdorf, the treacherous German (who, in a later edition and in a different political climate, is converted to Marakinoff, the Russian devil); Lakla, the handmaiden (personification of good), and Yolara, dark priestess of evil.

Along with them are such stock chillers as frog men, dwarf men, and dead-alive men, and the love scenes make no concession to a world climbing out of Victorian prudery.

Yet the novel holds magic for its readers. It is an honest story. It evokes more than a hint of the strangest mysteries, and the imagination of the author never falters in his brilliant preoccupation with the unearthly, the terrifying, and the bizarre. It also promises rich, colorful, heroic action and it keeps that promise. The age-old struggle between good and evil, with the cleavage sharply differentiated, forms the basis of the plot. In this contest, the reader is thrilled by flights of imaginative fantasy equal to the best of H. Rider Haggard.

Greatest victory of all, Merritt transcended the coldness and dehumanization that frequently accompany pure fantasy. His word pictures shape a mood.

Humanity shines from this work. For every stock character there is a brilliantly original one of his own creating. The Shining One, a robot of pure force with fantastic powers, becomes believable as its intelligence acquires humanlike drives of personal pride and desire for achievement and power. The Silent Ones, ageless godlike men from an ancient civilization which created The Shining One—now aloof and inscrutable—call upon ancient science to thwart the ambitions of this strange thinking force and its dreadful omniscience. When they have destroyed their creation: "No flames now in their ebon eyes—for the flickering fires were quenched in great tears, streaming down the marble white faces."

Basic patterns for other Merritt novels were established in *The Moon Pool*. Later stories would always be built on the conflict of light against darkness. There would always be a beautiful priestess of evil, and the villains would be memorable, brilliantly characterized. Forms which are generally symbols of repulsion—the frog men in *The Moon Pool*, the spider men and some women in "The Snake Mother," Ricori, the gangster, in *Burn, Witch, Burn!*—are converted by literary sorcery into sympathetic and admirable characters.

Sam Moskowitz, "The Marvelous A. Merritt," *Explorers of the Infinite: Shapers of Science Fiction* (Cleveland: World Publishing Co, 1963), pp. 194–95

E. F. BLEILER   If one wanted to characterize Merritt in simple terms, one could call him the most romantic (in the late-nineteenth century sense of the word) major science fiction and fantasy writer of his day. This romantic quality was highly regarded, and Merritt was one of the authors most frequently imitated by young writers.

Today, we are more apt to find things in Merritt's writing, particularly his early writing, that should not be imitated, but admitting weaknesses should not preclude seeing strengths. He had a fine imagination, and each of his stories was innovative in significant ways. He had the knack of treating each motif as a fulfillment, exhausting its potential. Thus, one can take sentimental treatment of survival after death no further than "Three Lines of Old French."

Merritt could be an exciting writer, and he could digress from the pulp milieu in unusual ways. He was an excellent craftsman when he wanted to be, and his skills evolved as he grew older. If he was always concerned with love and dualism (good versus evil) he constantly varied their embodiments.

Yet despite these strengths, the ultimate feeling today is that Merritt was for the most part an unsatisfying writer. Perhaps the problem was lack of literary integrity, a too great cleaving to the attitudes and wish fulfillments of his fleeting audience, with the result that his stories are filled with now-dated material. If he was cleverer than most of his colleagues in doing this, he has paid a higher price in the end, for what appealed to the readers of the Munsey pulp magazines of the 1920's may strike readers of the 1980's as itself a fantasy world.

In many instances, Merritt carried out his emotional topicality to such an extent that when the Zeitgeist changed, the older position was difficult to accept or even ludicrous or repellent. Such is the case with "Three Lines of Old French," which today seems obscene, a deliberate attempt by a very intelligent writer to play upon feelings of bereavement arising out of World War I.

Perhaps there was an element of cynicism in Merritt's work that his contemporaries did not see. Could a professional newspaperman high in the Hearst empire be other than intellectually hardboiled? Or was there perhaps a situation like that of William Sharp and Fiona Macleod, where Sharp, a professional journalist, wrote florid, mushy stories about the Hebrides under the pseudonym of Fiona Macleod, and threatened to stop writing if the secret was revealed? Was Merritt equally wrapped up in his work? We do not know.

Is any of Merritt's work worth reading today, other than as historical documents? The mythic quality of *Dwellers in the Mirage*, with its formal structuring and inner drama, is still vital. A sense of peril emerges from *Burn, Witch, Burn!* and *Creep, Shadow!* is an excellent suspense story. There are also moments in the other major works. As for the rest of Merritt's fiction, it belongs back in the 1920's and 1930's, perhaps occasionally to be stroked for nostalgia, but maintainable only by taxidermy.

> E. F. Bleiler, "A. Merritt," *Supernatural Fiction Writers*, ed. E. F. Bleiler (New York: Charles Scribner's Sons, 1985), Vol. 2, p. 842

RONALD FOUST   *Dwellers in the Mirage* derives its unique force from its use of mythic archetypes as well as from its peculiarly personal quality. Here, the reader senses, is Merritt's fictional autobiography, the book that completes the psychological odyssey that all his earlier work prepared him to make. Once again, Merritt bases the action on the mythic archetype of the journey. The protagonist, Leif Langdon, travels not only spatially within the novel's various setting (the Gobi desert, Alaska and the land of the Mirage), but also backward through time as he atavistically regresses from his modern identity to that of a prehistoric ancestor, Dwayanu, ruthless warrior priest of the ancient Ayjirs. While these spatial and temporal journeys are highly entertaining devices which allow Merritt to create some of his most colorful descriptions of warfare and carnage, they are secondary to the motif of the inward journey; that is, to the theme of the bewildered individual's quest for identity and individuation. At the beginning of his quest the protagonist exists in a painful condition of multiplicity of which he is only partially aware. His conscious ego-identity (that of the decent rational man), created for him by his modern environment, is suddenly attacked at intervals with increasing force by an atavistic personality, a savage and seemingly alien self that has been buried in his subconscious all of his life. As this id-identity gains strength, it presses for release and finally attempts, with temporary success, to usurp control of his consciousness; the repressed "alien" self seeks, in effect, to possess the hero, to become his identity. Psychologically considered, the ancient concept of Fate can be understood as the success or failure of the individual's attempt to coordinate the competing claims of these two identities and finally to subordinate the anarchic demands of the unconscious to the more moderate and rational needs of consciousness. The novel's power derives in part from the way in which Merritt uses the Jungian archetype of the night-sea journey—the perilous quest to achieve some goal which takes the hero inward to a confusing psychological maze of conflicting demands—as a basis for an exploration of the universal theme of man's divided nature.

In *Dwellers in the Mirage*, this theme is symbolized by the multiple identities of the protagonist, whose first name is a pun establishing him as an archetypal Everyman. The fiction's ultimate purpose will be to confront Leif (the ego-identity) with Dwayanu (the id-identity) and to pit them in a contest for mastery of the Self. The stakes are high since Dwayanu represents nothing less than the universal force of anarchic un-reason. His temporary capture of Leif's personality mid-way in the text liberates long-dormant energies and initiates an atrocity that deeply scars the protagonist after he has ultimately mastered Dwayanu and returned to his modern identity. The archetypal modern for Leif's character, then, is that of the Gemini, the divided and eternally warring Twins, which Merritt has modernized by treating them as two aspects of the divided psyche of his protagonist.

But *Dwellers in the Mirage* is more than a mere manipulation of literary and mythic archetypes. It is Merritt's best science romance because it is his most personal; the unity of its effect, which saves it from the problem of the double-structure that plagued his earlier work, derives from the sustained emotional sincerity of its tone and from the loving but, for Merritt, relatively unsentimental treatment of its characters. It is not only his best science romance, however; it is also his last. The novel gives the impression of gathering together and exhausting the preoccupations of the earlier fictions and of freeing Merritt of a demon of his unconscious with which he was earlier unable to come to grips.

Ronald Foust, A. Merritt (Mercer Island, WA: Starmont House, 1989), pp. 55–56

◈ *Bibliography*

The Moon Pool. 1919.

The Ship of Ishtar. 1926.

Seven Footprints to Satan. 1928.

The Face in the Abyss. 1931.

Dwellers in the Mirage. 1932.

Through the Dragon Glass. 1932.

Burn, Witch, Burn! 1933.

Creep, Shadow! 1934.

Three Lines of Old French. 1939.

The Story behind the Story. 1942.

The Metal Monster. 1946.

The Fox Woman ⟨with *The Blue Pagoda* by Hannes Bok⟩. 1946.

The Black Wheel (with Hannes Bok). 1947.

The Fox Woman and Other Stories. Ed. Donald A. Wollheim. 1949.

The Challenge from Beyond (with C. L. Moore, H. P. Lovecraft, Robert E. Howard, and Frank Belknap Long). 1954.

❖ ❖ ❖

Mervyn Peake
1911–1968

MERVYN PEAKE was born on July 9, 1911, in Kuling, China, where his parents were missionaries. Peake spent most of his childhood in Tientsin, attending the Tientsin Grammar School and absorbing the traditions of both the British community there and the Chinese towns and countryside, which he explored in spite of his delicate health. His family retired from missionary service and returned to England in 1922, settling in a large Victorian house built in the Gothic style in Wallington, Surrey; Peake attended a school for the sons of missionaries, Eltham College in south London.

At an early age Peake demonstrated a talent for both drawing and writing, and in 1929 he left Eltham to study art at the Royal Academy Schools. He exhibited his work in several London galleries during the 1930s. In 1933, however, he failed his examinations and was refused readmittance to the Royal Academy. For the next two years he lived mainly on the island of Sark, in the Channel Islands, working at a private gallery there. In 1935 he returned to London to work on his painting and writing, teaching part-time at the Westminster School of Art; there he met a painter, Maeve Gilmore, whom he married in 1937 and with whom he had three children. Peake's first book, an illustrated children's story entitled *Captain Slaughterboard Drops Anchor*, was published in 1939.

When the war broke out, Peake attempted to gain an appointment as a war artist, but, although he remained in the army from 1940 to 1942, his art projects were repeatedly rejected. After spending six months in an army hospital recovering from a nervous breakdown, he was finally transferred to a unit of artists in 1943. He was sent to Birmingham to draw a picture of a cathode ray tube, and this experience with glassblowing would lead later to the writing of a collection of poems entitled *The Glassblowers* (1950). At the end of the war he traveled to Germany where he provided the army with drawings of the concentration camp at Belsen.

After the war Peake returned to the island of Sark and pursued his writing career. He had been working on the first of his three fantasy novels set in

Gormenghast, *Titus Groan,* since 1939, and it was published in 1946. It was followed by *Gormenghast* in 1950 and *Titus Alone* in 1959. A novelette, "Boy in Darkness" (first published in 1956), is also part of the Gormenghast cycle. Peake also wrote another children's book, *Letters from a Lost Uncle (From Polar Regions)* (1948), and a mainstream novel, *Mr. Pye* (1953). His several plays written in the 1950s were staged throughout England but were on the whole poorly received.

Peake continued to be a much sought-after book illustrator, and among the many volumes he illustrated are Lewis Carroll's *The Hunting of the Snark* (1941), Coleridge's *The Rime of the Ancient Mariner* (1943), the Brothers Grimm's *Household Tales* (1946), Stevenson's *Dr. Jekyll and Mr. Hyde* (1948), and Balzac's *Droll Stories* (1961).

Peake returned to London with his family in 1949, working at the Central School of Art in Holborn. In 1951 he moved to a house in Kent, but the next year he returned to his family home in Wallington upon the death of his father. During the mid-1950s his health began to deteriorate. The third volume of the Gormenghast cycle was much hampered by his illness, and notes survive for a projected fourth volume. Eventually Peake was diagnosed as having Parkinson's disease and, after spending several years in hospitals, he died on November 17, 1968. Around the time of his death a renewed interest in fantasy fiction led to the republication of his Gormenghast trilogy. His wife assembled *Peake's Progress* (1978), a large volume of his uncollected writings and drawings, as well as several separate editions of his illustrations.

▨ *Critical Extracts*

HENRY REED   In the face of *Titus Groan* I feel like a soldier who has sworn so much that he has no words left with which to describe the act of shame. I mean that I should like to describe the book as *fascinating,* but the semantic of the word has become so disgustingly eroded that it is inconceivable that it any longer conveys any meaning. I am therefore forced to say that Mr. Peake's first novel holds one with its glittering eye. It begins by saying: Part One: Gormenghast. No part two is discoverable throughout the entire length of the book (well over four hundred modern pages) and the hero is much younger even than Tristram Shandy by the time the book ends; he has in fact not spoken up to that point. The reader is left to anticipate further volumes. I hope they will come; I do not think I have ever so much enjoyed a novel sent to me for review.

The book, which is about the ancient family of Groan, who live in a vast castle in an unidentifiable landscape and at an unnamed time, is as nearly pure story-telling as any book I have read since childhood. I admit that every now and then I was uneasily conscious that by the contrast of the megalomaniac aristocrats and the hut-dwellers at their gates, a contemporary contrast might be adumbrated; and the internal struggle for power inside the castle itself might also "imply" something. But I shut these thoughts out as often as I could, and chide myself for being a victim of the intellectual inhibitions of my time. In any case even a Marxist might find so riotous an embellishment of his favourite themes a little frivolous. ⟨. . .⟩

Titus Groan, though long and Gothically detailed, is not wayward; it has a genuine plot in the strictest sense, and it persuades you to read on simply in order to know what will happen; in spite of its setting, there is nothing particularly dream-like about it. Its gallery of characters is wonderful. The old nurse, Nannie Slagg, appears oftener than can be easily put up with, and the mysterious Keda, with her two lovers who kill each other, is not a success: she recalls, rather strongly, Meriam, the hired girl in *Cold Comfort Farm*; though her part in the action will doubtless later be revealed as indispensable. Otherwise the characters are a joy: Swelter, Flay, the Prunes-quallors, Steerpike, Barquentine, the Countess, and not least the thwarted and deluded twins, Cora and Clarice. ("I like roofs," said Clarice; "they are something I like more than most things because they are on top of the houses they cover, and Cora and I like being over the tops of things because we love power, and that's why we are both fond of roofs.") The book is also remarkable for its gigantic set-pieces of action. Steerpike's daylong climb over the great roofscape of Gormenghast, and the final conflict of Flay and Swelter in the Hall of Spiders, are magnificently thrilling.

Henry Reed, "New Novels," *New Statesman and Nation*, 4 May 1946, p. 323

ROBERTSON DAVIES   No brief description of Mervyn Peake's books can give a satisfactory idea of their quality. The plot is simple: Gormenghast is a huge and remote earldom ruled by the family of Groan; the Groans are ruled by complex, inherited ritual, and the days of the Earl and his family are lived in strict accordance with the orders of a master of ceremonies; change is unthinkable. To the scholarly seventy-sixth Earl, Sepulchrave, and his bird-loving Countess, is born a son, Titus. In time the child inherits his father's title and rebels against the circumstances of his life. At last he leaves Gormenghast behind him and goes out into the world, which he finds fully as arbitrary, as dominated by irrationality, as packed with eccentrics, as the family domain. In the end young Titus re-visits his home, only to leave it again, knowing that he will never be free of it in his heart.

Such a skeleton of the plot gives no idea of the richness of the books. Gormenghast is peopled with fantastic creations; the castle is a city in itself, riddled with passages that everyone has forgotten, people who are rarely seen, containing even a complete boys' school, with a large staff, as one of its lesser appurtenances. The Earl is its titular head, but the real rulers are Hay, the valet, Swelter, the chef, and Sourdust, the master of ceremonies— succeeded in time by his son Barquentine, a malignant dwarf. The loneliest and most neglected creature is the Lady Fuchsia, the Earl's older child and one of the most interesting heroines in modern fiction. The atmosphere of Gormenghast is that of Fuseli's drawings come to life.

As sometimes happens in novels full of highly coloured characters, the central figure is the one least successfully brought to life. Titus Groan is a minor creation in this army of oddities. Mervyn Peake's best character, in my opinion, is Steerpike, who begins as a kitchen-boy at Gormenghast, and by a hair-raising career of intelligence, craft and ruthlessness, rises at last to be master of ceremonies and real ruler of the castle. Steerpike is a magnificent adventurer, and in the third volume *Titus Alone* we feel the want of him very badly.

This is a long novel, and Mervyn Peake is not able to keep his invention at the highest pitch all through it. He is a painter as well as a writer, and his extended passages of description are masterly—but now and then they are a drag on the action. You must take this long book as you find it; here is no neatly carpentered, simple tale, but a great, walloping gallimaufry of imagination, thrilling adventure (the fight between Flay and Swelter, in which Earl Sepulchrave perishes, is the best fight I know of in modern fiction), poetry, humour and sheer inventive exuberance. It asks for an unusual response in its readers, but it rewards them with riches so strange and wonderful that they are worth twenty times the effort.

Robertson Davies, "The Gormenghast Trilogy" (1960), *The Enthusiasms of Robertson Davies,* ed. Judith Skelton Grant (New York: Viking, 1990), pp. 201–2

JOHN BATCHELOR   Despite the sad state of its latter part, *Titus Alone* is an important addition to the two earlier Titus books, and apart from the masterly handling of Titus's own moral growth its most interesting and original feature is the creation and presentation of Muzzlehatch. This friend is an anarchist, a pirate by inclination with the flavour of the sea surrounding much that he does, a self-contained mature man whose solid friendship with the boy and whose mature love for Juno do not conflict with a comfortable self-knowledge. As he drives home Muzzlehatch reflects, unblushingly, on his own imperfections:

> His unfaithfulness; his egotism; his eternal play-acting; his
> gigantic pride; his lack of tenderness; his deafening exuberance;
> his selfishness. (Chapter 33, 2nd edition)

His self-centredness is healthy and unashamed, like that of the spivs and soldiers who fascinated Peake in his 'Head-Hunting' poems of the 1930s and the war, and one can see Muzzlehatch as the successor to these aliens, the last and richest portrait in a series which includes Long John Silver, Captain Slaughterboard, the sailor in *The Rhyme of the Flying Bomb*, 'Caliban' (in a poem in *The Glassblowers*), those vigorous male extroverts who inhabit their skins with confidence and are at peace with themselves.

John Batchelor, *Mervyn Peake: A Biographical and Critical Exploration* (London: Duckworth, 1974), p. 122

RONALD BINNS   'There comes a time when the brain, flashing through constellations of conjecture, is in danger of losing itself in worlds from which there is no return', Peake commented in *Boy in Darkness*. Before the progress of mental illness necessitated permanent hospitalisation Peake did manage largely to complete *Titus Alone*. The chapters are much shorter, and the world that Titus, now twenty, discovers outside Gormenghast, is radically different to anything previously experienced in his homeland. Gormenghast conjured up an ancient, feudal world, and evil contained itself in the single figure of Steerpike. By contrast, in the unidentified world of *Titus Alone* we get a vision of the future, more science fiction than Gothic romance, more urban and contemporary than the temporally and geographically remote society of Gormenghast. Titus enters a world of cars, slums, police, prostitution, prisons, courts and asylums, at the heart of which lies the sinister factory, a place of death and evil, surrounded by the stench of burning bodies. This last feature, together with the dying girl, Black Rose, reveals that Belsen still preyed on Peake's mind, though it's worth noting the ambivalence of Titus's response to the suffering girl: ' "I can't sustain her. I can't comfort her. I can't love her. Her suffering is far too clear to see. There is no veil across it: no mystery: no romance. Nothing but a factual pain, like the pain of a nagging tooth." ' This seems to be Peake speaking as much as Titus, expressing his anguish at a world which had cruelly violated the fancies of his tranquil earlier life. A realistic portrayal of Belsen was outside the scope of his imagination; instead he placed his memories of the camp inside the larger, despairing vision of a futuristic, highly technological totalitarian society.

The characterisation in *Titus Alone* is impoverished in comparison with the earlier two volumes of the trilogy. Muzzlehatch reincarnates Flay, and the beautiful, demonic Cheeta is reminiscent, more than just in name, of the cunning beast-humans of *Boy in Darkness*. It seems significant that the other main character, Juno, the first woman whom Titus has a sexual relationship with, should turn out to be a kind of mother-substitute, twice his age and at the other extreme from the wispy 'Thing'. The final scene in the novel serves as a reminder of the theme of repressed or displaced sexuality which runs through the trilogy. At the end a vast, foul explosion (perhaps Peake had the atom bomb in mind) obliterates the factory. Titus survives and flees, returning one day, by accident, to the very edge of his domain, arriving back at the cave where his attempted rape of the 'Thing' expelled him for ever from the world of imagination and romance. At the close of the trilogy the outcast Titus, unlike David Copperfield, has still not met a woman who is his equal. He seems doomed to perpetual solitude; as ⟨Leslie⟩ Fiedler puts it, for this kind of romance protagonist 'it is hard to imagine a real acceptance of adult life and sexuality, hard to conceive of anything but continuing flight or self-destruction'. From Peake's sketchy jottings for a fourth volume it seems, indeed, that he merely envisaged further picaresque adventure, further flight. But if Titus is still in some ways a child at the end of *Titus Alone* he is nevertheless a particularly twentieth-century figure: unhoused, a refugee whose responses are 'no longer clear and simple', a youth whose burden of knowledge is one of 'tragedy, violence and the sense of his own perfidy'.

Ronald Binns, "Situating Gormenghast," *Critical Quarterly* 21, No. 1 (Spring 1979): 30–32

JOSEPH L. SANDERS   In "Boy in Darkness," Titus is just fourteen
years old, still imprisoned within the castle's ritual. He already knows that
he hates "the eternal round of deadly symbolism," and on the night of his
fourteenth birthday he instinctively seizes the chance to escape. His flight
takes him into a nightmarish country outside the castle. There, captured
by two grossly ugly, semi-human creatures, the Goat and the Hyena, Titus
is carried toward their master, the Lamb—in the person of whom Peake
simultaneously attacks religion and science.

The religious implications of the Lamb are first apparent. The Lamb lives
alone, blind, in an underground apartment lit by candles and carpeted in
blood-red (cf. Revelation 7:14, 12:11). His face is "angelically white" (cf.
1 Peter 1:19), and his hands move "in a strangely parsonic way." The Lamb
is, of course, a traditional religious symbol of innocence and purity; Christ
is described as "the Lamb of God" (John 1:29). In Peake's story, too, the
Goat mumbles to himself that the Lamb " 'is the heart of life and love, and
that is true because he *tells* us so.' " So the Goat and the Hyena treat the
Lamb with religious awe, as they pray to him: " 'O thou by whom we live
and breathe and are!' " (cf. Revelation 5:13). Their awe is justified; though
he did not create them in the first place, the Lamb *has* made them what
they are. Specifically, the Lamb has changed the natures of all living things,
shaping them to resemble the beasts they are most like spiritually. With
the change they have died except for the Goat and the Hyena who have
survived because of "their coarseness of soul and fibre." Most recent to die
was the Lion, who "only an age ago, had collapsed in a mockery of power. . . .
It was a great and terrible fall: yet it was merciful, for, under the macabre
aegis of the dazzling Lamb, the one time king of beasts was brought to
degradation." Thus the Lamb has ironically fulfilled an image from popular
religion, by making the lion lie down with the lamb. Now, as he surveys
Titus, Lamb's hands flutter "like little white doves," another symbol of
spiritual virtue. While the boy sleeps, the Lamb waits, lusting to change
his nature too, but with "his hands together, as though in prayer."

The host of specifically religious suggestions and images, in a story that
until now has been devoid of such concern, suggests very strongly that Peake
is here referring to the Christian religion as a debasing influence. Peake's
treatment of Gormenghast's ritual shows that he dislikes any system of
values imposed on the individual from outside, offering him nothing directly
relevant for himself and encouraging him in whatever weakness he possesses.
So, here, the Lamb can break down but not build; despite his worshippers'

praise, he does not really understand how to keep his creatures alive. Still the Lamb glories in his power. True, in changing men he has destroyed them, denying them freedom to develop for themselves; to the Lamb, however, that is incidental to his own gratification.

In addition to religion, however, Peake attacks modern technnology. However different faith in religion and faith in science appear, they can function in the same way for their believers. When religion is employed systematically to manipulate and nullify human beings, it functions as a science for the priests who operate it; by the same token, when science gives man the satisfaction of godlike control over human beings, it serves a religious purpose for him. The country beneath which the Lamb lives is littered with the waste and debris of science and industry. Underground, also, is a dead wilderness of metal: "there had been a time when these deserted solitudes were alive with hope, excitement and conjecture on how the world was to be changed. But that was far beyond the skyline. All that was left was a kind of shipwreck. A shipwreck of metal . . . vistas of forgotten metal; moribund, stiff in a thousand attitudes of mortality; with not a rat, not a mouse; not a bat, not a spider. Only the Lamb." The Lamb belongs in this setting. He, too, like those who worked in metal and stone thrives on change, though like that of the others it is a sterile, ego-directed change only. He hungers excitedly for more living things to alter according to his desires.

Joseph L. Sanders, " 'The Passions in the Clay': Mervyn Peake's Titus Stories," *Voices for the Future*, ed. Thomas D. Clareson and Thomas L. Wymer (Bowling Green, OH: Bowling Green University Popular Press, 1984), Vol. 3, pp. 97–98

GORDON SMITH   ⟨Peake's⟩ book illustrations fell into several groups. There are his own original creations, like *Captain Slaughterboard Drops Anchor* or *Letters from a Lost Uncle*; there are books like *Treasure Island, Alice in Wonderland* and *The Hunting of the Snark*, which were all long familiar and particularly 'sib' to his imagination; and there are collections almost as much to hand, like *Ride a Cock-Horse* and *Grimm's Household Tales*. All these are superbly successful. But he was also superb treating less familiar subjects, like *Witchcraft in England* by Christina Hole. When Mervyn illustrated a book, he first soaked himself in the text, until he felt almost a part of it. This was particularly true of Dickens and the drawings he did for *Bleak House*. Each book he read was an education, and Dickens was revelation. The sheer sweep of his creativeness, the vividness of his description, the liveliness of his conversations, the fantastic quality of his imagination and his human oddities: all these struck sympathetic chords in Mervyn's own mind, and had, as he himself insisted, a considerable influence upon what he was already engaged in writing, the 'Gormenghast' trilogy.

> Gordon Smith, *Mervyn Peake: A Personal Memoir* (London: Victor Gollancz, 1984), p. 100

ANTHONY BURGESS   Peake has been praised, but he has also been mistrusted. His prose works are not easily classifiable; they are unique as, say, the books of Peacock or Lovecraft are unique. Moreover, he has too many talents: he is a fine poet and a highly original draughtsman. The Peake style in book illustration is inimitable, and it has been greatly imitated. He has, in his total mastery of the literary as well as the pictorial art, only one peer—Wyndham Lewis. Their aims in both arts could not be more dissimilar, but Peake and Lewis come together in an approach to descriptive writing which owes a great deal to the draughtsman's trade. If their books seem slow-moving, that is because of the immense solidity of their visual contents, the lack of interest in time and the compensatory obsession with filling up space. *Titus Groan* is aggressively three-dimensional. Look at the opening description of Gormenghast, where the term 'a certain ponderous architectural quality' exactly conveys what we are in for. But around the solidity is an extra dimension, one of magic, showing the poet as well as the draughtsman: 'This tower, patched unevenly with black ivy, arose like a mutilated finger from among the fists of knuckled masonry and pointed blasphemously at heaven.'

This sounds like 'Gothic' writing, but the term is inadequate. As we read *Titus Groan*, we seem to be given clues directing us towards the daylight of a literary category, but all the keys change into red herrings. Take the names of the characters, for instance—Nettel ('the octogenarian who lived in the tower above the rusting armoury'); Rottcodd, curator of the Hall of the Bright Carvings; Flay, Swelter, Steerpike, Mrs Slagg, Prunesquallor. These are fitting for a Peacock novel, for Dickens or for a comic children's story. They are farcical, but the mood is not one of easy laughter or even of airy fantasy: the ponderous architectural quality holds everything down, and we have to take the characters very seriously, despite their names. Nor is it appropriate to think in terms of a gallery of glorious eccentrics (a very British concept). Nobody flies away from a centre of normality; everybody belongs to a system built on very rigid rules.

> Anthony Burgess, "Introduction," *The Gormenghast Trilogy* by Mervyn Peake (Woodstock, NY: Overlook Press, 1988), pp. 2–3

TANYA J. GARDINER-SCOTT   *Gormenghast* was written between 1948 and 1949 on the island of Sark, and won the Royal Society of Literature award for 1951, along with Peake's book of poetry, *The Glassblowers*. It is a more easily accessible novel in terms of plot and organization than *Titus Groan*, as Peake has already familiarized the reader with his descriptions of setting, most of his characters, the seeds of action and the Castle itself. Only Titus seems to age as a character, from seven to seventeen, in the course of the novel; the other characters develop according to the directions suggested in *Titus Groan*, causing an impression of stasis and change at a different level from that in the first Titus book. The only major new characterization is that of the Professors.

Having set his scenes and introduced most of his characters in *Titus Groan*, to some extent a preface for the action of *Gormenghast*, Peake can focus on specific themes—of loyalty, evil, menace and, most importantly, freedom. He does this through a combination of set descriptive pieces and action, with the proportion of action considerably higher than in *Titus Groan*. As in that novel, the Castle is a location both physical and psychic, a reflector and enhancer of the moods of its inhabitants, a character in its own right gathering to resist the forces of change (as embodied in Steerpike and culminating in his death and the restoration of order)—thus, as ⟨John⟩ Batchelor points out, the title of the novel. Peake focusses on specific blocks of time—Titus' day of escape, his night with Flay and return the following morning to the Castle; the morning to evening cycle of the Poet's ceremony; the day of Irma's party; the day Steerpike visits the Aunts and kills Barquentine; the evening of his flight with Fuchsia and the following morning's tracking of him to the Aunts' bodies; the Ceremony of the Carvings, Titus' escape and return to the Castle; the sequence when Fuchsia dies and Steerpike is finally killed—and he has chapters (45 and 51–52, for example) where he telescopes the passing years and Steerpike's schemes. But the action is essentially sequential, although within the sequences plots are juxtaposed, time becomes subjective according to the state of mind of the character (for example, the schoolroom scene in chapter 14), and Titus and Fuchsia both have flashbacks to earlier days.

The novel opens with a fine prose poem that sets up the distinction between the private and public roles of Titus, childhood and Earldom. The Biblical rhythms of the prose, the sentence fragments, the reversals of sentence order and the compelling images of labyrinth, shadow and architecture make it a dramatic opening, suitable to Titus' centrality and his own sense of the dramatic as played out with Steerpike in the novel. The atmosphere is of mystery and agelessness and the intermingling of time and space—"there are days when the living have no substance and the dead are active." This blurring of fantasy and reality sets the tone of the novel, some of the action of which is carried on inside the characters' heads, haunted heads, as suggested in this fusing of the past and present that opens it—"an arabesque in motion whose thoughts were action, or if not, hung like bats from an attic rafter or veered between towers on leaflike wings." Peake surveys the dead/exiled and the living in a summation that brings the reader up to date with all that has happened in *Titus Groan* and conveys a sense of the intervening five-and-a-half years before the opening of this next novel. Batchelor calls the effect "rough but strong, like the opening of a folk-tale"; indeed, folktale and allegory are two of the genres Peake fragmentarily exploits in his telling of the tale.

Tanya J. Gardiner-Scott, *Mervyn Peake: The Evolution of a Dark Romantic* (New York: Peter Lang, 1989), pp. 99–100

PHILIP REDPATH   In many ways *Titus Groan* is reminiscent of Sterne's *Tristram Shandy*. In both works there is a slow, leisurely progress, an almost total absence of the titular hero, and an ending that is open, promising more. In *Tristram Shandy* the narrator is menaced by death. He attempts to escape it by fleeing to the Continent. But in fact all of the running is done through the writing of the novel. To write takes longer than to live, and if Tristram can continue writing about his life before death became a threat, he can continue to exist in the written space of the novel. By the end of the book Tristram (the subject) and Tristram (the narrator/writer) have not chronologically coincided. At least one of them, therefore, will survive. By the time he came to write *Titus Alone*, illness was seriously threatening Peake physically and mentally. He had moved Titus out of the imaginative space of Gormenghast into a world more recognizably that of the real, modern world of himself and his readers. But this was the world in which Peake was dying. *Titus Alone* therefore chronicles a desperate attempt to return to the imaginative realm of Gormenghast in which the mind divorced from the sick body could exist. The problem was that, in many respects, Gormenghast was a mental *and* physical reaction. The mind could not be divorced in Cartesian terms so completely from the body. Peake admitted that *Titus Groan* was something he had to purge from his body "rather like having to be sick." When he tried to reconstruct Gormenghast he found himself prevented by his sick body and the toll his illness took on his concentration. *Titus Alone* can thus be read as a commentary on the imaginative feat of *Titus Groan* and *Gormenghast* and on the impossibility of returning to the world created in them. The tragic irony is that Gormenghast is a world created of words, it is self-sufficient and can continue to exist without its architect. If it is a solipsist's dream come true, it also turned into Peake's nightmare.

Although there are three Titus books, the work is not properly a trilogy. *Titus Alone* is unfinished in that it is composed of fragments which its author would have worked out and expanded into a more acceptable form than that which we now have. The fragments that comprise the one hundred and twenty-two short chapters are indicative of Peake's failing powers of concentration, but it was concentration that was required if the castle was to be rebuilt. Because of illness Peake had to stop writing, and death took him forever out of Gormenghast. Titus's escape from the castle is a form of self-imposed banishment from the area Peake felt so threatening to his sanity. But as Mr Flay, a reluctant exile from Gormenghast, implies in the second book, illness and banishment in this context are closely related: " 'Ill, Lordship? No, boy, no . . . but banished.' " Peake's own self-banishment from his kingdom was also accompanied by illness. ⟨. . .⟩

Gormenghast is not a reaction against reality: it constitutes an imaginative reality—the reality of language. The black marks on the white page may be no more than a network of signifiers which are open and available to all readers, but writing also guarantees a certain concreteness, a state of permanence. What Peake's books will always signify is Gormenghast and its existence as a signified in the minds of the readers. Titus, therefore, does not need to return to Gormenghast; without even seeing it at the end of

Titus Alone he can turn away assured of its existence, its autonomy, and its permanence:

> His heart beat out more rapidly, for something was growing . . .
> some kind of knowledge. A thrill of the brain. A synthesis. For
> Titus was recognising in a flash of retrospect that a new phase of
> which he was only half aware, had been reached. It was a sense of
> maturity, almost of fulfilment. He had no longer any need for
> home, for he carried his Gormenghast within him.

Peake could also turn from Gormenghast, certain that if he could no longer inhabit it it was because of a failure of the physical body and not of the imagination.

Philip Redpath, "Mervyn Peake's Black House: An Allegory of Mind and Body," *Ariel* 20, No. 1 (January 1989): 68–69, 73

Bibliography

Captain Slaughterboard Drops Anchor. 1939.

Shapes and Sounds. 1940.

Rhymes without Reason. 1944.

Titus Groan. 1946.

The Craft of the Lead Pencil. 1946.

Letters from a Lost Uncle (From Polar Regions). 1948.

Drawings. 1949.

Gormenghast. 1950.

The Glassblowers. 1950.

Mr. Pye. 1953.

Figures of Speech. 1954.

Titus Alone. 1959.

The Rhyme of the Flying Bomb. 1962.

Poems and Drawings. 1965.

A Reverie of Bone and Other Poems. 1967.

A Book of Nonsense. 1972.

Selected Poems. 1972.

Drawings. 1974.

Writings and Drawings. Ed. Maeve Gilmore and Shelagh Johnson. 1974.

Twelve Poems 1939–1960. 1975.
Boy in Darkness. 1976.
Peake's Progress: Selected Writings and Drawings. Ed. Maeve Gilmore. 1978.
Sketches from Bleak House. Ed. Leon Garfield and Edward Blishen. 1983.

M. P. Shiel
1865–1947

MATTHEW PHIPPS SHIEL was born on July 21, 1865, on the island of Montserrat in the West Indies. He was the son of an Irish preacher, Matthew David Shiel, and Priscilla Ann Shiel, who had previously had eight daughters. At the age of fifteen Shiel was crowned king of the small island of Redonda, and successors to this title retain control of it. His novel *Contraband of War* (1899) is partially set on Redonda. Shiel attended Harrison College, Barbados, from 1881 to 1883. In 1885 he sailed to England and enrolled at King's College, London, but apparently left without a degree. He also studied medicine for a few months at St. Bartholomew's Hospital.

Shiel had begun writing as a boy; at the age of twelve he had written a full-length novel. Around 1890 he began a career in journalism. His first book, *Prince Zaleski* (1895), contained three long stories about an eccentric detective. Shiel also wrote several adventure novels with Louis Tracy under the pseudonym Gordon Holmes. *Shapes in the Fire* (1896) was a well-received story collection that contained "Vaila," a tale Shiel later rewrote into "The House of Sounds" (in *The Pale Ape and Other Pulses*, 1911), which H. P. Lovecraft considered one of the best horror stories ever written. He married Carolina Garcia Gomez in 1898, but she died a few years later after giving birth to a daughter.

By the turn of the century Shiel had become a prolific novelist. Among his works are several novels—*The Yellow Danger* (1898), *The Yellow Wave* (1905), and *The Dragon* (1913; later titled *The Yellow Peril*)—about the possibility of an invasion of Europe by Asians. Aside from several historical novels (*Cold Steel*, 1899; *The Man-Stealers*, 1900), murder mysteries (*The Weird o' It*, 1902; *The Evil That Men Do*, 1904), and romantic adventure novels (*Unto the Third Generation*, 1903; *The Lost Viol*, 1905), Shiel's best-known works are two fantasies: *The Purple Cloud* (1901), an apocalyptic novel about the destruction of the human race, and *The Lord of the Sea* (1901), about a man who gains control of all the oceans of the world.

From 1913 to 1923 Shiel published little; he appears to have been working unsuccessfully on plays, which were neither published nor produced. During this period he was living alternately in London and Paris. He married Lydia Fawley around 1918; they separated in 1929. By the 1920s Shiel's productivity increased again: he published several mystery novels (*How the Old Woman Got Home*, 1927; *Dr. Krasinski's Secret*, 1929; *The Black Box*, 1930), a collection of tales (*Here Comes the Lady*, 1928), and revised several of his earlier novels for a new edition published by Victor Gollancz. *The Young Men Are Coming!* (1937) is a science fiction novel. Although Shiel scorned organized religion, he was fascinated by the figure of Jesus, and several of his novels (*The Last Miracle*, 1906; *This Above All*, 1933) are on religious themes. Late in life he was working on a long treatise entitled *Jesus*.

Shiel spent his last years at a home called L'Abri in Horsham, Sussex. A young man named John Gawsworth became fascinated with his work and assisted in Shiel's later writing, collaborating on a volume of stories, *The Invisible Voices* (1935), and later editing a posthumous collection of Shiel's *Best Short Stories* (1948) and a volume of essays, *Science, Life, and Literature* (1950). Shiel died on February 17, 1947. Much of his voluminous work is now forgotten, but *The Purple Cloud* and some short stories retain a following for their bizarrerie of conception and exoticism of style.

◈ *Critical Extracts*

ARTHUR RANSOME   I knocked, and went into the most dishevelled room it is possible to imagine. There was a big bed in it, unmade, the bed-clothes tumbled anyhow, several broken chairs, and a washing-stand with a basin out of which someone had taken a bite. The novelist, in a dressing-gown open at the neck, and showing plainly that there was nothing but skin beneath it, was writing at a desk, throwing off his sheets as fast as he covered them. A very pretty little Irish girl, of about nineteen or twenty, picked them up as they fell, and sorted them, at the same time doing her best to quiet the baby who sprawled all over her, as she sat on the floor. They stood up when I came in, and the novelist tried to apologise for the disorder, but the baby howled so loudly that it was impossible to hear him.

"Take it out!" he shouted to the girl, and she obediently picked it up and carried it out of the room. ⟨. . .⟩

I saw him more than once there later, and always the room was in the same condition, the child howling, the wife pretty, untidy as ever, the great man unwashed but working. How he could work! Sheet after sheet used to drop from his desk. Sometimes when I called upon him he would be in the middle of a chapter, and then he would ask me to sit down and smoke, while his pen whirled imperturbably to the end. He could write in any noise, and he could throw off his work completely as soon as the pen was out of his hand. He was quite contented in the lodging-house, living with wife and child in a single room. He seemed more amused than annoyed by its inconveniences. "After all," he would say, "I have to pretend to superb intellect, and the pretence would be exposed at once if I let such things worry me."

Arthur Ransome, "A Novelist," *Bohemia in London* (New York: Dodd, Mead, 1907), pp. 256–57, 260

H. P. LOVECRAFT   Speaking of ⟨W. Paul⟩ Cook, he hath just lent me two books, one of which is Bram Stoker's last production, *The Lair of the White Worm*. ⟨. . .⟩ The other volume Cook lent is a very different— oh, how different!—proposition, since it contains what both Cook and I solemnly declare to be a peerless masterpiece—the finest horror-story of the generation, and by a living and almost wholly unknown author. The book is a collection of weird tales by M. P. Shiel, and is called—after the opening story—*The Pale Ape*. Some of the things are mediocre, though all are smooth. One is diabolically clever, though hardly weird. Three or four are superfine—"Huguenin's Wife", "The Bride", "The Great King", and "The House of Sounds". Yes—this last is the masterpiece! How can I describe its poison-grey "insidious madness"? If I say that it is very like "The Fall of the House of Usher", or that one feature mirrors my own "Alchemist", (1908) I shall not even have suggested the utterly unique delirium of arctic wastes, titan seas, insane brazen towers, centuried malignity, frenzied waves and cataracts, and above all hideous, insistent, brain-petrifying, Pan-accursed cosmic SOUND . . . God! but after that story I shall never try to write another of my own. Shiel has done so much better than my best, that I am left breathless and inarticulate. And yet the man is virtually unknown in America—and almost so in his native Britain.

H. P. Lovecraft, Letter to Frank Belknap Long (7 October 1923), *Selected Letters: 1911–1924*, ed. August Derleth and Donald Wandrei (Sauk City, WI: Arkham House, 1965), p. 255

CARL VAN VECHTEN   My first impressions of Shiel were rather mixed. I think, indeed, that this might be anybody's experience, unless he happens to be lucky enough to hit first upon one of the better novels, *The Lord of the Sea*, for example, for the work of this imaginative adept is curiously uneven—not a little of it bearing the mark of undue haste in execution—and its intelligent perusal and appraisement is further complicated by the fact that this author from year to year has varied his "tone," style and form yielding to the mood of the new matter presented. Unfortunately, I did not start out with the best books. I began with *Prince Zaleski*, published in that same Keynote Series which originally harboured *The Great God Pan* and *The Three Impostors* ⟨by Arthur Machen⟩, and I could honestly say that I liked it, but the next two volumes that I read—I shall not mention their names here—almost caused me to forsake the quest. However, book-sellers whom I had put on the scent continued to dispatch new packages which I automatically opened. I do not recall the exact number of books by Shiel I had examined with mounting enthusiasm before I stumbled upon *The Purple Cloud*, but I do remember that when, at one sitting, I had finished reading this extremely long novel at four a.m., I cried aloud with the morning stars.

Nevertheless, if they are lucky enough to begin with one of the better of Shiel's romances, most readers, I fancy, will find it necessary to acquaint themselves with several others before they can appreciate with any exactitude the magic of this writer or can capitulate to his special charm. Any novice in the matter, to be sure, should be perfectly aware at once of the vitality and glamour, the presence of the grand manner, in *The Lord of the Sea*, but whether he will see further than this, at first, I am not so sure, for Shiel, apparently, to an early reader, is a mere maker of plots, a manufacturer of wild romances in the manner of Jules Verne or of the Dumas of *Monte-Cristo*. It is only a little later that one perceives that here there is a philosophic consciousness, a sophisticated naïveté, an imaginative au delà, of which the plot is only the formal expression. Shiel, I feel convinced, will satisfy any admirer of *The Count of Monte-Cristo*, but, in the end, he will also satisfy any reader who cares for George Meredith or Herman Melville, two writers, as unlike as the Poles in themselves, with whom the author of *The Lord of the Sea* has a certain esoteric affinity, and gradually it will further become evident that Shiel may be compared more reasonably with the H. G. Wells of the early romances, and even with W. H. Mallock, than with the creator of *Twenty Thousand Leagues Under the Sea*.

Carl Van Vechten, "Matthew Phipps Shiel" (1924), *Excavations: A Book of Advocacies* (New York: Alfred A. Knopf, 1926), pp. 150–52

THOMAS EARLE WELBY   The two main merits of such of his tales as I read twenty odd years ago were the largeness of the central idea and the flaming romanticism of the style. Both merits are very rare in work of the kind. Writers of mystery or adventure stories, or, more broadly, of serial melodrama, usually pride themselves on their ingenuity; and if they have ingenuity, the stories may 'intrigue,' as the cant phrase goes, or excite us; but the trick of the thing, once explained, is explained away; whereas Shiel's central idea remains in the mind long after the reader knows what the issue is. Fantastic, gruesome, what you will, it really is an idea. And like most genuine ideas, it is of a massive simplicity.

Then there is the flushed romantical style, breaking out into an extravagant efflorescence. Romanticism run mad, it might be said. But frequently there is, amidst the hot colouring and the frenetic vigour, a surprising propriety of simile and metaphor. Take this, from a melodramatic passage:

> With anguished gradualness, as a glacier stirs, tender as a nerve
> of each leaf that touched me, I moved, I stole, toward her through
> the belt of bush, the knife behind my back—stealthy though
> slow—till there came a restraint, a check—I felt myself held
> back—had to stop—one of the sheaves of my beard having
> caught in a limb of prickly-pear.

The amount of things said in those few lines is matter for wonder.

'As a glacier stirs, tender as a nerve of each leaf that touched me': those are words that would have been applauded in Stevenson, because his way of writing invited readers to be on the alert for felicities. But here, in Shiel, the similes are not merely new and remarkable; they are very much to the purpose, and convey the icy cruelty and nervous agitation of the dual man. And the grotesque check to his murderous progress is an invention reconciling us to the purpose of his evil self by its reminder of the savagery into which he has fallen as supposedly, for all purposes till this encounter actually, the one survivor of a poisoned earth.

> Thomas Earle Welby (as "Stet"), "M. P. Shiel," *Back Numbers* (London: Constable, 1929), pp. 100–101

MARY ROSS   With the gusto his readers have learned to anticipate eagerly, M. P. Shiel ⟨in *The Purple Cloud*⟩ paints one of the most captivating romantic dreams of mankind—a cosmos stricken in which a sole survivor starts again to work out the myth of the first man. His narrator is a young physician who had been engaged in an Arctic expedition; when the purple cloud came he was at the North Pole itself, looking for the first time with humanity's eyes on the secrets that eternity had kept inviolate. Only there, in intolerable cold, did the deadly volcanic gas spare a man, for at that low temperature it was precipitated as rain. And as he pushed southward, past the companions of his expedition, unaccountably dead, he realized slowly that he had come back to a world where flowers still bloomed, where man's inventions stood as monuments on every hand, but in which man himself and all other breathing creatures lay dead amid a faint scent of peach blossoms. ⟨. . .⟩

Back in 1901, for purposes of romance, M. P. Shiel postulated that ships should be run by liquid air. But his Adam lacks the magic carpet which has actually come into being. He runs up and down in ships and trains and motor cars, week-ending in Gallipoli to get salycilate of soda, dashing to Constantinople for wine, but never does he have—nor apparently imagine— an airplane. However, even with the North Pole discovered and airplanes achieved, there is no whit less of appetite, I imagine, for the cosmic fairy tales which people have told from time immemorial to soothe, divert and justify themselves. How Adam Jeffson ran riot in his world and found, eventually, his Eve, and by her was civilized again, is first-rate foolery, potent nepenthe to any one harassed by traffic regulation, income tax blanks, or more fundamental immediate realities. If you would summon up a really glowing and persuasive orgy of the imagination, here is Aladdin's lamp to do your bidding.

Mary Ross, "A World for a Toy," *New York Herald Tribune Books*, 4 May 1930, p. 14

FRED T. MARSH   *The English Review* is quoted as saying of M. P. Shiel, "Had Carlyle shared Coleridge's penchant for laudanum, he might have written thus." And *The New York Evening Post* once said, "A genius drunk with the hottest juices of our language." Arthur Machen puts it: "He tells us of a wilder wonderland than Poe dreamed of." Mad, drunk or apocalyptic, Mr. Shiel would seem to be deserving of his blurbs, of the spirit that prompted them anyway, if not of the letter. In *The Young Men Are Coming* you observe an Irishman making a fairyland of science and politics, finding the "little people" in the astro-physical heavens, making mysticism of mathematical formulae and with Irish fancy and recklessness scattering himself about in what to my more sober way of thinking is on the whole distressing. I think he is mad. But there is some poetry and some virtue if little method in his madness.

Fred T. Marsh, [Review of *The Young Men Are Coming!*], New York Herald Tribune Books, 12 December 1937, p. 10

EDWARD SHANKS   I would say a few words more about *The Purple Cloud*. Books about the future are liable to become dated. The contemporary world moves forward into the period which they purport to describe and they lose their meaning. This book would appear to date itself with some definiteness. When it was written the North Pole was still unreached, and the recent failure of Nansen to reach it was still lively in the public mind. That failure did make credible the fancy which inspired Shiel, the idea that there was something mystically forbidden about this particular spot on the surface of the earth. Now not one but several men have trodden the ice of the Pole and we are told that it is destined to be the Clapham Junction of the airlines of the future. But who cares a rap about this when he reads Shiel's account of Adam Jefferson's journey or regards it as anything but a proper and adequate prelude to the tremendous fantasy which follows? This book was a legend, an apocalypse, out of space, out of time.

In speaking of Shiel, it is difficult to avoid giving the impression that he was a 'one-book' man. To some extent at any rate, that he must always be. There is a parallel case which is worth mentioning. Herman Melville will always first and foremost be the author of *Moby Dick*. For as many generations ahead as one can see critics and readers will continue to pay at any rate lip-service to that one book. But among the readers thus influenced some will always seek in other books the qualities however attenuated or frustrated which made that one great.

So it will be with Shiel. The gold which shows so richly in his finest work can be seen in all the others and there will always be readers anxious to seek it out. They will be rewarded. For the first and last thing to be said about him is that he had the character of a poet and a prophet—a prophet, I mean, in the Old Testament manner. His vision always approached the apocalyptic, just as his style often approached (sometimes, one has to own, too closely) the dithyrambic. He believed intensely in what he saw, whether it was a depopulated world or a world set right by the application of an economic theory. He may—I could not tell—have attempted to compromise with the demands made on authors who desire popular success. If he ever did, his own indomitable inner self kept on breaking in. I doubt whether it would be possible to read a whole page of any of his books without recognizing the author.

> Edward Shanks, "The Address of Edward Shanks at the Funeral of Matthew Phipps Shiel" (1947), cited in A. Reynolds Morse, *The Works of M. P. Shiel Updated: A Study in Bibliography* (Dayton, OH: Reynolds Morse Foundation/JDS Books, 1980), Vol. 2, Part 2, pp. 469–70

SAM MOSKOWITZ   Shiel's last important work of fiction was *The Young Men Are Coming*, and it is at once one of his most imaginative and one of his most damning novels. A sort of super flying saucer lands in England and fantastic flaming-haired creatures whisk away an aging Dr. Warwick. They travel three times the speed of light to the first moon of Jupiter. There, the unhatched egg of one of the space creatures engages Dr. Warwick in a prolonged discussion on philosophy, science, sociology, and religion. Dr. Warwick is given a draught of immortality and a parting message from the space creatures:

> Farewell. I bear you this message from the Egg's Mother; that she sets a detector to resonance with your rays: so, if in an emergency worthy of her notice you, having on your psychophone, send out your soul in worship to her, she still journeying in this eastern region of worlds, your wish will reach her.

Returned to earth and immortal, Dr. Warwick organizes the "young men" into a group of virtual storm troopers to defeat the "old men" who are planning a "fascistic" movement. The political goal of the "young men" is to overthrow religion and substitute science (reason) in its place.

A revolutionary war ensues. To win over the people, Dr. Warwick tells them he will perform a *scientific* "miracle" and challenges religion to duplicate, top, or stop him. He sends a message out to the space creatures to create a universal storm, thereby illustrating the power of science over religion. They respond with a globular hurricane which sinks land masses, drowns or kills millions, and inadvertently destroys the air fleet of the "old men" who have the "young men" just about licked in a fair fight.

As far as bloodshed is concerned, Shiel scoffs at the notion that "the next war will wreck civilization." Wars are merely "inconveniences," he avers, concluding, "*Cursed* are the meek! For they shall *not* inherit the earth."

Sam Moskowitz, "The World, the Devil, and M. P. Shiel," *Explorers of the Infinite: Shapers of Science Fiction* (Cleveland: World Publishing Co., 1963), pp. 155–56

DON HERRON   Mr. ⟨A. Reynolds⟩ Morse, Shiel's bibliographer, calls *How the Old Woman Got Home* "real Shiel." That it is—a fast-moving, idiosyncratic novel, in a style only M. P. Shiel ever used. For the Shiel devotee, this book ranks among his best. For the mystery fan, however, it presents many problems. ⟨. . .⟩

The mother of hero Caxton Hazlitt is kidnapped; reason unknown. A couple of suspicious characters have been noticed in the neighborhood by Hazlitt, but he is preoccupied with finding a hand-to-mouth living, eating in soup kitchens, searching for work—then suddenly he comes into miraculous wealth, is installed in a luxurious townhouse . . ., and forgets about his mother for a few chapters. When Hazlitt is informed that the door of his mother's apartment has been found ajar, with the old woman gone:

> "Really?" went Hazlitt; then in a moment, throwing it off him:
> "Well, but she is there all right. I will see her on—Tuesday say."

Even when her abduction is confirmed, Hazlitt allows hismelf to be drawn away to Europe on a trip, to be interrupted in his effort to find the old woman countless times, usually for speechifying on Science and politics. Shiel said of *How the Old Woman Got Home* that it had the "distinction, that in it is given . . . my political system." The chapters of exposition on his system, given in conversation among the characters, halt the action like a collision with a brick wall. Words and intellectual concepts rush on at breakneck pace. But movement toward finding the old woman, solving the mystery, stops.

Shiel clearly was not writing a simple mystery. To carp over this or that point as if he were engaged in writing a true whodunit would be petty enough criticism. Possibly the reason Shiel, once he became established as an author, chose to work in so many different genres was so that he could convey his concepts on Science to several different audiences, readers who might not come across them otherwise. Therefore Shiel spread the word on Science to those who read mysteries, those who read romance, those who read adventure, in case some of these readers did not read in all fields. But if Hazlitt falls short as a desirable hero for a mystery, and he does, he is equally unfit to be a Shielian overman. In Hazlitt the contradictions of Shiel himself are embodied. Shiel, so enamoured of Science, who spent his life not as a scientist but as a writer of popular fiction. Shiel, obsessed with the idea of the overman who conquers all with his abilities, who spent the last years of his life in poverty and virtually forgotten. A man with great ideas that did not manifest themselves in his actual existence. Hazlitt in the novel also mouths all the right words; he does nothing else right. The overman is a superior figure, trained, able to take care of himself in any contingency—yet Hazlitt *earns* nothing by means of his own effort. His wealth in the novel is *given* to him. When he is imprisoned at one point his escape attempts fail; and the last attempt, which might have proven successful, comes too late: his rescuers break in the door. Only at the very end of the novel does Hazlitt take truly *purposeful* action, and then he blunders ruinously. Hazlitt's ineffectual presence as the main character destroys this book as a mystery, and only the sleuthing of Mary Semper, a woman who lives in Mrs. Hazlitt's neighborhood, provides a rallying point. Mary Semper is coolly logical, never misses a beat, a fine detective figure all in all, but her scenes are much too brief to offset Hazlitt's persona.

How the Old Woman Got Home is great fare for those interested in Shiel's ideas, in his monumental command of language, but it shows that mere style—however fast-paced the wording—does not make up for the lack of sleuthing action, which is the substance of a mystery. And regretfully Shiel's characters are motivated by hidden relationships, as in *The Lost Viol,* and not by dark enough forces to produce a murder. Without murder, a mystery novel does not provide many thrills.

> Don Herron, "The Mysteries of M. P. Shiel," *Shiel in Diverse Hands: A Collection of Essays,* ed. A. Reynolds Morse (Cleveland: Reynolds Morse Foundation, 1983), pp. 189–90

BRIAN STABLEFORD   To a considerable extent, the concerns of M. P. Shiel were the common concerns of the more serious writers of early British scientific romance. He wrote several future war stories and one disaster story. He was interested in evolutionary philosophy and socialism. He was deeply suspicious of the hold which religious ideas had over the minds of his contemporaries. One could say the same of Wells and of Beresford, modifying hardly a word. To all these matters, however, he brought a determined idiosyncrasy of viewpoint which isolated him as a writer.

Although his particular complex of ideas was his alone, the individual parts of it were firmly rooted in nineteenth century thought. More often than not, they were rooted in aspects of nineteenth century thought that were themselves eccentric and which have since lost any fashionability or credibility they once had. Shiel's economics is the economics of Henry George rather than of Marx; his evolutionism is the evolutionism of Spencer rather than of Darwin. Even his dogged insistence on being reckoned a deist rather than an agnostic or an atheist cannot conceal the fact that his anticlericalism is allied to the ideas of Thomas Henry Huxley, Auguste Comte and Ludwig Feuerbach. Thirty-seven years of living in the twentieth century had not shaken Shiel's commitment to these ideas when he summarised his position in *The Young Men Are Coming.* No doubt he would have wanted to be reckoned a young man in spirit, but in fact he had not escaped from the trap of age.

The genuinely original aspect of Shiel's philosophical system is to be found in his social and moral philosophy. The character of his commitment to socialism is very different from Wells' commitment to Fabianism, and though he borrowed his economic theory from Henry George (or, perhaps, came to the same conclusions on his own) his political rhetoric is very different from George's.

For Shiel, the exploitation of the working classes by capitalists and landlords was not bad simply because it *was* exploitation. He was not at all interested in lifting the yoke of misery from the workers simply to make them *comfortable*. Exploitation was bad, for Shiel, in precisely the way that nineteenth century religiosity was bad: *because it stifled scientific inquiry.* It was bad for the mind, rather than for the body. The injustice of the system was a minor matter, for Shiel; the suffering of individuals was of no consequence. What mattered was that evolution was being held back. ⟨. . .⟩

We are, of course, perfectly free to decide that Shiel's brand of moral collectivism is itself an evil, and given that it is embedded in a highly suspect metaphysical system we might even be tempted to dismiss it as absurd, but we cannot say that it is incoherent or that Shiel was inconsistent in his advocacy of it. It is the presence of this underlying pattern of thought that enlivens so many of Shiel's plots, and makes them both fascinating and disturbing. More than any other leading figure in the history of British scientific romance he presents an imaginative challenge to the reader. His work does not have the imaginative fertility of Wells' speculative fictions, but it is not so easy to take up an intellectual position relative to his: he is harder to engage in intellectual dialogue.

> Brian Stableford, "The Politics of Evolution: Philosophical Themes in the Speculative Fiction of M. P. Shiel," *Shiel in Diverse Hands: A Collection of Essays,* ed. A. Reynolds Morse (Cleveland: Reynolds Morse Foundation, 1983), pp. 390–91

E. F. BLEILER   Shiel's overall literary stature is highly ambiguous. Eminent literary figures like Rebecca West, Bertrand Russell, John Middleton Murray, and L. P. Hartley have praised his work, but a modern reader is likely to be more impressed with Shiel's defects: melodramatic plots, weak development, difficulties with form, cardboard characters, and a message that is flattered if called an eccentric variety of socialism. How can these contrary estimations be reconciled?

The answer, probably, is that Shiel is a writer's writer, by which one means that a fellow artist can admire certain aspects of technique. Shiel's imagination was remarkable and his stylistic virtuosity enormous. No one else could match Shiel's use of the decorated style of the 1890's. He had a remarkable gift for handling assonances, and his mind was so programmed that he was perpetually "conscious of each consonant and of every (accented) vowel-sound" ("On Reading"). ⟨. . .⟩

At the moment, the cultus of Shiel is not very strong, and his devoted followers are few in number. As for Shiel the writer—the novelistic daredevil who decorated his writing like Tiffany glass, who plotted like Cecil B. DeMille and chronicled flamboyant Napoleons—who smashed mankind in purple prose, drew horrible monsters from beyond death, hid Jesus comfortably in Tibet, shattered the landed aristocracy of England, pulled diamonds from the sky—while he never fulfilled his early promise, his best work is not dead. *The Purple Cloud* remains the best "last man" novel; *The Lord of the Sea* is a fine, overloaded fantasy of history in the manner of Alexandre Dumas, *père; How the Old Woman Got Home* is a demonstration of virtuosity; and the stories of *Shapes in the Fire* are the best things of their sort since Poe.

E. F. Bleiler, "M. P. Shiel," *Supernatural Fiction Writers,* ed. E. F. Bleiler (New York: Charles Scribner's Sons, 1985), Vol. 1, pp. 366–67

▣ *Bibliography*

Prince Zaleski. 1895.

The Rajah's Sapphire. 1896.

Shapes in the Fire: Being a Mid-Winter-Night's Entertainment in Two Parts and an Interlude. 1896.

An American Emperor (with Louis Tracy). 1897.

The Yellow Danger. 1898.

Contraband of War: A Tale of the Hispano-American Struggle. 1899, 1914.

Cold Steel. 1899, 1929.

The Man-Stealers: An Incident in the Life of the Iron Duke. 1900, 1927.

The Lord of the Sea. 1901, 1924.

The Purple Cloud. 1901, 1929.

The Weird o' It. 1902.

Unto the Third Generation. 1903.

The Evil That Men Do. 1904.

The Yellow Wave. 1905.

The Lost Viol. 1905.

The Late Tenant (with Louis Tracy). 1906.

The Last Miracle. 1906, 1929.

The White Wedding. 1908.

The Isle of Lies. 1908.

By Force of Circumstances (with Louis Tracy). 1909.

This Knot of Life. 1909.

The Pale Ape and Other Pulses. 1911.

The House of Silence (with Louis Tracy). 1911.

The Dragon ⟨The Yellow Peril⟩. 1913.

The Hungarian Revolution: An Eyewitness's Account by Charles Henry Schmitt (translator). 1919.

Children of the Wind. 1923.

How the Old Woman Got Home. 1927.

Here Comes the Lady. 1928.

Dr. Krasinski's Secret. 1929.

The Black Box. 1930.

This Above All. 1933.

Say Au R'voir But Not Goodbye. 1933.

The Invisible Voices (with John Gawsworth). 1935.

⟨Poems.⟩ Ed. John Gawsworth. 1936.

The Young Men Are Coming! 1937.

Best Short Stories. Ed. John Gawsworth. 1948.

Science, Life, and Literature. Ed. John Gawsworth. 1950.

The Good Machen. 1963.

Xélucha and Others. 1975.

Prince Zaleski and Cummings King Monk. 1977.

The New King. Ed. A. Reynolds Morse. 1980.

Clark Ashton Smith
1893–1961

CLARK ASHTON SMITH was born on January 13, 1893, in Long Valley, California, the only son of an Englishman, Timeus Smith, and a California native, Fanny Gaylord. In 1902 Smith's father purchased a tract of land outside of Auburn, California, where he built a house that had no electricity or running water. Smith completed grammar school but withdrew from high school after a few days, declaring his intention to be a poet. Later he refused a Guggenheim scholarship to the University of California at Berkeley. Smith became, however, prodigiously self-educated by reading the dictionary and the *Encyclopaedia Britannica* through at least twice.

As an adolescent Smith wrote many stories influenced by Poe, William Beckford, and the *Arabian Nights*, including a 100,000-word unpublished novel, *The Black Diamonds*. He sold his first stories to the *Black Cat* in 1910 at the age of seventeen, after which he abandoned fiction for fifteen years, concentrating instead on poetry. *The Star-Treader and Other Poems* (1912) created a stir in California literary circles, and Smith was hailed as a "boy genius" akin to Keats, Shelley, and Swinburne. Much of this early verse sings rhapsodically of the boundless gulfs of the universe, especially a long poem, *The Hashish-Eater; or, The Apocalypse of Evil*, contained in Smith's third volume, *Ebony and Crystal: Poems in Verse and Prose* (1922). Smith was greatly influenced by George Sterling, with whom he maintained an extensive correspondence between 1911 and 1926. Smith's later poetry volumes—*Odes and Sonnets* (1918), *Ebony and Crystal*, *Sandalwood* (1925), *The Dark Chateau* (1951), *Spells and Philtres* (1958)—failed to attract much attention outside the fantasy and science fiction communities. His poetry includes translations from French, particularly of Baudelaire, and poems written in French and Spanish. His *Selected Poems*, whose preparation Smith completed in 1949 but which was not published until 1971, includes more than 500 of his poems, but many remain uncollected and unpublished. His prose poems are considered among the finest in English.

Between 1913 and 1921 Smith suffered from various nervous illnesses that left him a semi-invalid. Recovering his health, Smith now found himself obliged to undertake various menial jobs—fruit picking, well digging, mining—to support himself. He contributed a column of pensées and aphorisms to the *Auburn Journal* between 1923 and 1926. Around this time Smith, although largely a recluse who never left the state of California, developed a reputation as a bohemian fond of wine, women, and unconventional social and philosophical beliefs. He carried on a lengthy relationship with a married woman, Genevieve K. Sully, and perhaps had liaisons with other women in Auburn.

In 1922 Smith came into contact with H. P. Lovecraft, and the two writers remained close correspondents until Lovecraft's death in 1937. It was perhaps from Lovecraft's example that Smith resumed the writing of fiction: in 1925 he wrote "The Abominations of Yondo," and a few years later he began writing voluminously for the weird and science fiction pulp magazines, notably *Weird Tales* and *Wonder Stories*. In such tales as "The City of the Singing Flame" (1931) and "The Monster of the Prophecy" (1932) he effected a distinctive union between pure fantasy and science fiction. Many of his tales fall into cycles using a common setting. Among the most notable of these are the tales of Averoigne (a mythical region in medieval France), Poseidonis (an island off the coast of Atlantis), the lost continents Zothique and Hyperborea, and the remote planet Xiccarph. Smith's first volume of tales was the self-published *Double Shadow and Other Fantasies* (1933).

Smith's fiction writing was inspired in part by the need to support his parents, who suffered increasing health problems in their later years. When they died (his mother in 1935 and his father in 1937), Smith's output of fiction declined sharply and he turned his attention to painting and sculpture. All his major collections of tales—*Out of Space and Time* (1942), *Lost Worlds* (1944), *Genius Loci* (1948), *The Abominations of Yondo* (1960), *Tales of Science and Sorcery* (1964), and *Other Dimensions* (1970)—are largely drawn from his stories of the 1930s. These volumes were published by Arkham House, whose founder, August Derleth, maintained a close correspondence with Smith from the late 1920s to Smith's death.

In his later years Smith suffered increasing neglect, as his writing fell out of fashion with the developing fields of fantasy and science fiction. Some of his artwork was, however, displayed at local galleries and museums. He married Carol Jones Dorman, a divorced mother of three children, in 1954.

He wrote less and less with the passage of time, and he died on August 14, 1961, in Pacific Grove, California. His work, however, continues to attract a small cadre of supporters. His literary executor, Roy A. Squires, issued many small chapbooks of Smith's work, notably the poem cycle *The Hill of Dionysus* (1962). His few essays were collected as *Planets and Dimensions* (1973); his *Letters to H. P. Lovecraft* appeared in 1987; his complete prose poems were published in 1988; and a large volume of his uncollected stories, fragments, and synopses, *Strange Shadows*, was edited by Steve Behrends in 1989.

Critical Extracts

AMBROSE BIERCE   Kindly convey to young Smith of Auburn my felicitations on his admirable "Ode to the Abyss"—a large theme, treated with dignity and power. It has many striking passages—such, for example, as "The Romes of ruined spheres." I'm conscious of my sin against the rhetoricians for liking that, for it jolts the reader out of the Abyss and back to earth. Moreover, it is a metaphor which belittles, instead of dignifying. But I like it.

He is evidently a student of George Sterling, and being in the formative stage, cannot—why should he?—conceal the fact.

Ambrose Bierce, Letter to George Sterling (8 August 1911), *The Letters of Ambrose Bierce*, ed. Bertha Clark Pope (San Francisco: Book Club of California, 1922), pp. 180–81

GEORGE STERLING   Who of us care to be present at the *accouchement* of the immortal? I believe that we so attend who are first to take this book in our hands. A bold assertion, truly, and one demonstrable only in years remote from these; and—dust wages no war with dust. But it is one of those things that I should most "like to come back and see."

Because he has lent himself the more innocently to the whispers of his subconscious daemon, and because he has set those murmurs to purer and harder crystal than we others, by so much the longer will the poems of

Clark Ashton Smith endure. Here indeed is loot against the forays of moth and rust. Here we shall find none or little of the sentimental fat with which so much of our literature is larded. Rather shall one in Imagination's "mystic mid-region" see elfin rubies burn at his feet, witch-fires glow in the nearer cypresses, and feel upon his brow a wind from the unknown. The brave hunters of fly-specks on Art's cathedral windows will find little here for their trouble, and both the stupid and the over-sophisticated would best stare owlishly and pass by: here are neither kindergartens nor skyscrapers. But let him who is worthy by reason of his clear eye and unjaded heart wander across these borders of beauty and mystery and be glad.

George Sterling, "Preface," *Ebony and Crystal: Poems in Verse and Prose* by Clark Ashton Smith (Auburn, CA: Auburn Journal, 1922), p. [ix]

DONALD A. WANDREI   Imagination is his god, beauty his ideal; his poems are an offering to both. He is the poet of the infinite, the envoy of eternity, the amanuensis of beauty. For even as beauty was deity to Keats and Shelley, so it is to him, and in its praise has he written. But he has not celebrated it as an abstract term or an aesthetic quality, but as a more tangible substance. He has constructed entire worlds of his own and filled them with creations of his own fancy. And his beauty has thus crossed the boundary between that which is mortal and that which is immortal, and has become the beauty of strange stars and distant lands, of jewels and cypresses and moons, of flaming suns and comets, of marble palaces, of fabled realms and wonders, of gods, and daemons, and sorcery. Time and Space have been his servants, the universe his domain; with the stars his steeds and the heavens his tramping ground, he has wandered in realms afar; and he has found there a wondrous beauty and a strange fear, the goal of his early dreams and the enchanted road to greater, all manner of things illusory and fantastical.

Some of his poems are like shadowed gold; some are like flame-encircled ebony; some are crystal-clear and pure; others are as unearthly starshine. One is coldly wrought in marble; another is curiously carved in jade; there are a few glittering diamonds; and there are many rubies and emeralds aflame, glowing with a secret fire. Here and there may be found a poppy-flower, an orchid from the hot-bed of Hell, the whisper of an eldritch wind, a breath from the burning sands of regions infernal. The wizard calls, and at his imperious summons come genie, witch, and daemon to open the portal to the haunted realms of faery; and their wonder is transmuted so that those who can open the door may listen to the murmuring waters of Acheron, or watch the passing of a phantom throng; and the fen-fires gleam; and the slow mists arise; and heavy perfumes, and poisons, and dank odors fill the air. A marble palace rises in the dusk, a treasure-house of gold, and ebony, and ivory; soft lutes play within; fair women, passionless and passionate, wander in the corridors; silks and tapestries adorn the walls, and fuming censers burn a rare incense. And fabulous demogorgon and hippogriff guard the golden gateway to the hoarded wealth. The sky is black. But now and again white comets blaze, or suns of green, of crimson, of purple, flame across the firmament with silver moons. The sky is burning. Stars hurtle to destruction or waste away. All mysteries are uncertained. One may watch a landscape of the moon, the seas of Saturn, the sunken fanes of old Atlantis, wars and wonders on some distant star.

There is no place in the poetry of Clark Ashton Smith for the conventional, the trite, the outworn. It is useless to search his work for offerings to popular desire. Some authors pander to the public taste; their books may have a huge sale, but die with the author. Some writers have skill and ability but desire wealth or immediate fame; their work has not so great a popularity but endures longer. A very few have what is called "genius." They write primarily for themselves, or with a certain small group of people who know literature in mind. They are artists, word artists; and they fashion their prose or poetry with care and labor. They are seldom appreciated in their lifetime, and never have widespread popularity, but the highest minds of every age enjoy their work. These are ones who speak to us across the ages, who will speak across the ages to come. It is to this class that Clark Ashton Smith belongs. One will examine his poems in vain for the commonplaces that have so largely crept into our literature; and by so much as he has avoided ephemeral and written of immortal things, by so much the longer will his work endure.

Donald A. Wandrei, "The Emperor of Dreams," *Overland Monthly* 84, No. 12 (December 1926): 380–81

H. P. LOVECRAFT Of younger Americans, none strikes the note

of cosmic terror so well as the California poet, artist, and fictionist Clark

Ashton Smith, whose bizarre writings, drawings, paintings, and stories are the delight of a sensitive few. Mr. Smith has for his background a universe of remote and paralysing fright—jungles of poisonous and iridescent blossoms on the moons of Saturn, evil and grotesque temples in Atlantis, Lemuria, and forgotten elder worlds, and dank morasses of spotted death-fungi in spectral countries beyond earth's rim. His longest and most ambitious poem, "The Hashish-Eater", is in pentameter blank verse; and opens up chaotic and incredible vistas of kaleidoscopic nightmare in the spaces between the stars. In sheer daemonic strangeness and fertility of conception Mr. Smith is perhaps unexcelled by any writer dead or living. Who else has seen such gorgeous, luxuriant, and feverishly distorted visions of infinite spaces and multiple dimensions and lived to tell the tale?

H. P. Lovecraft, "Supernatural Horror in Literature" (1927), *Dagon and Other Macabre Tales*, ed. S. T. Joshi (Sauk City, WI: Arkham House, 1986), p. 412

CLARK ASHTON SMITH   In writing fantastic science tales, two themes have attracted me more than others, and have seemed to offer the amplest possibilities and the deepest stimulus to imagination: the interplanetary and the inter-dimensional themes. Among those of my stories that can be classed, more or less accurately, as science fiction, the majority have dealt either with worlds remote in space, or worlds hidden from human perception by their different vibratory rate or atomic composition. ⟨. . .⟩

Among my several inter-dimensional stories, I think "City of Singing Flame" is the best. I owe its inspiration to several camping sojourns amid the high Sierras, at a spot within easy walking distance of the Crater Ridge described by Angarth and Hastane. The Ridge is a wild eerie place, differing wholly in its geology and general aspect from the surrounding region, exactly as pictured in the story. It impressed my imagination profoundly, suggesting almost at first sight the contiguity of some unknown, invisible world to which it might afford the mundane approach and entrance. And, since I have never explored the whole of its area, I am not altogether sure that the worn, broken column-ends found by the story's narrators do not really exist somewhere among the curiously shaped and charactered stones that lie in such strange abundance there!

All fantasy apart, however, it seems to me that the theory of interlocking worlds is one that might be offered and defended. We know nothing of the ranges of vibration, the forms of matter and energy, that may lie beyond the testing of our most delicate instruments. Spheres and beings whose atomic structure removes them from all detection may float through or beside the Earth, no less oblivious of our existence than we of theirs. Transit between planes of space, though filled with obvious material difficulties, is at least more readily comprehensible than time-travelling.

Clark Ashton Smith, "Planets and Dimensions" (1940), *Planets and Dimensions: Collected Essays of Clark Ashton Smith*, ed. Gary K. Wolfe (Baltimore: Mirage Press, 1973), pp. 56–57

FRANCIS T. LANEY   I had of course heard a great deal about Clark Ashton Smith, and seen many pictures of him, but none of this had prepared me adequately for the man himself. ⟨. . .⟩ Smith is extremely shy at first, but as he gradually comes to feel that he is among friends who will not ridicule his mode of life and thought, he unbends, and becomes one of the most gracious hosts and entertaining conversationalists I have ever known.

We spent the afternoon drinking wine, talking, and being shown Smith's collection. His books, a choice and varied lot, including many surpassingly beautiful illustrated editions, are very much worth examining, but the real stab came from the surprisingly large quantity of artwork, mostly the creation of Smith himself. His sculptures, using the small boulders picked up in his yard, are somewhat known to fantasy lovers, several of them having been shown on the dust jacket of *Lost Worlds* and in the illustrations in ⟨H. P. Lovecraft's⟩ *Marginalia*. There were far more of them, however, than I had imagined—at least a hundred.

But the high point of the afternoon came when Smith brought out a stack of original drawings and paintings at least two feet thick. Perhaps 25 or 30 of them were commercially published ones, including the originals of most of Smith's drawings from *Weird Tales*, and the Finlay original from ⟨Lovecraft's⟩ "The Thing on the Doorstep". ⟨. . .⟩ There were also several early Boks, including a couple of wonderful unpublished ones, and an unpublished Roy Hunt drawing of Tsathoggua.

Smith's own drawings and paintings, every one of them unpublished, made up the rest of the stack. Nothing of his that has been published gives any inkling of the man's stature as an artist. In technique, of course, he

lacks a good deal, being entirely self-taught. But he more than makes up
for it with subtle and bizarre ideas, by a surprisingly good sense of form and
structure, and above all by his unconventional and often superlative use of
color. Most of the paintings are done in showcard paint, or something very
much like it; they tend to be garish, but yet there is a certain use of restraint
that makes even the most unrestrained ones quite acceptable. Perhaps twenty
show entities from the Cthulhu Mythos; the remainder are extraterrestrial
landscapes, divided about equally between non-human architecture and
alien plant life.

> Francis T. Laney, *Ah, Sweet Idiocy!* (Los Angeles: Francis T. Laney & Charles Burbee,
> 1948), pp. 27–28

FRITZ LEIBER   I can hardly think of a Smith story, the principal
theme of which is not death. The very fine "The End of the Story" and a
few other tales of Averoigne chiefly champion paganism. The even better
"The City of the Singing Flame" shows a passionate concern for life battling
doom which is absent from most of the tales, where Smith is simply the
devoted chronicler of death, ever ready with his fabulous forms and colors
and sounds to do the Grisly Lord gorgeous honor. 〈. . .〉

Smith is *sui generis,* one of the most uninfluenced and original writers I
know of. A germ from Poe, a little fire from George Sterling, perhaps an
acid drop from Bierce, the color and cruelty of Eastern legends—nothing
else in literature contributed to him, except in the most general or minor
fashion. The few tiny borrowings between him and Lovecraft were merely
playful expressions of a literary friendship. 〈. . .〉

A few days ago I mentioned Smith to Harlan Ellison, a tough and
metropolitan writer. He instantly said, "Did you know that 'The City of
the Singing Flame' started me writing science fiction?" Perhaps the influence
of Smith on other writers is deeper and more far-reaching than I have
guessed. The more a writer stands alone—Melville, for example—the slower
posterity is to put him at his rightful level.

> Fritz Leiber, "Letter," *Emperor of Dreams: A Clark Ashton Smith Bibliography* by Donald
> Sidney-Fryer (West Kingston, RI: Donald M. Grant, 1978), p. 103

JEAN MARIGNY   Clark Ashton Smith's work scarcely corresponds
to the definitions customarily given to the genre of the fantastic. In fact,

only in a small number of tales like "The Hunters from Beyond" can there be found that "strange, almost unbearable irruption into the real world" which Roger Caillois has mentioned. Smith is fond of plunging his reader directly into an unreal world which is not necessarily opposed to the reassuring world of everyday reality. This is particularly true in the tales of the Averoigne, Hyperborea, and Zothique cycles. The reader enters head first into these imaginary worlds; he must accept their norms and can rely upon them entirely, knowing in advance that all rational explication of the narrated events will be vain. We do not, as a general rule, find in Smith that ambiguity, that uncertainty which according to Todorov is the central condition of authentic fantasy. Moreover, if we agree with Lovecraft that fantasy is inseparable from pain and horror, we must acknowledge that Smith places himself well within this conception. He excels, in fact, in descriptions of macabre or horrible scenes like the drowned and half-eaten corpses who come back to life in "Necromancy in Naat," or the hordes of mummies, skeletons, and decomposed corpses who emerge from their tombs in "The Empire of the Necromancers."

There is a latent sadism in these tales of Smith—he is fond of visibly describing scenes of torture or of particularly cruel vengeance. Smith, however, never reaches the limits of the unbearable—in contrast, for example, to Stoker—and he never founders in the cheap eroticism of a good number of his contemporaries. Smith is, moreover, much less effective when he embarks upon traditional fantastic themes: his vampires, werewolves, and lamias are not very terrifying and incite us more often to laughter. What is most lacking in Smith is that profound conviction as to the powers of the forces of Evil which we find in a Lovecraft, a Blackwood, or a Machen, or again that pathological obsession which is at the heart of Poe's work.

Clark Ashton Smith's literary art is situated on another level: it is an art above all visual, in which the writer takes the place of a painter, and his pen the place of a brush. Where other authors are content for the most part to suggest, Smith is fond above all of describing with a riot of detail rarely equalled. His extraordinary lands peopled with disquieting monsters, his Dantesque abysses, his evocations of *danses macabres*, his cosmic visions stamped with a strange poetry raise him to the level of the great creators of Fantasy, and he sometimes chances, in this precise regard, to surpass his mentor and friend Lovecraft.

Jean Marigny, "Clark Ashton Smith and His World of Fantasy" (1978), tr. S. T. Joshi, *Crypt of Cthulhu* No. 26 (Hallowmass 1984): 7–8

RAY BRADBURY   Rereading these tales many years later, I realize one of the reasons why they have stayed with me for such a long while: they are, above all, sensually compelling. One of the first things a fiction writer must learn is the business of enclosing his characters, and therefore his readers, in a scene, an atmosphere, providing a frame of reference. Once you have trapped your readers in sights, sounds, smells, and textures, you have them just about where you want them. From that point on, no matter how high, wide, or grotesque the miracles you introduce, your readers will be unable to resist them. CAS has rarely strayed far from this first writer's law. Take one step across the threshold of his stories, and you plunge into color, sound, taste, smell, and texture—into language.

    Ray Bradbury, "Introduction," *A Rendezvous in Averoigne: Best Fantastic Tales of Clark Ashton Smith* (Sauk City, WI: Arkham House, 1988), pp. ix–x

---

S. T. JOSHI   The prose poem has traditionally ⟨. . .⟩ been designed, it seems, to exemplify the great dictum of Oscar Wilde (himself a master prose poet): "The artist is the creator of beautiful things." Beauty—the beauty of love or passion, of Nature, of a novel mood, image, or conception, or merely the self-created beauty of language—is the desideratum. That Smith accomplishes this goal in all these ways needs no demonstration. Simile is frequently the dominant mode for an entire prose poem, and one of the "Litany of the Seven Kisses"—"I kiss thy cheeks, where lingers a faint flush, like the reflection of a rose upheld to an urn of alabaster"— must rank as one of the most exquisite images in all literature. Whereas nearly any sort of prose fiction requires a certain modicum of realism, the prose poem is under no such restriction; and the plethora of poeticisms rarely causes surfeit here, as it occasionally does in Smith's fiction.

    Like the best poetry, many of Smith's prose poems can be read as a facet of his philosophy. In some cases this is more obvious than others: Smith the bitter atheist is revealed in the grim colloquy of "The Corpse and the Skeleton", while "The Touch-Stone" lays bare (perhaps a little too obviously) "the common illusions, the friendly and benign images that make our existence possible". But Smith is at his best when he inserts the philosophical message subtly and unobtrusively; and "From the Crypts of Memory" ⟨. . .⟩ is perhaps the finest of his prose poems for its poignant depiction of the weight of accumulated history that hangs over us all. It is we who dwell "beneath the palls of twilight and silence thrown about the towering tombs and monuments of the Past", and when we die we will know "the years as a passing of shadows, and death itself as the yielding of twilight unto night". ⟨. . .⟩

Next to poetry, the prose poem is the most concentrated form of expression in literature. It is a rarely used form because it requires supreme command of both poetry and prose—their separate rhythms, imagery, and structure; and although Smith learned much about the form from such French masters as Baudelaire and Huysmans, it is not unwarranted to deem Smith the greatest prose poet in English. His poetry may be his most monumental achievement, his prose his most popular; but his relatively few prose poems, all as finely chiselled as a sculpture of Bernini or Canova, may perhaps be his most flawless and satisfying work.

> S. T. Joshi, "Introduction," *Nostalgia of the Unknown: The Complete Prose Poetry* by Clark Ashton Smith, ed. Marc Michaud, Susan Michaud, Steve Behrends, and S. T. Joshi (West Warwick, RI: Necronomicon Press, 1988), pp. vii–viii

STEVE BEHRENDS   Smith's interest in prose lay in the glittering surface of the writing, not the intellectual or thematic depths. He revelled in exoticism and the ultra-human, in coined names, in descriptions of unearthly flora and strange, vapor-hung sunsets. An early critic, Arthur Hillman, wrote that "Clark Ashton Smith may be a Prophet of Doom, but he is robed in hues of gorgeous purple and gold. Although the fatalistic acceptance of the utter humanity [of the universe] runs like a sombre thread through his tapestries, all are beautiful." Carrying this imagery further, Smith might be likened to a maker of fine carpets (of the flying variety, to strain the metaphor), who, to insure the sale of his product, at times employed conventional patterns, but whose delight came from the rich color of his thread and the delicate perfection of his weave.

His prose writings partake of skills developed earlier as a poet. A favorite technique involved is the heavy use of metaphor and simile, by which an object or scene is likened to something of purer or more intense emotional content. Smith's preference was to describe what something is *like*, rather than what it *is*, forsaking realism and exactitude for emotional power. As a result, his descriptive passages are imbued with meaning, and are *evocative* in the true sense of the word. The interplay of descriptions with story-lines, or the tensions underlying his scenes, ranges from the obvious (a wizard preparing to announce his curse is said to have lips "like a pale-red seal on a shut parchment of doom") to the more subtle (a group of dead sailors, the victims of an arctic demon, stare with eyes "like ice in deep pools fast frozen to the bottom"). And occasionally, the use of metaphor enables a description to presage or contain within itself some future scene or happening. For example, in "The Voyage of King Euvoran" a necromancer causes a stuffed bird to fly from the crown of a king and to head out over the sea; the utterance that accomplishes this reanimation is "shrill and eldritch as the crying of migrant fowl that pass over toward unknown shores in the night."

These and other literary techniques were employed to establish a definite atmosphere for each of the stories. Smith likened his authorial role to that of a sorcerer: he felt he was practicing a "verbal black magic . . . of prose-rhythm, metaphor, simile, tone-color, counter-point, and other stylistic resources, like a sort of incantation." The resulting prose-style (like the somewhat similar style of contemporary author Jack Vance) is instantly recognizable, and so great is the degree of continuity in Smith's writings that prime examples of this prose-style are easy to come by. But Smith himself gave us an explicitly characteristic—and deliberately self-parodic—exemplar of his writing. In 1934, by which time Smith had established himself as a major fantasy writer, he was asked by *Fantasy Magazine* to produce a characteristic piece of writing. The magazine's editors asked the "top writers" in the field to describe a lit cigarette in such a way that the author's identity would be instantly apparent. Smith's entry reads:

> Ignited in the rich and multi-hued Antarean dusk, the tip of the
> space pilot's cigarette began to glow and foulder like the small
> scarlet eye of some cavern-dwelling chimera; and an opal-grey
> vapor fumed in gyrant spirals, like incense from an altar of
> pagany, across the high auroral flames that soared from the setting
> of the giant sun.

Included in this exemplary paragraph are an allusion to classical mythology (the chimera), examples of his elaborate vocabulary ("foulder," "gyrant," "pagany"), and two instances of metaphor. And we note that the setting Smith chose for his "Cigarette Characterization" (as the magazine's series was called) is a grand, colorful, and exotic one.

Steve Behrends, *Clark Ashton Smith* (Mercer Island, WA: Starmont House, 1990), pp. 12–13

STEFAN DZIEMIANOWICZ   "The Colossus of Ylourgne", with its series of increasingly bizarre events culminating in the rampage of the most awesome monster to appear in Smith's fiction, comes closest of any of the Averoigne tales to evoking the sense of wonder in Smith's otherworldly fantasies. Here again, though, the plot is one concerned with human ambitiousness that results in overreaching and downfall. The story tells of Nathaire, an ugly and deformed sorcerer of "minikin stature" reviled by the citizens of Vyones. Hounded from the city, he takes up residence in nearby Ylourgne where he fashions a simulacrum as tall as the cathedral out of the skin and tissues of corpses into which he projects his soul. When the creature begins to ransack the countryside, the people of Averoigne discover one final surprise: *"the face of the stupendous monster . . . was the face of the Satanic dwarf, Nathaire—re-magnified a hundred times, but the same in its implacable madness and malevolence!"* Although Nathaire possesses the power of God in his ability to create a being in his own image, his handiwork is revealed here to be no more than a desperate act of psychological overcompensation by which he hopes to achieve the stature (literally) he was denied in life. Smith appears to be saying that even the sorcerers of Averoigne are unable to transcend their flawed humanity, a point he drives home symbolically in the final image of the monster dispatched by a sorcery that compels it to dig its own grave, lie down in it, and rot to pieces, even as Nathaire, now powerless to stop the process of natural corruption, protests vehemently.

> Stefan Dziemianowicz, "Into the Woods: The Human Geography of Clark Ashton Smith's Averoigne," *Dark Eidolon: The Journal of Smith Studies* No. 3 (Winter 1993): 6–7

Bibliography

The Star-Treader and Other Poems. 1912.

Odes and Sonnets. 1918.

Ebony and Crystal: Poems in Verse and Prose. 1922.

Sandalwood. 1925.

The Double Shadow and Other Fantasies. 1933.

Nero and Other Poems. 1937.

Out of Space and Time. 1942.

Lost Worlds. 1944.

Genius Loci and Other Tales. 1948.

The Dark Chateau and Other Poems. 1951.

Spells and Philtres. 1958.

The Abominations of Yondo. 1960.

The Hill of Dionysus: A Selection. [Ed. Roy A. Squires.] 1962.

Dónde Duermes, Eldorado? y Otros Poemas. 1964.

Tales of Science and Sorcery. 1964.

Poems in Prose. 1965.

Other Dimensions. 1970.

Fugitive Poems. [Ed. Roy A. Squires.] 1970. 4 vols.

Zothique. Ed. Lin Carter. 1970.

Hyperborea. Ed. Lin Carter. 1970.

Xiccarph. Ed. Lin Carter. 1971.

Selected Poems. 1971.

Planets and Dimensions: Collected Essays. Ed. Charles K. Wolfe. 1973.

Poseidonis: Tales of Lost Atlantis. Ed. Lin Carter. 1973.

The Fantastic Art of Clark Ashton Smith. Ed. Dennis Rickard. 1973.

Grotesques et Fantastiques. Ed. Gerry de la Ree. 1973.

Klarkash-Ton and Mostro Ligriv. Ed. Gerry de la Ree. 1974.

Fugitive Poems: Second Series. [Ed. Roy A. Squires.] 1974–77. 6 vols.

The Black Book of Clark Ashton Smith. [Ed. Rah Hoffman and Donald Sidney-
     Fryer.] 1979.

[*As It Is Written.* Ed. Will Murray. 1982.]

Letters to H. P. Lovecraft. Ed. Steve Behrends. 1987.

The Unexpurgated Clark Ashton Smith. Ed. Steve Behrends. 1987–88. 6 vols.

Nostalgia of the Unknown: The Complete Prose Poetry. Ed. Marc Michaud,
     Susan Michaud, Steve Behrends, and S. T. Joshi. 1988.

Strange Shadows: The Uncollected Fiction and Essays of Clark Ashton Smith. Ed.
     Steve Behrends, Donald Sidney-Fryer, and Rah Hoffman. 1989.

The Devil's Notebook: Collected Epigrams and Pensées. Ed. Donald Sidney-Fryer
     and Don Herron. 1990.

J. R. R. Tolkien
1892–1973

JOHN RONALD REUEL TOLKIEN, philologist, translator, and fantasy writer, was born on January 3, 1892, at Bloemfontein, Orange Free State (now South Africa), where his father was a banker. In 1895 Tolkien was taken to England by his mother for reasons of health, and his father, who had planned to join them shortly, died in South Africa the following year. In England Tolkien attended St. Phillip's Grammar School and King Edward's School. When his mother died in 1904, he and his younger brother Hilary were left in the guardianship of their local parish priest.

In 1911 Tolkien won a scholarship to study classics at Oxford University; however, he soon changed his area of study and in 1915 took a first in English. Upon graduation he entered the army and in 1916 married Edith Bratt; the couple later had four children. Tolkien fought in the Battle of the Somme, but in November 1916 he contracted trench fever and was invalided back to England.

In 1917, while convalescing, he began to write *The Book of Lost Tales*, a vast compendium of poetry, epic prose, chronology, and mythic detail concerning the world in which many of his later works of fantasy would be set. Although he never finished arranging this primary material for publication, since his death a great deal of it has been edited and published by his son, Christopher Tolkien, beginning with *The Silmarillion* (1977). More of this material remains unpublished; the work grew continuously throughout Tolkien's lifetime, and he was known to describe his published novels as relatively unimportant distractions from the business of primary background-creation.

After the war Tolkien returned to Oxford, where he joined the staff of the *Oxford English Dictionary*. In 1920 he became a Reader in English at Leeds University. His first scholarly publication, *A Middle English Vocabulary*, appeared in 1922, and in 1924 he was promoted to Professor of English Languages. In 1925 he produced an edition of *Sir Gawain and the Green Knight* in collaboration with E. V. Gordon and was elected Rawlinson and

Bosworth Professor of Anglo-Saxon at Oxford. He remained at Oxford until he retired in 1959, and from 1945 onward he was Merton Professor of English Language and Literature. At Oxford he became a member of the Inklings, a group of friends that included C. S. Lewis, Charles Williams, Dorothy L. Sayers, and Owen Barfield, to all of whom he read aloud his works in progress. In 1936 he delivered Oxford's annual Sir Israel Gollancz Memorial Lecture, which later saw print as the influential critical essay, "Beowulf: The Monsters and the Critics."

Tolkien's popular children's book *The Hobbit* (1937) proved to be only the preface to his phenomenally successful epic fantasy, *The Lord of the Rings*, published in three volumes as *The Fellowship of the Ring* (1954), *The Two Towers* (1954), and *The Return of the King* (1955). This trilogy draws deeply from Tolkien's study of Anglo-Saxon in both its invented language and its quasi-epic events; it is, in effect, a fantasy epic set in "Middle-earth," in the dim prehistory of the Earth, and involves the quest to destroy a ring of infinite power before it can fall into the hands of an evil Dark Lord, Sauron. Critics have praised the mythological scope and structure of the work, although some have deprecated its too clear-cut dichotomy between the forces of good and the forces of evil. As a Catholic, however, Tolkien felt this dichotomy very deeply, as did his colleagues in the Inklings.

Tolkien's shorter works of fantasy include "Leaf by Niggle" (1945), *Farmer Giles of Ham* (1949), *The Adventures of Tom Bombadil* (1962), and *Smith of Wootton Major* (1967). "On Fairy-Stories," a lecture delivered in 1939, discusses his theories of folklore and fantasy.

Tolkien died on September 2, 1973. Besides the volumes derived from his background notes on Middle-earth, other works published since his death include a set of modern English translations of *Sir Gawain and the Green Knight*, *Pearl*, and *Sir Orfeo* (1975), a selection of letters (1981), and a collection of lectures and essays, *The Monsters and the Critics* (1983).

🔲 *Critical Extracts*

J. R. R. TOLKIEN   To make a Secondary World inside which the green sun will be credible, commanding Secondary Belief, will probably require labour and thought, and will certainly demand a special skill, a kind of elvish craft. Few attempt such difficult tasks. But when they are attempted and in any degree accomplished then we have a rare achievement of Art: indeed narrative art, story-making in its primary and most potent mode. ⟨. . .⟩

To the elvish craft, Enchantment, Fantasy aspires, and when it is successful of all forms of human art most nearly approaches. At the heart of many man-made stories of the elves lies, open or concealed, pure or alloyed, the desire for a living, realised sub-creative art, which (however much it may outwardly resemble it) is inwardly wholly different from the greed for self-centred power which is the mark of the mere Magician. Of this desire the elves, in their better (but still perilous) part, are largely made; and it is from them that we may learn what is the central desire and aspiration of human Fantasy—even if the elves are, all the more in so far as they are, only a product of Fantasy itself. That creative desire is only cheated by counterfeits, whether the innocent but clumsy devices of the human dramatist, or the malevolent frauds of the magicians. In this world it is for men unsatisfiable, and so imperishable. Uncorrupted it does not seek delusion, nor bewitchment and domination; it seeks shared enrichment, partners in making and delight, not slaves.

To many, Fantasy, this sub-creative art which plays strange tricks with the world and all that is in it, combining nouns and redistributing adjectives, has seemed suspect, if not illegitimate. To some it has seemed at least a childish folly, a thing only for peoples or for persons in their youth. ⟨. . .⟩

Fantasy is a natural human activity. It certainly does not destroy or even insult Reason; and it does not either blunt the appetite for, nor obscure the perception of, scientific verity. On the contrary. The keener and the clearer is the reason, the better fantasy will it make. If men were ever in a state in which they did not want to know or could not perceive truth (facts or evidence), then Fantasy would languish until they were cured. If they ever get into that state (it would not seem at all impossible), Fantasy will perish, and become Morbid Delusion.

For creative Fantasy is founded upon the hard recognition that things are so in the world as it appears under the sun; on a recognition of fact, but not a slavery to it. So upon logic was founded the nonsense that displays itself in the tales and rhymes of Lewis Carroll. If men really could not distinguish between frogs and men, fairy-stories about frog-kings would not have arisen.

Fantasy can, of course, be carried to excess. It can be ill done. It can be put to evil uses. It may even delude the minds out of which it came. But of what human being in this fallen world is that not true? Men have conceived not only of elves, but they have imagined gods, and worshipped them, even worshipped those most deformed by their authors' own evil. But they have made false gods out of other materials: their notions, their banners, their monies; even their sciences and their social and economic theories have demanded human sacrifice. *Abusus non tollit usum.* Fantasy remains a human right: we make in our measure and in our derivative mode, because we are made: and not only made, but made in the image and likeness of a Maker.

> J. R. R. Tolkien, "On Fairy-Stories" (1939), *The Monsters and the Critics and Other Essays*, ed. Christopher Tolkien (London: George Allen & Unwin, 1983), pp. 140, 143–45

C. S. LEWIS   When I reviewed the first volume of this work ⟨*The Lord of the Rings*⟩, I hardly dared to hope it would have the success which I was sure it deserved. Happily I am proved wrong. There is, however, one piece of false criticism which had better be answered: the complaint that the characters are all either black or white. Since the climax of Volume I was mainly concerned with the struggle between good and evil in the mind of Boromir, it is not easy to see how anyone could have said this. I will hazard a guess. "How shall a man judge what to do in such times?" asks someone in Volume II. "As he has ever judged," comes the reply. "Good and ill have not changed . . . nor are they one thing among Elves and Dwarves and another among Men."

This is the basis of the whole Tolkinian world. I think some readers, seeing (and disliking) this rigid demarcation of black and white, imagine they have seen a rigid demarcation between black and white people. Looking at the squares, they assume (in defiance of the facts) that all the pieces must be making bishops' moves which confine them to one color. But even such readers will hardly brazen it out through the last two volumes. Motives, even on the right side, are mixed. Those who are now traitors usually began with comparatively innocent intentions. Heroic Rohan and imperial Gondor are partly diseased. Even the wretched Sméagol, till quite late in the story, has good impulses; and, by a tragic paradox, what finally pushes him over the brink is an unpremeditated speech by the most selfless character of all.

There are two Books in each volume and now that all six are before us the very high architectural quality of the romance is revealed. Book I builds up the main theme. In Book II that theme, enriched with much retrospective material, continues. Then comes the change. In III and V the fate of the company, now divided, becomes entangled with a huge complex of forces which are grouping and regrouping themselves in relation to Mordor. The main theme, isolated from this, occupies IV and the early part of VI (the latter part of course giving all the resolutions). But we are never allowed to forget the intimate connection between it and the rest. On the one hand, the whole world is going to the war; the story rings with galloping hoofs, trumpets, steel on steel. On the other, very far away, two tiny, miserable figures creep (like mice on a slag heap) through the twilight of Mordor. And all the time we know that the fate of the world depends far more on the small movement than on the great. This is a structural invention of the highest order: it adds immensely to the pathos, irony, and grandeur of the tale.

This main theme is not to be treated in those jocular, whimsical tones now generally used by reviewers of "juveniles." It is entirely serious: the growing anguish, the drag of the Ring on the neck, the ineluctable conversion of hobbit into hero in conditions which exclude all hope of fame or fear of infamy. Without the relief offered by the more crowded and bustling Books it would be hardly tolerable. ⟨. . .⟩

The book is too original and too opulent for any final judgment on a first reading. But we know at once that it has done things to us. We are not quite the same men. And though we must ration ourselves in our rereadings, I have little doubt that the book will soon take its place among the indispensables.

> C. S. Lewis, "The Dethronement of Power" (1955), *Tolkien and the Critics: Essays on J. R. R. Tolkien's* The Lord of the Rings, ed. Neil D. Isaacs and Rose A. Zimbardo (Notre Dame: University of Notre Dame Press, 1968), pp. 12–13, 16

EDMUND WILSON   The most distinguished of Tolkien's admirers and the most conspicuous of his defenders has been Mr. W. H. Auden. That Auden is a master of English verse and a well-equipped critic of poetry, no one, as they say, will dispute. It is significant, then, that he comments on the badness of Tolkien's verse—there is a good deal of poetry in *The Lord of the Rings*—but is apparently quite insensible through comparative lack of interest in this other department to the fact that Tolkien's prose is just as bad. Prose and verse are on the same level of professorial amateurishness. What I believe has misled Mr. Auden is his own special preoccupation with the legendary theme of the Quest. ⟨. . .⟩ It is indeed a tale of a Quest, but, to this reader, an extremely unrewarding one. The hero has no serious temptations; is lured by no insidious enchantments, perplexed by no serious problems. What we get here is a simple confrontation—in more or less the traditional terms of British melodrama—of the Forces of Evil with the Forces of Good, the remote and alien villain with the plucky little home-grown hero. There are streaks of imagination: the ancient tree-spirits, the Ents, with their deep eyes, twiggy beards, rumbly voices; the Elves, whose nobility and beauty is elusive and not quite human. But even these are rather clumsily handled. There is never much development in the episodes; you simply go on getting more of the same. Dr. Tolkien has little skill at narrative and no instinct for literary form. The characters talk a story-book language that might have come out of Howard Pyle, and as personalities they do not impose themselves. At the end of this long romance, I had still no conception of the wizard Gandalph, who is made to play a cardinal role. I had never been able to visualize him at all. For the most part such characterizations as Dr. Tolkien is able to contrive are perfectly stereotyped: Frodo the good little Englishman; Samwise, his dog-like servant, who talks lower-class and respectful, and never deserts his master. These characters who are no characters are involved in interminable adventures the poverty of invention displayed in which is, it seems to me, almost pathetic.

Edmund Wilson, "Oo, Those Awful Orcs!" (1956), *The Bit Between My Teeth: A Literary Chronicle of 1950–1965* (New York: Farrar, Straus & Giroux, 1966), pp. 328–29

CATHARINE R. STIMPSON   Many find Tolkien's moral vision serious and impeccable. Surely men ought to be both courageous and charitable. Surely men ought not to be haughty and selfish. Of course, the good is creative. Of course, evil is corroding, then corrupting, and finally canceling. However, Tolkien seems rigid. He admits that men, elves, and dwarfs are a collection of good, bad, and indifferent beings, but he more consistently divides the ambiguous world into two unambiguous halves: good and evil, nice and nasty. Any writer has the right to dramatize, not to argue, his morality. However, Tolkien's dialogue, plot, and symbols are terribly simplistic. A star always means hope, enchantment, wonder; an ash heap always means despair, enslavement, waste. Readily explicable, they also seem to conceal intellectual fuzziness and opaque maxims. Moreover, Tolkien gives way to a lust for miracles. Wizards, weapons, and thaumaturges, leaping in and out of the action at Tolkien's will, are as sophisticated as last-minute cavalry charges in the more old-fashioned Westerns.

Behind the moral structure is a regressive emotional pattern. For Tolkien is irritatingly, blandly, traditionally masculine. Not only does he apparently place more faith in battles than in persuasion, but he makes his women, no matter what their rank, the most hackneyed of stereotypes. They are either beautiful and distant, simply distant, or simply simple. Although the adoration of dwarf Gimli for elf queen and mother figure Galadriel neatly parodies the excesses of courtly love, some of Tolkien's men do worship their women. However, their devotion is callow, shallow, and mawkish. More often women are ignored, unless, like the hobbit Rosie Cotten, they are a necessary adjunct to a domestic scene, or, like the warrior lass Éowyn, a necessarily fillip for the plot. 〈. . .〉

It is hardly surprising that Tolkien generally ignores the rich medieval theme of the conflict between love and duty. Nor is it startling that the most delicate and tender feelings in Tolkien's writing exist between men, the members of holy fellowships and companies. Fathers and sons, or their surrogate figures, also receive attentive notice. When Tolkien does sidle up to genuine romantic love, sensuality, or sexuality, his style becomes coy and infantile, or else it burgeons into a mass of irrelevant, surface, descriptive detail. Unlike very many good modern writers, he is no homosexual. Rather, he simply seems a little childish, a little nasty, and evasive.

Catharine R. Stimpson, *J. R. R. Tolkien* (New York: Columbia University Press, 1969), pp. 18–20

PAUL H. KOCHER   If *The Hobbit* is a quarry it is one in which the blocks of stone lie scattered about in a much looser and less imposing pattern than that in which the epic assembles those which it chooses to borrow. For example, Bilbo's enemies are serial, not united under any paragon of evil, as is to happen in the epic. *The Hobbit*'s trolls, goblins (orcs), spiders, and dragon know nothing of one another and are all acting on their own. They are certainly not shown to be servants of the nameless and nebulous Necromancer, whose only function in the story is to cause Gandalf to leave Bilbo and company to confront exciting perils unaided for a time. Nor ⟨. . .⟩ is that magician linked in any way with the Ring, which comes out of nowhere belonging to no one. Also, as there is no alliance on behalf of evil so there is none against it. Dwarves, elves, and men act mainly for their selfish interests, often at cross-purposes, until a coalition is forced upon them by a goblin army hostile to all at the very end. Even then the issue is relatively localized and not worldwide in its ramifications.

Some of the places later to be brilliantly visualized in the epic appear for the first time in *The Hobbit*, but its geography tends to be rudimentary and uncertain and it is not given a continental context. ⟨. . .⟩ In fact, since Bilbo's world is never called Middle-earth until we run across a reference to the constellation of the Wain (stars in the Great Bear) in its northern sky, we may be pardoned for wondering whether it is any place in particular, assuming, of course, that we have not read the epic. Tolkien has not yet learned to take the pains he later takes to make us accept this world as our own planet Earth and the events of his story as a portion of Earth's distant prehistory.

The case is the same for the individual characters and the races in *The Hobbit* who will reappear in *The Lord of the Rings*. Tolkien's abrupt leap from a children's tale to an epic of heroic struggle requires a radical elevation of stature for all of them. As the Necromancer of *The Hobbit* is not yet Sauron, Gandalf is not yet Gandalf. The wizard of the child's story who "never minded explaining his cleverness more than once," who is "dreadfully afraid" of the wargs, who tricks Beorn into accepting thirteen unwanted dwarves into his house, and the like, needs nothing short of a total literary resurrection to become the messenger sent by the Valar to rally the West against Sauron. ⟨. . .⟩

Much of this need for upgrading the characters and the plot of *The Hobbit* arises from Tolkien's treatment of them in many situations of that tale as seriocomic. He evidently believes that the children will enjoy laughing at them sometimes, as a relief from shivering in excitement sympathetically with them at others. In truth, *The Hobbit* is seldom far from comedy. Tolkien begins by making Bilbo the butt of Gandalf's joke in sending the dwarves unexpectedly to eat up all his food, proceeds on to the lamentable humor of the troll scene, hangs his dwarves up in trees, rolls them in barrels, touches the riddle scene with wit, makes the talk between Bilbo and Smaug triumphantly ridiculous, and tops it all off with Bilbo's return home to find his goods being auctioned off and his reputation for respectable stupidity in ruins. It must be acknowledged that the comedy is not invariably successful and that Tolkien's wry paternal manner of addressing his young listeners does not always avoid an air of talking down, which sets the teeth on edge. Nevertheless, *The Hobbit* was never meant to be a wholly serious tale, nor his young audience to listen without laughing often. In contradistinction, *The Lord of the Rings* does on occasion evoke smiles, but most of the time its issues go too deep for laughter. In the interval between the two stories the children are sent off to bed and their places taken by grownups, young or young at heart, to hear of a graver sort of quest in which every human life is secretly engaged.

Paul H. Kocher, *Master of Middle-Earth: The Fiction of J. R. R. Tolkien* (Boston: Houghton Mifflin, 1972), pp. 30–33

DEREK S. BREWER   One of the fine things in *The Lord of the Rings* is the increasing horror of Frodo's journey, especially after he and Sam are on their own. The effectiveness of the journey is partly found in the interweaving of the adventures of the other members of the Company with those of Frodo, and Tolkien shows great skill in inventing significant and varied narrative events; but the main power, naturally enough, lies with the Ring-bearer himself. The paradox of this particular quest is that what is most wanted is most against the grain. Not only must good struggle against evil: not only must Frodo labour through miserable physical circumstances: but there is for the hero a struggle within himself, to do what he must do, but can hardly bear to do. No subtle or realistic characterisation is needed to show this situation, yet it reaches down into our deepest sense of identity. Tolkien is extraordinarily good at creating that visionary dreariness in the world, that sinking of the heart that comes, for example, to an unprofessional soldier, when the orders for the attack are received, but which recurs often enough in ordinary existence, from the most trivial examples to the greatest. We have to do something, of our own choice, that we do not want to do. There is in human consciousness a deep sense that the ultimate goodness of the universe requires an ultimate sacrifice of the self that would usually seem to be the ultimate personal disaster. ⟨. . .⟩ Self-sacrifice is most poignant when it is entirely solitary; when apparently no one can ever know of the lonely painful deed that has been ungladly volunteered, and that has apparently been of no avail. This solitary heroism is Frodo's, and the more convincing in that Tolkien does not totally isolate him physically, since Sam remains with him for various purposes of the narrative. But Frodo becomes progressively withdrawn even from Sam. In the last stages of the journey to the Crack of Doom Tolkien succeeds in creating the sense of physical difficulty and cost that romance sometimes fails to achieve. He realises most vividly the appalling landscape, the aching struggle towards the repellent yet desired objective, barely relieved by the blessed brief oblivion of exhausted sleep. This is a hopelessness which is not despair; an assertion of the will which denies the self. No doubt Tolkien's war-experience contributed to the imagery, but it is of the nature of literature to enable us to create such experiences in our own minds out of the very much smaller, but perhaps not less significant events, in our own individual lives, when any kind of moral and physical achievements have been sought. Very little in life is achieved without some self-sacrifice and some strain. One of the virtues of romance is that its remote adventures can so well symbolise quite ordinary and usual predicaments.

Tolkien achieves the final perfect twist to the Quest when he makes Frodo, at the very brink of success, relinquish it. This seems to me a fine comment on the feebleness of the human will. Then Gollum springs forward, the despised, hated, barely tolerated, yet pitied enemy, and bites off both ring and finger, to fall himself into the Crack of Doom. Even evil may do good in its own despite, may even be given a pitiful satisfaction. It is a splendid narrative turn, unexpected yet true, full of interest in itself, yet also symbolically significant of a view of life. It is entirely within the rules of the romance, yet entirely translatable into the terms of our own world.

Derek S. Brewer, "The Lord of the Rings as Romance," J. R. R. Tolkien, Scholar and Storyteller: Essays in Memoriam, ed. Mary Salu and Robert T. Farrell (Ithaca, NY: Cornell University Press, 1979), pp. 256–57

JANET MENZIES   The Lord of the Rings has now itself become a circumstance of daily life. The craze of the '60s and '70s is a seminal influence in the '80s. The blockbusting film *Star Wars* shows many signs of its influence. It concerns the epic theme of good fighting evil, and the movements and *gestes* of mankind caught up in the age-long struggle. There are wizards, too, in the shape of Jedi knights. Darth Vader is Saruman, a wizard turned to evil, and his adversary is Obi Kenobi, a Gandalf figure whose own death is eventually a triumph over evil. ⟨. . .⟩

The 'new romantic' pop wave also shows a Tolkienish desire for heroic figures. Adam Ant went back to fairy-tale roots for his Prince Charming; and Toyah's preoccupations are with white horses galloping across a Mordor-like plain. Costumes are those of Norse war-lords, noble savages, Arthurian knights, princes and princesses: the heroes of earlier times. So many of today's pop videos could be the very landscape of Middle-earth; they show an impersonal, changed world of fantasy.

They possess the same concrete appreciation of a potent physical world which Tolkien inspired in me. This is not simply a response to having been brought up in a Tolkien generation. Nor does it wholly reflect the adolescent love of sensations. Today's experience is impersonal; Tolkien provides the trappings of heroism. His externalized outlook leads us into the abstract world of the *geste*. 'This means nothing to me' is a repeated phrase (listen to Ultra Vox's song 'Vienna') which voices a recognition of the baselessness of our situation. Actions are felt intensely, but they remain cold and remote; events are enthralling, but formalistic. ⟨. . .⟩

As a child *The Lord of the Rings* meant everything to me; coming back to it as an adult I find it superficially attractive but ultimately unsatisfying. It is a book of and for adolescence. Of its author I can only say that Tolkien showed me how to perceive the world, but he did not convey to me an understanding of it.

Janet Menzies, "Middle-earth and the Adolescent," *J. R. R. Tolkien: The Far Land*, ed. Robert Giddings (London: Vision Press, 1983), pp. 70–71

CHRISTOPHER CLAUSEN   In fact *Lord of the Rings* is a novel, one drawn from many disparate sources but a novel nonetheless, embodying most of the technical features associated with novels since the eighteenth century—even a realistic novel for most of its length, provided that "realism" is understood as a set of conventions for the delineation of plot and character rather than as a theory about the world. It is furthermore an identifiably modernist novel, one that incorporates myth and a variety of elements from the distant literary past in a self-conscious way to achieve a wholly new creation. In conception, it bears a closer resemblance to *The Waste Land* than to any medieval Arthurian work. Although it is set in a remote period of imaginary history ⟨. . .⟩ the alert reader is never allowed to forget the twentieth century and its dilemmas of totalitarian power, technological obliteration, and individual choice. With occasional exceptions, the source-hunting to which *Lord of the Rings* has driven baffled scholars and critics is as futile as the footnoting of T. S. Eliot's literary allusions. The meaning of the book (a complicated meaning, reducible to no simple set of assertions) has to do with twentieth-century problems and is directed at twentieth-century readers.

It is precisely the contemporary significance of *Lord of the Rings*, however subliminally apprehended, that has led to the polarization of opinion about it. Of all the attacks made on it, the most implausible is the charge of escapism. Far from encouraging us to take refuge in a world of dreamy Elves, *Lord of the Rings* is a book with moral and social designs on its readers. A comparison with *The Silmarillion*, which really is dominated by dreamy Elves, is enlightening. That book, which Tolkien worked on desultorily for half a century and never finished, was a disappointment to everyone but a few fanatics when the author's son Christopher published a version of it in 1977. What it lacks is human concerns that have any bearing on contemporary life. *Lord of the Rings* is altogether a different kind of work, and in praising or attacking it critics tend not surprisingly to focus on the moral and social positions which it seems to embody. Those who admire the book praise it for showing us powerful examples of heroism, courage, loyalty, determination, and—an explicitly twentieth-century virtue—environmental sensitivity. Those who attack it do so because they consider it authoritarian, militaristic, snobbish or worse in its apparently unquestioning acceptance of hereditary inequalities, condescending at best in its portrayal of women, shallow in its characterizations, and above all morally simplistic in its description of a war to the death between good and evil.

> Christopher Clausen, "J. R. R. Tolkien: The Monsters and the Critics," *The Moral Imagination: Essays on Literature and Ethics* (Iowa City: University of Iowa Press, 1986), pp. 88–90

KATHARYN W. CRABBE   *The Silmarillion*, Tolkien's posthumously published account of the First Age of the world, is the densest, the most difficult, and for the general reader the least attractive of all his works. As a backdrop to *The Lord of the Rings* and *The Hobbit*, *The Silmarillion* is perhaps the most essential of Tolkien's works; at the same time it is the least able to stand alone as a unified vision. Although individual tales from this chronicle of the earliest age of Middle-earth may be exquisite, or majestic, or horrifying, *The Silmarillion* as a whole has neither unity of tone nor unity of style. In addition, the number of characters is simply staggering. So while *The Silmarillion* is Tolkien's most ambitious project, it is in many ways his most flawed performance. ⟨. . .⟩

Like the poem *Beowulf*, which Tolkien studied and loved, *The Silmarillion* is not really a narrative in the sense that it tells a story in a straightforward and sequential manner. Instead, the collection of tales with its cross-references, modifications, and contradictions is presented as a mythology which, having come from divers hands and divers places, cannot be expected to achieve any great degree of inner consistency. The pose of the narrator, then, as a translator or as an editor obviates criticism of the lack of unity in the work.

To say, however, that *The Silmarillion* lacks narrative unity is not to say that it lacks structure. Indeed, the work is highly structured, taking the form of a triptych, a three-paneled picture often used as an altarpiece. This structure seems to have been part of Tolkien's own plan for the work, for Christopher Tolkien notes in the Foreword that the first and third panels "are included according to my father's explicit intention."

The large central section, the *Quenta Silmarillion*, or "History of the Silmarils," is flanked on one side by the story of the creation in the *Ainulindalë* and the *Valaquenta*, and on the other by the story of the decline of the elves and the rise of men in the *Akallabêth* and *Of the Rings of Power and the Third Age*. As in an actual triptych, the central panel is the largest and carries the most meaning, but the two side panels provide a context for the central panel, give a perspective on it, and direct the eye toward it. The relative emphasis to be placed on the three panels is a function not only of size but of orientation, for the central panel is focused straight ahead and so seems independent, while the side panels make connections with the central panel and defer to it. Thus by placement of the parts and by proportion, *The Silmarillion* is an account of the history of the elves of Middle-earth. It is, at the same time, a symbolic representation of the fall of man because it is in the nature of myths to link gods, demigods, and men.

Katharyn W. Crabbe, *J. R. R. Tolkien* (New York: Continuum, 1988), pp. 112–15

◈ Bibliography

A Middle English Vocabulary. 1922.

Sir Gawain and the Green Knight (editor; with E. V. Gordon). 1925.

Beowulf: The Monsters and the Critics. 1936.

Songs for the Philologists (with others). 1936.

The Hobbit; or, There and Back Again. 1937.

Farmer Giles of Ham. 1949.

The Fellowship of the Ring. 1954.

The Two Towers. 1954.

The Return of the King. 1955.

Ancrene Wisse: The English Text of the Ancrene Riwle (editor). 1962.

The Adventures of Tom Bombadil and Other Verses from the Red Book. 1962.

Tree and Leaf. 1964.

The Tolkien Reader. 1966.

The Road Goes Ever On: A Song Cycle. 1967.

Smith of Wootton Major. 1967.

Sir Gawain and the Green Knight, Pearl, and Sir Orfeo (translator). Ed. Christopher Tolkien. 1975.

The Father Christmas Letters. Ed. Baillie Tolkien. 1976.

The Silmarillion. Ed. Christopher Tolkien. 1977.

Pictures. Ed. Christopher Tolkien. 1979.

Unfinished Tales of Númenor and Middle-Earth. Ed. Christopher Tolkien. 1980.

The Old English Exodus (translator). Ed. Joan Turville-Petre. 1981.

Letters. Ed. Humphrey Carpenter and Christopher Tolkien. 1981.

Mr. Bliss. 1982.

Finn and Hengist: The Fragment and the Episode. Ed. Alan Bliss. 1982.

The Monsters and the Critics and Other Essays. Ed. Christopher Tolkien. 1983.

The Book of Lost Tales. Ed. Christopher Tolkien. 1983–84. 2 vols.

The Lays of Beleriand. Ed. Christopher Tolkien. 1985.

The Shaping of Middle Earth. Ed. Christopher Tolkien. 1986.

The Lost Road and Other Writings: Language and Legend Before The Lord of the Rings. Ed. Christopher Tolkien. 1987.

The Return of the Shadow. Ed. Christopher Tolkien. 1988.

The Treason of Isengard. Ed. Christopher Tolkien. 1989.

The War of the Ring. Ed. Christopher Tolkien. 1990.

Sauron Defeated: The End of the Third Eye. Ed. Christopher Tolkien. 1992.

Morgoth's Ring: The Later Silmarillion, Part One: The Legends of Aman. Ed.
Christopher Tolkien. 1993.

Poems. 1993. 3 vols.

Charles Williams
1886–1945

CHARLES WALTER STANBY WILLIAMS was born in London on September 20, 1886, to a middle-class Anglican family. In 1894 his family moved to St. Albans, and Williams attended St. Albans Grammar School. He was confirmed as an Anglican in 1901, and throughout his life he retained his devotion to the Church of England. For two years beginning in 1902 Williams attended University College, London (now the University of London), but his family's financial difficulties forced him to leave before completing his course of study. Williams worked for four years as a clerk at the Methodist Bookroom; then, in 1908, he became an editor at the London office of Oxford University Press, where he worked for the rest of his life. The same year he met Florence Conway, whom he married in 1917; they had one son.

During his twenties Williams developed an interest in magic and the occult and joined the Hermetic Order of the Golden Dawn; although he remained a member only briefly, many of the Hermetic concepts to which he was exposed would later appear in his writing.

Throughout his career Williams considered himself primarily a poet, and in his early years he published only poetry, beginning in 1912 with the collection *The Silver Stair*. His first novel was *Shadows of Ecstasy*, written in 1925; but Williams was unable to find a publisher for it, and it did not see print until 1933. *War in Heaven*, his first published novel, appeared in 1930, by which time he had already built a minor reputation as a poet, critic (*Poetry at Present*, 1930), and editor (*A Book of Victorian Narrative Verse*, 1927; *The Oxford Book of Regency Verse*, 1928); but it is for his novels that Williams is best remembered today. They include *Many Dimensions* (1931), *The Place of the Lion* (1931), *The Greater Trumps* (1932), *Descent into Hell* (1937), and *All Hallows' Eve* (1945). These distinctive works utilize a complicated series of symbols and supernatural or fantastic events to convey the core of Williams's philosophical and religious thought. They became quite popular in the 1930s and attracted some influential admirers, among them T. S. Eliot, C. S. Lewis, and W. H. Auden.

Aside from his novels, Williams gained some recognition for his plays, many of them—including *The Masque of the Manuscript* (1927), *Thomas Cranmer of Canterbury* (1936), and *Judgement at Chelmsford* (1939)—on religious themes. His *Collected Plays* appeared in 1963. Williams also wrote biographies of Sir Francis Bacon (1933), James I (1934), and the Earl of Rochester (1935). *He Came Down from Heaven* (1938) is an important statement of Williams's theological beliefs, while *The Descent of the Dove* (1939) is an informal history of the Christian church. *Witchcraft: A History of Black Magic in Christian Times* (1941) is a study of the interrelationship of witchcraft and Christianity.

Soon after the outbreak of World War II the staff of the London branch of Oxford University Press was relocated to Oxford, and there Williams was introduced by C. S. Lewis to the Inklings, a group of writers who met regularly to read to each other from their works-in-progress. Along with Lewis and J. R. R. Tolkien, Williams rapidly became one of the three dominant members. Through Lewis he also became a lecturer on English poetry at Oxford University, which awarded him an honorary M.A. in 1943. Williams died suddenly on May 15, 1945, in Oxford after a seemingly minor operation.

▦ *Critical Extracts*

UNSIGNED   "It is impossible to describe this novel," the publishers say of *The Place of the Lion*. No one is likely to challenge that statement; the book is not only impossible to describe, it is almost equally impossible to understand. This is the first work of Mr. Williams to be published in America and in certain respects it introduces a writer of genuine gifts, certainly one who cannot be shoved into a corner and thereafter ignored. But the fantasy Mr. Williams has written is hoist on the petard of its own symbolism and very often comes to resemble nothing so much as learned nonsense.

One cannot enjoy or appreciate the fantastic, as E. M. Forster pointed out, unless one is willing "to pay a little extra"—to accept, in other words, whatever is initially improbable or incredible in the picture presented. That the reader's imagination must cooperate, no intelligent person will deny or resent. But the soul of good fantasy lies in its imaginativeness, in its ability to enlarge the possibilities of life with broad, free strokes, and any attempt to intellectualize the fantastic, to explain it, to encumber it with reasons and details can only work harm. Thus, it is all right to introduce an animal who talks, but it is all wrong to educe pseudo-scientific reasons which "justify" the talking. Fantasy is lost so soon as it calls attention to itself. And that is the reason why *The Place of the Lion* is not a success and so often seems close to nonsense. The heavy frame of learning which Mr. Williams has placed around his picture; the religious, intellectual and spiritual implications which he attempts to deduce from it, quite ruin the picture's value. ⟨. . .⟩

The mind simply cannot grapple with Mr. Williams's hierarchy—physical, intellectual, spiritual—of symbols; at least it cannot grapple with them in terms of creative literature. As mental exercise the thing, perhaps, can be done. But the fantasy grows dull and the erudite symbolism grows unintelligible; our wits are so overworked that our emotions have no opportunity for expression. The whole thing is a great deal of a pity, for there is no doubt that Mr. Williams, besides being imaginative and well-read, is also witty and extraordinarily gifted in the use of words. Individual scenes are superbly vivid, but there are too few of them. The book is impressive enough, but in a meaningless and unsuccessful way. It is to be hoped that in future Mr. Williams will confine himself to life on one plane rather than half a dozen.

Unsigned, "A Learned Fantasy," *New York Times Book Review*, 1 May 1932, p. 18

T. S. ELIOT   To ⟨Williams⟩ the supernatural was perfectly natural, and the natural was also supernatural. And this peculiarity gave him that profound insight into Good and Evil, into the heights of Heaven and the depths of Hell, which provides both the immediate thrill, and the permanent message of his novels.

While this theme runs through all of Williams's best work, it is made most apprehensible in this series of novels, from *War in Heaven* to *All Hallows' Eve*. Not having known him in his earlier years, I do not know what literary influences were strongest upon him at the beginning. I suspect some influence from Chesterton, and especially, in connection with the novels, an influence of *The Man Who Was Thursday*. If this influence is present, it is most present in the first novel, *War in Heaven*, and becomes fainter in the later work. ⟨. . .⟩ But I suggest a derivation only to point a difference. Chesterton's *The Man Who Was Thursday* is an allegory; it has a meaning which is meant to be discovered at the end; while we can enjoy it in reading, simply because of the swiftly moving plot and the periodic surprises, it is intended to convey a definite moral and religious point expressible in intellectual terms. It gives you *ideas*, rather than *feelings*, of another world. Williams has no such "palpable design" upon his reader. His aim is to make you partake of a kind of experience that he has had, rather than to make you accept some dogmatic belief. This gives him an affinity with writers of an entirely different type of supernatural thriller from Chesterton's: with writers as different as Poe, Walter de la Mare, Montague James, Le Fanu and Arthur Machen. ⟨. . .⟩

The stories of Charles Williams, then, are not like those of Edgar Allan Poe, woven out of morbid psychology—I have never known a healthier-minded man than Williams. They are not like those of Chesterton, intended to teach the reader. And they are certainly not an exploitation of the supernatural for the sake of the immediate shudder. Williams is telling us about a world of experience known to him: he does not merely persuade us to believe in something, he communicates this experience that he has had. When I say that we are persuaded to believe in the supernatural world of Charles Williams, I do not mean that we necessarily give complete credence to all the apparatus of magic, white or black, that he employs. There is much which he has invented, or borrowed from the literature of the occult, merely for the sake of telling a good story. In reading *All Hallows' Eve*, we can, if we like, believe that the methods of the magician Simon for controlling mysterious forces could be used with success by anyone with suitable natural gifts and special training. We can, on the other hand, find the machinery of the story no more credible than that of any popular tale of vampires, werewolves, or demonic possession. But whether credulous or incredulous about the actual kinds of events in the story, we come to perceive that they are the vehicle for communicating a para-normal experience with which the author is familiar, for introducing us into a real world in which he is at home.

T. S. Eliot, "Introduction," *All Hallows' Eve* by Charles Williams (New York: Pellegrini & Cudahy, 1948), pp. xiv–xvi

GEORGE P. WINSHIP, JR.   In general, the theme of Charles Williams is the Christian faith, seen from a rather special and individual point of view. It may be that the majority of nominally Christian countries no longer hold to or even recognize Christian doctrine, although they are sympathetic to what they consider Christian sentiments. Williams confronts his readers with strange assertions and startling images, such as that of the Emperor.

In *The Greater Trumps*, ⟨. . .⟩ he uses Tarot cards to stand for the correspondences in the real world between natural elements or ideas and human beings. One card is the Emperor, the token on papyrus of Order in the civil realm. A few pages after he appears on the card, a character sees him again as a policeman directing traffic ⟨. . .⟩ The vision of a disciplined world, to Williams, is a Christian theme. He accepts authority and even hierarchy as consonant with the true nature of things, the same hierarchy that Dante, and before him the so-called Dionysius, delighted to describe in heaven. In his verse Williams used hazel rods as symbols of measurement, or rhythm in verse, and of order generally, including the punishment of unruly servants. Slavery, corporal punishment, and even the authority of the civil police are repellent to the modern liberal imagination, and this revulsion of our society against any manifestation of hierarchy is a condition which not only Christians but elected magistrates must recognize and deal with. It may be that Williams rests too much poetic weight upon the rather trivial figure of a policeman; but the novelist could retort that it is the central task of poetry, especially in the genre of prose fiction, to reveal the deeper implications of the commonplace. ⟨. . .⟩

⟨. . .⟩ When he writes at his best, which is magnificently, it is in passages of such strange, uncanny action that when quoted in isolation they sound simply bad. More mundane pages are usually clear, but not always: astonishingly for a professional editor, Williams has some trouble with grammar. On the larger scale he is better, although he learned slowly how to compose a novel. The later stories are admirably planned. The symmetry of paired characters in *The Greater Trumps* and *Descent into Hell* evinces a firm sense of design. Characterization is perhaps not important in stories of this particular type, but he has one rare excellence. It is recognized that good people are the most difficult to create in fiction and that Williams excels in presenting sanctity. But surely his greatest talent, and that upon which his authority as an honest witness must rest, is his ability to present to our

imagination what is denied by our presuppositions, to make real what lies
beyond reality.

> George P. Winship, Jr., "The Novels of Charles Williams," *Shadows of Imagination:*
> *The Fantasies of C. S. Lewis, J. R. R. Tolkien, and Charles Williams*, ed. Mark R.
> Hillegas (Carbondale: Southern Illinois University Press, 1969), pp. 118–20, 123–24

HUMPHREY CARPENTER

'I saw Shakespeare', he wrote in a
poem,

> In a Tube station on the Central London:
> He was smoking a pipe:
> He had Sax Rohmer's best novel under his arm
> (In a cheap edition)
> And the *Evening News*.
> He was reading in the half-detached way one does.
> He had just come away from an office
> And the notes for *The Merchant*
> Were in his pocket,
> Beginning (it was the first line he thought of)
> 'Stil quiring to the young-eyed cherubins',
> But his chief wish was to be earning more money.

This poem shows Williams's total disregard for the conventional distinc-
tions of time and space, the natural and the supernatural, and his habit of
setting extraordinary events against mundane backgrounds. If he wanted to
talk about seeing Shakespeare, why should it not happen in a Tube railway
station? If he wished to write a novel about the magical properties of the
Stone of Suleiman, then let it be set in modern London and let the partici-
pants include the Lord Chief Justice and his secretary. (This was *Many
Dimensions*, published in 1931, and including in the character of the secretary
Chloe something of a portrait of 'Celia'.) Or if the plot was to concern the
appearance in the material world of 'huge and mighty forms', the Platonic
archetypes themselves, then let those archetypes appear in the most ordinary
landscape that he knew, the Hertfordshire countryside surrounding St
Albans. (This was *The Place of the Lion*, published in the same year.) And,
if his subject was to be the Tarot cards and their supernatural relation to
the 'eternal dance' of the universe, let the terrifying results of the use and
abuse of those cards be experienced by a modern middle-class citizen at a
house on the South Downs. (This was *The Greater Trumps*, published in
1932. *Shadows of Ecstasy* was eventually issued a year later.)

These novels were all concerned with the rightful and wrongful use of power. And here somebody reading them may find himself in some confusion, for Williams's ideas of right and wrong often seem extremely odd. In *Shadows of Ecstasy* it is disturbing to find the 'hero' Roger Ingram becoming a disciple of the 'villain' Considine. In *War in Heaven* it is at first puzzling to discover that Williams seems to have almost as much enthusiasm for the cause of the black magicians as for the Archdeacon and his friends. And in *The Greater Trumps*, when Aaron Lee and his grandson Henry use the Tarot cards to raise a great storm by which they hope to murder a man, Williams seems to take sides with them as much as with Coningsby, their intended victim. What has happened to his moral sense?

The answer is that in these novels he was not principally concerned with moral issues. The question of the nature of good and evil occupied his mind, but he did not discuss it in depth in the novels, reserving it for his religious dramas and his theological study *He Came Down from Heaven*. For the moment he was content to leave it somewhat on one side, and to judge the characters in his novels not by such terms as 'good' and 'bad' but by differentiating their attitudes to the supernatural. Low in the scale come such people as Damaris Tighe in *The Place of the Lion*, who merely *studies* the history of supernatural beliefs without considering what she herself should believe. Low too in the scale are those—and there are many in the novels—who desire to use supernatural powers for their own ends; but though this may be evil it does show a proper awareness of those powers. Higher are those persons such as Lord Arglay in *Many Dimensions* and Sir Bernard Travers in *Shadows of Ecstasy* who are true agnostics, having decided neither to believe nor to disbelieve but to remain with open minds; and their unruffled scepticism, characteristic of one aspect of Williams himself, in its way admits that belief is possible. Highest of all come those few— there is rarely more than one in each novel—who commit themselves fully to the supernatural, resigning themselves utterly into its hands, even if the result is (as it sometimes is) physical death.

Humphrey Carpenter, *The Inklings: C. S. Lewis, J. R. R. Tolkien, Charles Williams, and Their Friends* (Boston: Houghton Mifflin, 1979), pp. 95–96

GLEN CAVALIERO   ⟨. . .⟩ Williams was not an instinctive novel-ist, in the generally accepted sense of that term. His two final novels succeed because in them he ceased trying to be one. For what is most memorable in all of them is the sense of the transcendent as it shines through the world of space and time. In this respect the books are genuinely original and impressive. Especially striking is the way in which the supernatural manifestations are seen as being precisely that—super-natural. They do not engage with the world of appearances, they take it over. There is none of that uneasy intrusion of the paranormal in terms of the normal that we find in the average occult novel, as in Dennis Wheatley's *The Devil Rides Out* (1935) or Aleister Crowley's partly satirical and wholly floundering *Moonchild* (1929). And through his narrative technique Williams, not himself a mystic, is able to present dramatically the conclusion of all visionary experience that spiritual reality co-inheres in material reality. So too he is able to coin, in terms of his various myths, memorable epigrams of redemption, such as 'The Way to the Stone is in the Stone', 'The Knowledge of the Angelicals' and 'The Knowledge of the Dance'. A language for religious experience is being evolved that is specifically symbolic and allusive: no confusion between appearance and reality being raised by or about it, the balance between belief and scepticism can be verbally contained.

The logical outcome of this process is found in *Descent into Hell*. Williams's treatment of occult themes had been moving towards an all-inclusive vision that may be termed multispatial. The debate in *Shadows of Ecstasy* as to the nature and true term of romantic experience concludes with the affirmation of unity set forth initially and dramatically in the four succeeding books, and acted out and set forth definitively in the final one. Parallel to the more selective exploration of division-in-unity leading to unity-in-division carried out in the criticism, biographies and plays, we find Williams using the novel form to enlarge his vision in more general and more widely referential terms.

The novels themselves occupy an ambiguous place in his total output. On the one hand, they are certainly his most well-known and popular writings, and are arguably his most original contribution to the literature of his time. On the other hand, when set alongside novels written out of other traditions than the metaphysical or occult, they dwindle into triviality. Only when read in the context of his total output does their significance become apparent.

The first six reveal an evolving awareness of human power-drives as they are confronted with the inevitable constrictions of human existence. Starting with the consciousness of sublimity, of endless possibility, of romantic yearning, Williams's thought leads inexorably to a consideration of the providence of God. A convinced Christian, he was never a facile one. He did not embrace religious belief because it consoled or even inspired him: rather, he saw it as the necessary accommodation of the self to fact. In his criticism, biographies and plays he concentrates on personal experience; but in the novels the individual dramas are given a wider setting. The metaphysical imagery provides an impersonal set of counters with which to set out the rules of the game.

> Glen Cavaliero, *Charles Williams: Poet of Theology* (Grand Rapids, MI: William B. Eerdmans, 1983), pp. 164–65

ALICE MARY HADFIELD   More than any other of his books, the early novels have produced speculations about Charles Williams's desire for power and capacity for cruelty. Much of it springs from those who do not follow Williams's own critical rule of attending to what words actually say and deriving conclusions only from them. Fortunately, we now have more source material.

The manuscript of the drama scribbled in 1902 when he was sixteen and a half, shows a juvenile idea of power—the Prince's campaigns and victories, the number of his armed forces, lists of his household and plans for his country (including a canal 500 miles long). It is the kind of fantasy of power that most of us have in youth and carry over into adult life, till we slowly allow it to be replaced by reality. Perhaps, however, few are so sensible as to keep no traces of 'If only. . . .' Certainly to the vivid and ranging imagination of a young man like Charles, they would come easily enough, and persist longer.

Fifteen years later, bubbling with ideas, emotions and words, he had to show for them one book of poetry published, another accepted, and a minor editorial job. In 1917 he married, so taking one leap forward, and joined the Order of the Golden Dawn, so taking another.

Marriage took him further into love, religion, poetry, and to *The Outlines of Romantic Theology*. The Golden Dawn took him into a wider world of people he would not otherwise have met, of study of new ways of power, and of participation in rituals. It could well have been the Masons; it happened to be the Golden Dawn.

Thus when he began to write novels the two levels of his life combined. Their underlying structure derived from religion, romantic love, and his work; their superstructure from his interest in the workings of material and magical power; their excitement from the clash between the two. Some of the story bases are, one cannot help feeling, a trifle corny: an African High Executive (surely a throwback to 1902 with a touch of Rider Haggard); the Stone of Suleiman; the Tarot cards. Platonism and the Grail are far better. But the corniness does not matter, for it provides the accidents of the stories, not the essence.

> Alice Mary Hadfield, *Charles Williams: An Exploration of His Life and Work* (New York: Oxford University Press, 1983), p. 103

KATHLEEN SPENCER   *Shadows of Ecstasy*, the first novel Williams wrote, does not introduce the fantastic at all, even in dialogue, until the fifth chapter, some seventy pages into the book, and does not give narratorial confirmation until the eleventh chapter (out of fourteen). By contrast, his last novel, *All-Hallows' Eve*, opens with the consciousness— both reported thoughts and actions, and free indirect speech—of a young woman named Lester Furnival who lives in London at the end of World War II: on the fifth page of the text, she suddenly realizes that she is dead. Yet her consciousness remains intact, and we enter into it periodically until the very end of the novel. The ordinary "real" world and living characters do not enter the story until the second chapter. Another peculiarity of this volume is that from the very beginning the narrator commits himself to the actuality of the fantastic events, telling things about the occurrences that the characters do not know—unlike the earlier novels when he leads up to that stage gradually. It is as if, at the end of his life, Williams had developed a new confidence in his story, or his audience, or both.

The rhythm and pace of his presentation may vary from novel to novel, but the goal does not. In all of his novels, more so than in most examples of the fantastic, Williams is writing about events which, despite the opinions of his own culture to the contrary, he believed to be possible. That is, it was not his own fictional evocations of the supernatural in which he believed but rather the conception of the universe upon which his fictions were based: a universe where the supernatural is real, coinherent in the natural world, and governed by laws allowing readers to comprehend it. This belief goes a long way to explain the special quality of Williams's novels, the kind of stories he chooses to tell, the heroes he selects, the assured, confident tone of the narrative and, above all, his choice of genre—the fantastic, which blends the ordinary real world with incredible characters and events.

The fantastic genre can be used for many purposes besides the one Williams chose, which was, at least in part, to give his audience a vivid experience of the numinous world in which he believed. Other nineteenth- and early twentieth-century writers use the genre for this same purpose, as a sort of pleasant propaganda for Spiritualism or Theosophy or magic. Some fantastic tales are just for the fun of the marvelous adventure or provide the special pleasures of the ghost story, the delightful frisson of being (safely) scared witless. Other tales, like most of what Tobin Siebers calls the Romantic Fantastic (a more precise term for the works Todorov discusses under the label of the fantastic), use the genre more seriously to explore the problems of subjectivity through the device of unreliable narrators and the unusual states of consciousness—madness, frenzy, hallucination, dream—with which many Romantic artists were obsessed.

Whatever the purpose to which the fantastic has been put, the sort of analysis to which I have here subjected Williams's novels can be a useful approach to any fantastic text. The pace at which the narrative hints at and then confirms the fantastic, the source of that confirmation and its reliability, or whether the text ever commits itself at all (as in Todorov's sense that the true fantastic consists of those texts which refuse to commit themselves to the actuality of the events being described) can provide sensitive clues to the central concerns of the text and can suggest reasons why the author has chosen the fantastic as the appropriate genre for the tale.

> Kathleen Spencer, "Naturalizing the Fantastic: Narrative Technique in the Novels of Charles Williams," *Extrapolation* 28, No. 1 (Spring 1987): 72–73

DENNIS L. WEEKS   While existentialism plays an important part in the underlying philosophies of Williams's life and work, the most significant idea behind his writing is the theory of Coinherence and Substitution. ⟨. . .⟩

Coinherence demands that we realize that all people, who have existed in the past, those people existing now, and individuals who will yet live in the future, are bound together by some common bond. ⟨. . .⟩ Thus, Coinherence is time/event related.

Many Dimensions is perhaps the novel which best exemplifies the time/ event assumption in Coinherence because Williams makes blatant use of the stone and its types to move people through time and space without apparent adherence to physical laws. Williams is not the first person to write about what appears to be science fiction, at the very least fantasy, by using the stone in this special way. For the origin of movement through time, we must look to Plato and Aristotle as they explore the idea of materiality and intelligence in their discussions of angels as "prime movers" to the celestial bodies. ⟨. . .⟩

Coinherence, as Williams matured his conception of it to the point that he was able to write the seven steps for the Companions of the Coinherence in 1937, also assumes that all people moving toward Coinherence are on a path. This path, as previously determined, is best illustrated in Brea's altar painting, "Paradise," with its pilgrims on their way toward heaven.

Brea's painting also assumes, by the pilgrims moving away from heaven, that Coinherence has two pathways—one toward heaven and Coinherence, and one path leading away from Coinherence. It is the pathway toward Coinherence that Williams's good characters eventually end up moving along. The opposite pathway is reserved for his evil characters, who have made their conscious choice to tread this road, eventually reaching damnation.

Whether the movement is toward Coinherence or damnation, Williams has identified the entire progress toward Coinherence by the collective title of "the redeemed City," which means all generations past, present, and future. The City is the metaphor that Williams uses to denote those individuals who are coinhered with the Godhead. Coinherence is, thus far, a combination of time/event reality and movement, upon recognition of the self in relation to Unity (Williams's term for God), toward Coinherence. There is, however, the idea of Substitution that must be tied into Coinherence for a complete understanding of Williams's theories. Substitution springs out of the catalyst of love. In the case of Substitution's relationship to Coinherence, love is altruistic, as seen for example in *Descent into Hell* and *All Hallows' Eve*.

In *Descent into Hell*, Peter Stanhope is able to substitute himself, that is, bear the burden of worry, for Pauline Anstruther, who lives in constant fear of meeting her doppelganger, who, she does not realize, represents past generations searching for Coinherence. There is no reason for Pauline to understand that her double is, ironically, her salvation, for Pauline must first understand Substitution as an unselfish act completed for her by Peter Stanhope. ⟨. . .⟩

⟨. . .⟩ Williams saw Coinherence as a building process that is based upon his seven steps and explained in his series of seven novels. There are, of course, many other themes in the novels that have been explicated by other critics. No other critic or study, however, has examined the novels as an outpouring of a deeply religious man who was committed enough in his beliefs to write seven books devoted to setting man upon the path of Unity in a century wracked by indecision and lack of faith. This was the goal of Charles Williams and one that is wrapped in a mystical shroud of fantasy and metaphysics which awaits the discerning reader who is willing to study and learn the seven steps toward Coinherence as they are explained in the novels.

> Dennis L. Weeks, *Steps toward Salvation: An Examination of Coinherence and Substitution in the Seven Novels of Charles Williams* (New York: Peter Lang, 1991), pp. 102–5

❖ Bibliography

The Silver Stair. 1912.
Poems of Conformity. 1917.
Divorce. 1920.
Poems of Home and Overseas (editor; with V. H. Collins). 1921.
Windows of Night. 1924.
A Book of Victorian Narrative Verse (editor). 1927.
The Masque of the Manuscript. 1927.
A Myth of Shakespeare. 1928.
The Oxford Book of Regency Verse (editor; with H. S. Milford). 1928.
The Masque of Perusal. 1929.
Poetry at Present. 1930.
Heroes and Kings. 1930.
War in Heaven. 1930.
Many Dimensions. 1931.
The Place of the Lion. 1931.
Three Plays. 1931.

The Greater Trumps. 1932.
The English Poetic Mind. 1932.
Bacon. 1933.
Reason and Beauty in the Poetic Mind. 1933.
A Short Life of Shakespeare by E. K. Chambers (editor). 1933.
Shadows of Ecstasy. 1933.
James I. 1934.
The Ring and the Book: The Story Retold. 1934.
Rochester. 1935.
The New Book of English Verse (editor; with others). 1935.
Thomas Cranmer of Canterbury. 1936.
Queen Elizabeth. 1936.
The Story of the Aeneid, Retold. 1936.
Stories of Great Names. 1937.
Henry VII. 1937.
Descent into Hell. 1937.
Taliessen through Logres. 1938.
He Came Down from Heaven. 1938.
The Descent of the Dove: A Short History of the Holy Spirit in the Church. 1939.
Judgement at Chelmsford: A Pageant Play. 1939.
The Passion of Christ (editor). 1939.
The New Christian Year (editor). 1941.
Religion and Love in Dante: The Theology of Romantic Love. 1941.
Witchcraft: A History of Black Magic in Christian Times. 1941.
The Forgiveness of Sins. 1942.
The Figure of Beatrice: A Study in Dante. 1943.
The Letters of Evelyn Underhill (editor). 1943.
The Region of the Summer Stars. 1944.
To Michal: After Marriage. 1944.
The House of the Octopus. 1945.
All Hallows' Eve. 1945.
Solway Ford and Other Poems by Wilfred Gibson (editor). 1945.
Flecker of Dean Close. 1946.
Arthurian Torso, Containing the Posthumous Fragment of "The Figure of Arthur."
        Ed. C. S. Lewis. 1948.
Seed of Adam and Other Plays. 1948.
The Image of the City and Other Essays. Ed. Anne Ridler. 1958.
Selected Writings. Ed. Anne Ridler. 1961.

Collected Plays. 1963.

Letters to Lalage: The Letters of Charles Williams to Lois Lang-Sims. Ed. Glen
        Cavaliero. 1989.

Outlines of Romantic Theology. Ed. Alice Mary Hadfield. 1990.

Essential Writings on Spirituality and Theology. Ed. Charles Hefling. 1993.